The Fight for Competitive Advantage

The Fight for
Competitive Advantage:

A Study of the United States
Domestic Trunk Air Carriers

WILLIAM E. FRUHAN, JR.
Assistant Professor of Business Administration
Harvard University

DIVISION OF RESEARCH
GRADUATE SCHOOL OF BUSINESS ADMINISTRATION
HARVARD UNIVERSITY
BOSTON · 1972

Preface

THIS STUDY was undertaken to examine how firms compete in an industry context. It deals specifically with the United States domestic trunk air carriers and the regulatory body (the Civil Aeronautics Board—CAB) which sets the rules for, and oversees, the competitive struggle among airline firms. The problems of competition and competitive strategy formulation are investigated with tools drawn from three very different conceptual approaches. By combining concepts from the fields of finance, policy, and industrial organization, I have reached conclusions that are quite different from earlier studies of interfirm competition.

These conclusions point out that the CAB, in its effort to maintain the financial health of existing competitors, has structured a competitive environment which includes some very undesirable and unnecessary features. Since these undesirable features of the competitive environment may wither naturally over an extended period of time, the research offers only modest hope that the CAB will find sufficient incentive to change its policy course.

This research study has provided material for a series of teaching cases, my doctoral dissertation, and finally this Division of Research publication.

Many people have made significant contributions to the progress of this study as it has evolved over time. At the dissertation stage, major contributions in the area of problem formulation and conceptual approach were made by Professors John H. McArthur, Joseph L. Bower, and Charles M. Williams.

Outside of academic life, there were also many people and organizations who were invaluable in the completion of this research effort at the dissertation stage. They include individuals from the airlines and the CAB, as well as the financial institutions that in one way or another have interests in airline problems. While the confidential nature of some of the material used in this study precludes my citing specific individuals and their firms by name, I should like to say that without the help of a few key people and firms, this research could never have seen the light of day in its present form. It is a somewhat remarkable phenomenon, in my estimation, that people in industry will discuss obviously sensitive subjects and make available internal material for an inquiry of this type when they have no way of knowing how the material may ultimately be used. With no prospect of benefit, and at substantial cost to themselves in terms of their time and the risk of personal embarrassment, a few individuals have aided this research effort immeasurably. For this assistance I shall long be grateful, and I hope that these industry people will never be discouraged from aiding young men with nothing to offer but the occasional challenge of some (as yet) untested idea.

As *The Fight for Competitive Advantage* progressed to its current state, the comments of other individuals proved to be extremely helpful. Professor George Eads of Princeton University; Professors William L. White, Robert R. Glauber, and Paul W. Cherington of the Harvard Business School; and Mr. Irving Roth, formerly Director of the Bureau of Economics of the CAB and now Vice President of United Air Lines, Inc.; all contributed in significant ways toward improving the final research product.

I wish to thank the Division of Research, Harvard Business School, and especially Professors Lawrence E. Fouraker (now Dean), and James P. Baughman, for their assistance in finding the resources to underwrite this research effort. Specifically, both for the Harvard Business School and for myself, I should like to acknowledge the generous financial support which The 1907 Foundation gave to this project. Without this aid and support, my work would certainly have progressed at a slower pace and contained less of a field orientation.

Rita Colella suffered nobly through the typing of several manuscript revisions. Hilma Holton was a more than understanding editor in guiding the author through the trauma of a first publication.

Finally my wife, Ginny, deserves special honors for enduring the environmental fallout which any research effort must inevitably produce. Ginny suffered through many lost weekends over the past several years with no lessening of spirit.

While many individuals have assisted me in this effort, I of course accept full responsibility for any and all errors of omission and/or commission.

Soldiers Field   WILLIAM E. FRUHAN, JR.
Boston, Massachusetts
December 1971

Table of Contents

List of Tables

List of Figures

The Fight for Competitive Advantage

Introduction

THIS BOOK WILL EXAMINE HOW FIRMS COMPETE in an oligopolistic industry, and the factors that are important to a competitively successful corporate strategy. The air transportation industry provides an interesting setting for such an investigation for three reasons. First, the industry has a history of unusually wide ranges in the relative profitability of individual firms, suggesting that effective strategy may have a high payoff. In testing the effectiveness of corporate strategy, a researcher should certainly pick an industry where substantial differences are observed in firm profitability, and the major U.S. airlines fulfill this prerequisite admirably.

By definition, firms in a regulated industry such as air transport are forced to operate with an array of competitive tools that are less numerous than those available to their unregulated counterparts. Where competitive activity is spread over fewer variables, its intensity must be more concentrated in those areas where it promises to be useful. A researcher seeking to identify and measure strategically important variables might thus expect to find his task greatly simplified by looking at a regulated industry. The airline example again provides this necessary degree of simplicity.

Finally, the airline industry provides a rich area for investigating competition since as of the early 1970s something has clearly gone awry in the competitive environment. Profits have all but disappeared in spite of numerous fare increases, and the carriers face a staggering financial burden brought on by large commitments to purchase new flight equipment. This burden promises to extend at least through the first half of the decade.

On a somewhat broader scale the competitive environment in air transportation offers a challenge for effective resource allocation of sufficient magnitude to merit some attention at the level of national policy making. It is difficult to see how attention at this level might be translated into socially beneficial actions, however, until national policy makers enjoy a clear understanding of the existing competitive dynamics in air transportation.

The Research Questions and Chapter Organization

The answers to three questions have been researched here:

(1) Why are some air carriers more profitable than others?
(2) How might the less profitable carriers act to improve their positions?
(3) How might public policy be adjusted so that an effective strategy at the corporate level would not only generate enhanced profitability for the firm, but also yield social benefits through a substantial saving in economic resources?

The book is divided into three parts. Part I (Chapter 1) provides a simple introduction to airline economics and finance. Part II (Chapters 2–5) relates solely to an examination of the competitive economic environment in air transportation. Part III (Chapter 6) shifts gears rather sharply, and examines how and by whom the competitive environment might be altered so as to (1) reward an effective corporate strategy via enhanced profitability and (2) discourage economically and/or socially wasteful competitive action. The strategies which are open to the participants with important roles to play in determining the industry's performance will be examined (1) to see how these alternatives relate to an efficient allocation of resources and (2) to see if the "best" strategies of each participant are necessarily in conflict, and if so, how this conflict might be resolved.

PART I—INDUSTRY BACKGROUND

Before plunging into the more significant issues examined by the book, the "nonairline" reader will find it useful to review some background material on the air transportation industry.

Chapter 1 provides sufficient information about the industry to build understanding in later chapters about why air carriers act in specific ways in an effort to gain a competitive advantage. It discusses the industry's market structure, its historic growth trend, and its current and projected financial structure as of 1971. The material on financial structure is broken down into the complementary problems of asset and liability management. Also, in this chapter particular emphasis is placed upon the following recurring industry problems: (1) enormous commitments for capital outlays which demand large infusions of external capital, (2) low industry profitability, and (3) hostile external capital markets. While this problem setting per se is not of central importance to the book, it illustrates an extremely interesting portion of the larger industry scenario which the book aims to define.

Part II—The Airline Competition Study

The first research question involving the problem of discovering and explaining why some air carriers are more profitable than others can be likened to the problem of explaining why some children have dark hair while others are blond. The problem is multilevel, and it ought to be answered in terms of the needs of the end-user of the information. The idly curious child might be satisfied with the answer, "Anne has black hair because her mother and father have black hair." A microbiologist's needs, in contrast, might require a response starting at the level of genes and working down to molecular structure and the sequence and spacing of atoms.

This book will deal with the question of airline profitability at many levels. In some chapters the detail will become so microscopic that the author runs the risk of having the reader lose sight of the link back to the initial problem.[1] This analytic detail is necessary, however, since the research findings relate to how carriers and/or the Civil Aeronautics Board (CAB)[2] can alter their decision making at the "atomc" (i.e., micro) level and thus produce changes in the competitive environment that promise to be quite obvious to the most casual observer of macro phenomena. Unlike the simple dyeing of hair, these changes could not be produced by directly operating on macro level problems.

A Relative Profitability Model of the Firm

The first research question (outlined earlier) was posed at a level of generality which removed it from researchable usefulness. This question now needs to be broken down into a number of manageable subunits which are narrower in scope and independently researchable.

The first area requiring investigation relates to variables which contribute to the separation of carriers along the relative profitability[3] dimension. What are the key variables in airline profitability? A researcher rarely veers far off the track in looking at unit costs, price, and volume, but can each of these factors in the profit equation be broken up further? Can important variables be identified in a manner which permits a numerical tag to be applied, or must the researcher be content with using qualitative judgmental variables like "overall beauty of stewardesses" as key elements in competitive advantage?

Once the important profit variables have been defined and quantified to some reasonable degree, the research effort can move on to a second area of inquiry.

---

[1] One rarely mentions black hair in a discussion of the sequence of atoms.

[2] The CAB (Civil Aeronautics Board) is a regulatory body constituted by the Congress of the United States and charged with regulating domestic (and some aspects of international) air transportation.

[3] A carrier's relative profitability in a given year is defined as its operating profit margin divided by the domestic trunk industry's operating profit margin.

This second area of interest relates to the degree of control each carrier management team can hope to exercise over those factors which have demonstrable profitability significance. The domestic trunk carriers operate in a regulated environment. Some of the traditional approaches used in building a competitive advantage in unregulated industries are not directly available to carrier managers for precisely this reason. In order to identify areas in which a competitive advantage might be built, it will be useful to place a tag on each of the important profit variables to show where direct control rests—with the Civil Aeronautics Board, or with carrier management.

Chapter 2 of this book assumes the task of defining and examining statistically[4] many of the factors which contribute to differences in relative profitability between carriers. Eleven variables are defined in the chapter. Nine of them are examined in detail since they seemed susceptible to some kind of quantification. Five of these nine variables are descriptive of the carriers' route structures, one relates to fare structure, and three relate to the manner in which carriers acquire and utilize their flight equipment. Since the routes flown by a carrier, and the fares charged for that transportation happen to be controlled by the CAB, this partitioning of variables accomplishes the "tagging" function necessary to show where control of each of the key strategic profitability elements resides.

In terms of sheer numbers, the CAB directly controls a majority of the significant profitability variables. More importantly, however, the statistical analysis in Chapter 2 indicates that the CAB-controlled variables are the ones of greatest overall competitive importance. The implication of the chapter is that in the long run the CAB has more direct control over a carrier's competitive position and relative profitability than does the carrier's own management. The decision makers paid by airline shareholders may thus be cast in the role of acting as a "second string" management team, with the CAB making most of the really important profitability decisions.

While the CAB has formal statutory control over most of the important profitability variables, this fact does not, in itself, imply that the carriers cannot with perfect propriety informally and/or indirectly exert influence in the way the CAB exercises its legal mandate. A new area of investigation will thus focus on the carriers' fight for competitive advantage in the areas where they lack direct control. This investigation will begin to outline some options relating to the second research question: How might the less profitable carriers act to improve their positions? My examination will be concerned with whether and/or when the carriers can exercise *indirect control,* or at least exert *significant influence,* on these important profitability variables. Where carriers' actions do have an impact, I will explore how indirect control is exercised. Where carriers' actions have no impact, I will lift up and explore the CAB's objectives in the exercise of its statutory powers.

---

[4] A statistical treatment of this topic is included primarily as corroborative evidence, which tends to confirm conclusions drawn by the author from field observation.

The Fight for Competitive Advantage—Fares

Chapters 3 and 4 address the question of how the carriers attempt to achieve a competitive advantage in the areas of fares and routes, respectively. Chapter 3 goes into considerable detail in analyzing (1) the process of changing industry fares, and (2) the jockeying for competitive advantage which occurs in response to this infrequent opportunity. The most significant conclusion of Chapter 3 is that the relative profitability payoff from achieving a competitive advantage in the area of fare structure is so high, and the interests of various carriers so totally in conflict, that alterations in the industry's fare structure must, of necessity, be coercive. The CAB by default, if not by design, is thus cast in the role of defining the industry's basic price policy. As the CAB is guided by policy objectives of its own choosing,[5] the opportunity for creative intervention by individual carriers in the CAB decision-making process is extremely low.

The Fight for Competitive Advantage—Routes

Chapter 4 carries the fight for competitive advantage to the arena of route awards. It concludes that the carriers have little influence either in the selection of markets needing added competitive service or in the selection of the specific carrier(s) to provide such service. The chapter further finds that the CAB uses its route authority to regulate (1) industry and (2) individual carrier profitability, and that in using routes to regulate the former, the CAB tends to encourage the carriers to purchase excessive numbers of aircraft.

The Fight for Competitive Advantage—Capacity and Equipment Purchases

Chapter 5 leaves the arena of direct CAB regulation and explores that area of competitive significance which carrier managers control completely, i.e., the *purchase* of equipment and *scheduling* decisions. The chapter examines in detail airline economics at the individual route level, and at the corporate level describes the complexity of the fight for competitive advantage in a rapidly growing oligopolistic industry. This portion of the book provides, perhaps, the most startling research conclusions. Severe overcapacity and general lack of profitability is found to be a predictable outgrowth of a combination of the industry's basic economics and the particular regulatory posture adopted by the CAB. The chapter concludes that occasional periods of satisfactory profit for the industry have resulted only from:

(1) Mistakes in traffic demand estimation by carrier managers.
(2) The unwillingness of lenders to advance additional credit to the industry when profits reach a dangerously low level.
(3) Supplier inability to meet the carriers' demands for new aircraft deliveries.

---

[5] Discussion of these specific objectives is deferred to Chapter 6.

Chapters 2 through 5 explore a trail which started with the first research question of why some air carriers are more profitable than others. This question forced the examination of certain key airline profitability variables. As a result of this research it is found that the CAB, both in law and in practice, exercises almost complete control over most of the variables which define a carrier's relative profitability. Little is said in these chapters about the overall goals, if any, guiding CAB decision making. In those important profitability areas controlled by management, the kinds of decisions encouraged by the economic and regulatory environment are found to be startlingly costly. This finding prompted an exploration of the "hows" and "whys" of the CAB's regulatory policy.

PART III—ALTERING THE COMPETITIVE ENVIRONMENT

Chapter 6 looks in some detail at the range of strategies available to the principal groups whose actions ultimately define the competitive environment in air transportation. These are the CAB, the Big 4 carriers, the Little 7 carriers, and the national administration.

The chapter first examines the CAB's apparent (though officially unacknowledged) regulation of intra-industry variance in firm profitability and asset size. It then explores ways in which the airline industry's very costly overcapacity spiral might be broken. The chapter concludes that the problem will, to a degree, be self-solving once the industry matures so that its growth on a long-term basis declines to the average level achieved by the GNP. It also suggests that this evolutionary problem-solving process could, and indeed should, be collapsed into a shorter period of time via mergers aimed at promptly equalizing carrier size (i.e., a domestic trunk industry comprised of about 6 participants) and potential profitability. Suggestions are also made regarding changes in CAB fare policies which, following these mergers, would operate to (1) reduce the attractiveness of playing the "capacity game" to the air carriers, and (2) allow any real "management quality" differences between carriers to escape the leveling impact of certain CAB policies. At the level of carrier management responsibility, the chapter argues that near the peak of the next industry profitability cycle, airline managers should take the opportunity to diversify substantially. Real opportunities would then exist to redeploy assets away from capacity duels into more productive business endeavors.

Chapter 6 brings us full circle, since it also answers a strategic question for the larger carriers. Once the "whys" of airline profitability have been discovered, the question of how to capitalize on the opportunities presented by the competitive environment remains. The chapter outlines how, preferably with CAB assistance but perhaps even without, the carriers making up the Big 4 might individually improve their relative profitability and simultaneously reduce in strength the forces encouraging overcapacity.[6] In so doing, the chapter hopefully answers research questions two and three.

---

[6] Consistent with the "hair color" analogy introduced earlier, the macro phenomenon of improved profitability would be achieved through the use of "atom level" decision changes.

As considerations of public policy and large firm profitability in an oligopolistic industry rarely point in the same direction, this is perhaps a research finding of some note.

In terms of options available to the national administration, the book concludes that the most efficient allocation of resources will probably be realized if this important participant in planning the future of air transportation simply makes a choice (conscious or unconscious) to ignore any *changes* in the number of air transport firm participants as long as the concentration among the top one or two carriers does not significantly increase. The notion that the public interest may best be served if one or more guardians of that interest fail to respond in a traditionally acceptable way to a reduction in the number of firms in an oligopolistic industry is a second research finding of some note.

CONCEPTUAL APPROACH

While Chapter 6 formally concludes the airline analysis, one aspect of the research not directly related to airline problems may be worth some additional discussion. That topic involves the conceptual approach used throughout the book.

It is difficult to look back on the problem of describing competition within an industry, even an industry as simple as air transportation, without being struck by the contrast between the richness of the competitive situation and the inadequacy of the conceptual models which are brought to bear individually by researchers in an effort to describe it. In the process of thinking about airline competition, it became clear to me that the traditional conceptual tools developed for business problem solving (particularly in the finance area which represents "home territory" for me) were not very useful in explaining the competitive interplay observed in the field. The phenomena observed in Chapters 1–6 which made up the total competitive environment in an industry had to be examined with a different perspective if these observations were to be explained in a sensible manner.[7]

The research effort undertaken in this book thus differs in approach from many studies of industry competition because, instead of relying on a single conceptual model, it attempts to weave elements of three distinctly different conceptual models[8] into a more complete and powerful tool for describing the competitive environment.

In preparing for a hike through uncertain territory (which any reader of new research should be prepared to undertake), the question of what to bring invariably arises. Having made the trip before, the author is in the enviable position, hopefully, of being able to provide some suggestions. My first thought in the

---

[7] Donaldson in *Strategy for Financial Mobility* (p. 12) has observed that research ought to try "to understand (the businessman's) operational frame of reference instead of imposing one on him. It means taking what is for many academicians the giant step of assuming that the average businessman is both intelligent and rational in what he does."

[8] These three models are described in some detail later in the Introduction.

role of advisor is that while the student of business administration undoubtedly possesses all the tools necessary for the trip I have planned, these tools may have never been arrayed previously in the same knapsack. Since to be forewarned is to be forearmed, the reader can thus look ahead to chapters in which portions of models from (1) finance, (2) business policy, and (3) industrial organization will be utilized, sometimes alternatively, sometimes in concert, but (I hope) always in proportion to their usefulness in illuminating complex issues in the competitive environment. The goal in this endeavor is thus to achieve a level of understanding in Chapters 1–6 that any of the three models used alone would have failed to produce. As Graham Allison has so ably demonstrated, when one fishes in familiar waters with different conceptual nets, the resulting catches can be quite different. "Which model an analyst employs *does* make a difference." [9]

The Models Employed

The particular phrasing of the research question "Why are some air carriers more profitable than others?" carries with it the challenge and the opportunity to integrate portions of these three overlapping yet distinct conceptual frameworks of business analysis and problem solving. The industry orientation of the research question invites an economic analysis modeled after the works of Chamberlain, Markham, Bain and Caves.[10] Such a research approach might focus on the relationships between industry conduct (market structure, price policy, cost structure, etc.) and industry performance (efficiency and profitability), and the public policy implications of these relationships.

The capital intense nature of the air transportation business coupled with a very erratic history of profitability and capital availability suggests the need to employ a second conceptual framework, the financial model, for analyzing interfirm competition. Both the volume and the nature of investments undertaken by each firm in an industry are, almost by definition, important competitive choices. The answers taken at the firm level to key financial questions posed by authors such as Solomon,[11] "Should an enterprise commit capital funds for certain purposes?" and "Do the expected returns meet financial standards of performance?" might thus carry us a long way toward resolving the basic research question.

Finally, the overall thrust of the research question relates to a firm's search for competitive advantage. This demands an analytic approach to strategy formulation which is found principally in writings of the business policy area.[12]

---

[9] Graham T. Allison, *Conceptual Models and the Cuban Missile Crisis,* p. 56.

[10] See for example, E. H. Chamberlain, *The Theory of Monopolistic Competition;* or J. W. Markham, *Competition in the Rayon Industry;* or J. S. Bain, *Barriers to New Competition;* or Richard E. Caves, *Air Transportation and Its Regulators.*

[11] E. Solomon, *The Theory of Financial Management,* p. 6.

[12] See for example, Learned, Christensen, Andrews, and Guth, *Business Policy;* or Bower, "Strategy as a Problem Solving Theory of Business Planning."

The Industrial Organization (Economic) Model

Aside from obvious strengths, each of the conceptual schemes mentioned has some distinct weaknesses in relation to the research question. The economic approach, for example, almost invariably fails to reach in and explore the process of making decisions at a level *within* a specific firm. The economist chooses (or is forced) to draw his research conclusions from aggregated data, and this choice masks much of the competitive interplay *between* and *within* firms operating in the industry. The economist who undertakes an industry study is thus cast in a role similar to that of the stockmarket technician who is eternally denied a look at the specialist's order book. In some cases this lack of decision-making detail at the level of the firm results in a product which is of little use in defining potential competitive strategies for the various firm managements (which this approach is admittedly not designed to accomplish). In other cases this research can lead the researcher to overlook or misinterpret evidence regarding the dynamics of competition (which this conceptual approach ought to avoid).

The Finance Model

The traditional analytic approach to decision making in the finance literature is quite different from that of the industrial organization (economic) literature. One gets the distinct impression from readings in finance that strategic firm decisions, particularly in the commitment of resources, are made in a competitive vacuum. The notion that firms operate *within industries* appears almost exclusively in the portfolio decision literature of capital markets and in the more recent writings in the capital structure area. There is almost a complete lack of industry consciousness elsewhere. While Joel Dean[13] defines 10 components for a firm's strategic decision making in the capital budgeting area (which include a "creative search for profitable opportunities" and the "projection and measurement of project worth"), the literature seems preoccupied with developing techniques for screening and selecting project portfolios from a set of well-defined alternatives. The need to understand businesses and the dynamics of competition *before* projects are defined is almost ignored in the *application* if not in the *formulation* of the analytic model.

In practice, the finance model as traditionally defined might be useful in decision making at the level of choosing the type[14] of aircraft to purchase, and whether to own or lease the aircraft in question. To go further in decision making, however, i.e., to decide the volume of aircraft a specific carrier should purchase, and how those aircraft ought to be deployed on specific routes, requires an understanding of the competitive dynamics of the industry. It is here that the researcher is

---

[13] Joel S. Dean, "Measuring the Productivity of Capital," *Harvard Business Review*, January-February 1954.

[14] For instance, route structure and market density considerations might make the Lockheed 1011 more attractive in ROI terms than the Boeing 747 for some carriers. This conclusion could be reached without ever looking at the competitive environment outside the firm.

faced with a crucial puzzle. In following the internal tracks left by a large capacity purchase decision for a trunk carrier, what does the researcher do when it
becomes evident that return on investment projections, while calculated for single
pieces of equipment as well as the aggregate package, simply don't count very
much in making the final purchase decision? The researcher's initial conclusion
might be that the carrier managers don't understand their business very well.
Donaldson's caveat (see footnote 7) coupled with a rough sampling of executive
backgrounds,[15] and personal discussions with air-carrier managers all argued
strongly, however, that it was the finance model, and not the managers, that lacked
analytic strength. The finance model, in practice,[16] appears to offer little insight
into describing, predicting, or generating understanding about the competitive
dynamics of the industry.

The Policy Model

   While the policy model attempts to integrate the economic and financial models
by introducing a rigorous environmental analysis, in practice the environmental
analyses within the field have been meager and quite qualitative in orientation.
The type of research required as a starting point for the policy model is expensive
and time consuming. Policy's contribution to business decision making lies clearly
beyond the stage of simply understanding a business. This "understanding" problem has thus been viewed, perhaps understandably, as the responsibility of some
other field. As a result, the policy model is concerned more with developing and
implementing rational strategies from an assumed set of resources, values, and
environmental conditions than in ascertaining the *actual state* of the important
variables within firms and industries.

   In essence, the financial and policy models both construct strategic alternatives
for individual business firms based on a set of assumptions about the environment
(especially competitive aspects of the industry) which neither field is particularly
concerned about verifying. The furtherance of understanding and the writing
about the basic businesses are left to the economists (or worse yet brokerage firms
who are about the only other writers with an industry orientation), who have designed their research for entirely different purposes, and who have analyzed data
which in many cases are irrelevant for solving a firm's strategic problem.

   In the process of examining the strategic questions facing the air transport
industry, this book suggests that an analytic approach which weaves together diverse threads from the economic, financial, and policy conceptual models will
enhance the power of research centered on the problem of gaining competitive
advantage at the level of the firm. This approach, which is sketched in the introduction, and developed in the body of the book, argues that:

---

[15] At the risk of appearing hopelessly provincial, I might point out that the 11 domestic
trunk carriers in 1969 employed 120 graduates of advanced programs of the Harvard Business
School, 70 of whom had MBA degrees. Of this total, 37 men ranked as vice presidents or higher.
   [16] In theory, of course, the finance model is still relevant in strategic decision making.

(1) The power of a firm's strategic planning in the shaping of competitive advantage proceeds from a thorough understanding of a business environment, and

(2) A thorough understanding of that environment demands the discipline and ability to pull together diverse analytic strands from the economic, financial, and policy conceptual models.

A demonstration of the analytic power of this approach to looking at industry competition may be viewed as a by-product of the research, but in reality it is a joint product. The research conclusions could not have been reached without the simultaneous appearance of the conceptual approach. For some readers, particularly those interested in the problems of doing research in the field of business administration (or who enjoy thinking seriously about strategic problems in business areas other than their own), the conceptual approach may prove to be of greater value than the airline analysis itself. If so, this excursion into the details of a conceptual approach to business problem solving will have been well worthwhile.

PART I

Industry Background

CHAPTER 1

The Air Transportation Industry
Its Market, Financial, Growth,
and Cost Structures

Market Structure

In 1968 the united states air transport industry included 38 airlines "certificated" [1] by the Civil Aeronautics Board (CAB), a regulatory agency of the federal government. Twelve of these air carriers, the eleven "domestic trunks" [2] plus Pan American World Airways received almost 90% of the industry's total revenue.

The revenue from air operations and revenue shares of the twelve major United States air carriers are shown in Table 1.1. Five of the carriers controlled over 70% of the group's total revenue, but the air transportation industry differed from many other basic American industries of comparable size in that no single company dominated the group.

---

[1] All carriers operating regularly scheduled flights over specific routes with aircraft weighing over 12,500 lbs. had to receive authority from the CAB to provide this service.

[2] The domestic trunk carriers served the larger communities with scheduled service over routes confined to the 48 contiguous states.

TABLE 1.1

TOTAL SYSTEM OPERATING REVENUES AND MARKET SHARES
DOMESTIC TRUNK CARRIERS AND PAN AMERICAN
(*Year Ended December 31, 1968*)

	System Operating Revenue (Millions of Dollars)	Revenue Share (Percent)
United	1,262	18.2
Pan American	1,030	14.9
American	957	13.9
TWA	948	13.7
Eastern	745	10.8
Delta	467	6.8
Northwest	416	6.0
Braniff	294	4.3
National	249	3.6
Western	222	3.2
Continental	208	3.0
Northeast	112	1.6
Total	6,910	100.0

SOURCE: U.S. Civil Aeronautics Board, *Air Carrier Financial Statistics*, December 1968.

FINANCIAL STRUCTURE: ASSET MANAGEMENT

Table 1.2 presents the combined balance sheet of the twelve major United States carriers. The group had assets of over $9 billion as of December 31, 1968, and the gross value of aircraft alone at that date amounted to 83% of the total figure. For this reason, the asset management function in air transportation could be redefined as the capital budgeting problem for flight equipment with little loss of detail. The asset management problem was reduced in complexity by the concentration of dollars into one or two asset categories, but this by no means made balance sheet problems trivial. Air transportation was clearly a capital intense industry; from a combination of figures in Table 1.1 and Table 1.2, it can be seen that flight equipment with a gross value of $8.0 billion and a depreciated value of $5.7 billion generated revenues of $6.9 billion. Given this degree of capital intensity, asset management constituted an area of key importance.

The volume of air transportation provided by United States air carriers grew rapidly during the decade ending with 1968 (Table 1.3).

Between 1958 and 1968 the annual compound growth rate of passenger traffic measured in terms of revenue passenger miles[3] was 14.2%. During the five-year period from 1963 to 1968 the growth rate was 17.8%.

---

[3] A revenue passenger mile is a measure of unit sales volume. It is equivalent to flying one paying passenger a distance of one air mile. An available seat mile is a unit of production. It

TABLE 1.2

COMBINED BALANCE SHEET
TOTAL DOMESTIC TRUNK CARRIERS AND PAN AMERICAN
(*December 31, 1968*)

Assets	(Millions of Dollars)	(Percent)
Current Assets	1,882	19.6
Investments	1,165	12.1
Operating Property & Equipment		
Flight Equipment (Gross)	7,986	83.2
Less Depreciation	2,334	(24.3)
Net Flight Equipment	5,652	58.9
Ground Equipment	936	
Less Depreciation	424	
Net Ground Equipment	512	5.4
Other Operating Property	215	2.2
Total Operating Property	6,379	66.5
Deferred Charges		
Total Deferred Charges	176	1.8
Total Assets	9,602	100.0

Liabilities	(Millions of Dollars)	(Percent)
Current Liabilities	1,447	15.0
Noncurrent Liabilities		
Long-term Debt*	4,456	46.5
Deferred Credits		
Deferred Federal Taxes	808	8.4
Stockholder Equity	2,891	30.1
Total Liabilities	9,602	100.0

* On December 31, 1968, these carriers had about $1 billion (at original purchase price) in additional flight equipment under long-term leases.

SOURCE: U.S. Civil Aeronautics Board, *Air Carrier Financial Statistics*, December 1968.

In a major industry study undertaken by the Air Transport Association (ATA) early in 1969, planners from the twelve major carriers projected a compound growth rate of 11.1% for the five-year period beginning with 1969.[4] This traffic growth rate would require a cumulative increase of 68% in the number of available seat miles of capacity the industry would have to provide by the end of 1973 if passenger load factors were to be maintained at the 1968 level.

represents one passenger seat flown one mile. The load factor is simply the percentage of available capacity that generates revenue, i.e., RPM/ASM.

[4] Air Transport Association of America, *Major U.S. Airlines, Economic Review and Financial Outlook 1969–1973,* June 1969.

TABLE 1.3

UNITED STATES DOMESTIC TRUNK AIRLINES

	(1) *Available Seat Miles (Billions)*	(2) *Revenue Passenger Miles (Billions)*	(3) *Passenger Load Factor (2)/(1) Percent*
1958	40.7	24.4	60.0
1963	67.6	36.4	53.8
1964	75.2	41.7	55.4
1965	88.7	49.0	55.2
1966	97.2	56.8	58.5
1967	124.1	71.0	57.2
1968	153.9	81.6	53.0

SOURCE: Air Transport Association of America, *Facts and Figures, 1969*.

Equipment Needs Translated into Cash Requirements

This projection of future traffic growth was not in itself particularly alarming when viewed against the pattern of the industry's growth over the prior ten years. The translation of this high rate of growth into cash requirements did, however, cause considerable concern within the industry. Expenditures for aircraft and ground equipment by the twelve major carriers between 1969 and 1973 were projected at $12.5 billion, an amount substantially greater than the total assets of the group at the end of 1968.

At first glance it is difficult to see how a 68% capacity expansion could have required an expenditure for flight and ground equipment equal to 155% of the gross stock of such equipment on the industry balance sheet at the end of 1968. The explanation has five parts. First, some of the new equipment purchased was simply *replacing* rather than *adding* to existing capacity. Nonjet aircraft would be entirely replaced by 1971, as would some of the early jets such as the Boeing 707 model first introduced in 1958.

Second, the investment per unit of capacity would increase substantially as the DC-10 and Boeing 747 jumbo jets entered service in 1970. Table 1.4 shows that the

TABLE 1.4

INVESTMENT PER DAILY AVAILABLE SEAT MILE

Year of Introduction	*1958*	*1966*	*1970*
Plane Type	B-707	DC-8-61	DC-10; Boeing 747
Aircraft Purchase Price	$5,000,000	$8,000,000	$20,000,000
Daily ASM Production	600,000	1,000,000	1,800,000
Aircraft Purchase Price/ Daily ASM Production	$8.30	$8.00	$11.10

SOURCE: Stuart G. Tipton, "Success Story of World Aviation," Air Transport Association of America, June 23, 1966.

investment per daily available seat mile of capacity would rise nearly 40% from a little over $8.00 for the Boeing 707 and DC-8 jets to over $11.00 for the DC-10 and Boeing 747.

Third, the cost of ground equipment needed to support the larger airplanes entering service was rising sharply. Of the industry's total capital expenditures from 1962 to 1966, 8.8% went for ground support equipment. Of the $12.5 billion capital expenditure planned for 1969–1973, $2.2 billion or 17.3% was for ground support equipment. Fourth, the $8 billion in gross flight equipment shown in Table 1.2 did not include about $1 billion in flight equipment leased by these carriers in 1968. Finally, the twelve carriers were purchasing equipment over and above the 68% capacity increase which would be necessary to sustain the passenger load factor experienced on both domestic and international operations in 1968.[5] By 1973, even if passenger traffic grew according to the airlines' projections, the aircraft capacity scheduled for delivery would reduce the industry's passenger load factor by roughly 3.2 percentage points (Table 1.5).

TABLE 1.5

ELEVEN DOMESTIC TRUNK CARRIERS AND PAN AMERICAN

	Projected Growth in RPMs	*Projected Percentage Point Change in Passenger Load Factor*
1969	13.2%	(.5)
1970	11.6	(.6)
1971	10.4	(1.4)
1972	10.4	(.1)
1973	9.8	(.6)
1969–1973	Average Growth Rate 11.1%	(3.2)

SOURCE: Air Transport Association of America, *Major U.S. Airlines: Economic Review and Financial Outlook, 1969–1973*, June 1969.

The projected expansion of the airlines' physical plant between 1969 and 1973 was clearly an enormous undertaking. In 1969 the $2.49 billion that the twelve major air carriers planned to spend represented almost 4% of the *total* projected capital spending of all United States business, up from less than 1% in 1963. In regard to the industry's expansion program, Stuart Tipton, President of the Air Transportation Association of America (ATA) stated:

No other major industry is expanding its investment base at such a rate as the airlines. No other industry is building, in effect, new plants every day of the year. The average price of a typical new factory is about one half million dollars, so it is as though the airlines were building 10 new factories every day.[6]

---

[5] An explanation for this phenomenon can be traced to the competitive environment—see Chapter 5.

[6] Stuart G. Tipton, "Air Transportation in 1967: The Opportunities and the Pressures," Air Transport Association of America, October 16, 1967.

Total Industry Cash Requirements

Although new commitments for aircraft and ground equipment were expected to represent the industry's major use of funds during the 1969–1973 period, additional resources would be needed to meet scheduled repayment of debt, dividends on common stock, and additions to working capital.

The air carriers had few difficulties projecting their funds *requirements* for the 1969–1971 three-year period. The $7.2 billion equipment expenditure was certain as a minimum,[7] since 90% of it represented firm commitments with aircraft manufacturers as of the beginning of 1969.

While the five-year projected expenditure of $12.5 billion for air and ground equipment was somewhat more speculative[8] than the three-year projection, most carriers felt committed to these purchases at least as a minimum.

The debt repayment figures needed for a funds requirement projection were also ascertainable since they were contractually fixed. Dividends could be expected to vary with profits, but a minimum payout of $96 million (the 1968 level) was viewed as firm. Working capital and other requirements were fairly predictable since they were a direct function of increased volume.

THE INDUSTRY'S INTERNAL CAPITAL SOURCES

The capital available to an air carrier came from a number of sources. Internally, a carrier was able to look to profits, depreciation, and tax deferrals or credits for funds generation. Externally, the carrier could rely on debt (or near-debt such as leases) plus the sale of equity securities. For the period 1969–1973 the ATA in June of 1969 estimated total industry cash requirements and sources under a

---

[7] Some industry spokesmen felt that the carriers' equipment expenditures would be considerably higher than $7.2 billion over the three-year period. During the 18 months spanning November 1967 to June 1969, the ATA made three surveys of planned carrier expenditures for flight and ground equipment.

Major United States Airlines Projected Expenditures
for Flight and Ground Equipment

	1969	1970	1971	1969–1971 Total
	(Millions of Dollars)			
November 1967 Estimate	2,164	1,979	1,490	5,633
June 1968 Estimate	2,344	2,180	1,918	6,442
June 1969 Estimate	2,494	2,432	2,235	7,161

As the more distant years approached, the cumulative totals got successively higher, lending some credence to the suggestion that actual spending would substantially exceed $7.2 billion.

[8] Of the $10.3 billion expenditure planned for flight equipment, 61% were firm orders, 17% were options, and 23% were orders planned but not yet announced. (It should be noted that "firm orders" could be canceled in some cases where delivery was still one or two years away for a relatively small penalty, e.g., $40,000 per plane.)

number of sets of assumptions. Estimates derived from this ATA data are presented in Tables 1.6 and 1.7.

The center portion of these figures assumed that[9]

(1) Yields (carrier revenue per RPM) would remain at the level achieved after a fare increase granted by the CAB effective February 20, 1969.
(2) Passenger load factors would decline by 3.2 percentage points between 1969 and 1973 as indicated in Table 1.5.
(3) The opposing effects of inflation cost increases and productivity savings[10] would be resolved in favor of net increases in total unit costs as shown below.

Year	Total Projected Unit Cost Increases (Percent)
1969	1.26
1970	2.05
1971	(.38)
1972	2.43
1973	2.31

This cost "tug of war" [11] between inflation and productivity, according to carrier estimates, would be won by inflation for the first time since 1959. (See Table 1.8.)

The center sections of Tables 1.6 and 1.7 depict a future course for the air transportation industry which could only be labeled a catastrophe. This portion of each exhibit is flanked on the right, however, by a slightly improved situation, and on the left by a dramatically improved picture.

The far right section of each exhibit recasts data of the middle section with a new assumption that the carriers suffer no erosion in passenger load factors. Without the burden of this extra capacity, after-tax earnings for the industry over the five-year period would be about $833 million higher.[12]

The far left section of Tables 1.6 and 1.7 finally assumes that by some combination of (1) fare increases, (2) higher than anticipated traffic growth, (3) lower than anticipated rate of inflation, and/or (4) higher than anticipated productivity savings, the carriers would be able to achieve the allowed 10.5% rate of return on investment. Under these favorable circumstances, carrier after-tax earnings for the five-year period would be more than $5 billion higher than they would have been given the assumptions of the middle section of the exhibit.

---

[9] The assumptions in (2) and (3) were supplied to the ATA by individual carrier managements who were not aware of the other carriers' estimates. The ATA aggregated the individual carrier expense and passenger load factor projections based on these individual carrier assumptions.

[10] Productivity savings generally resulted where "new generation" more efficient aircraft with lower operating costs were introduced into carrier fleets.

[11] An example of the debate on the future trend of airline unit costs can be found in J. J. Kerley and C. H. Brunie, "Industry Report, The Airlines," *The Institutional Investor*, March 1967.

[12] This is the difference between the sum of lines 1 and 4 for each section in Table 1.6.

TABLE 1.6

AIR CARRIER FINANCIAL REQUIREMENTS, 1969–1973

	Assumes Carriers Will Earn 10.5 Percent ROI (Millions of Dollars)						Assumes Constant Fare Yields, Inflated Unit Costs, Productivity Gains, and Passenger Load Factor Erosion (Millions of Dollars)						Assumes Constant Fare Yields, Inflated Unit Costs, Productivity Gains, and Constant Passenger Load Factor (Millions of Dollars)					
	1969	1970	1971	1972	1973	Total	1969	1970	1971	1972	1973	Total	1969	1970	1971	1972	1973	Total
Sources:																		
1 Earnings After Taxes Before ITC	603	684	747	787	817	3,638	322	51	(39)	(241)	(634)	(541)	348	110	107	(29)	(353)	183
2 Depreciation and Amortization	808	946	1,067	1,197	1,328	5,346	808	946	1,067	1,197	1,328	5,346	808	946	1,067	1,197	1,328	5,346
3 Deferred Taxes	350	386	387	388	407	1,918	343	—	—	—	—	343	356	41	53	—	—	450
4 Investment Tax Credit	163	155	150	167	171	806	(35)	—	—	—	—	(35)	(22)	42	54	—	—	74
5 Total Sources	1,924	2,171	2,351	2,539	2,723	11,708	1,438	997	1,028	956	694	5,113	1,490	1,139	1,281	1,168	975	6,053
Uses:																		
6 Aircraft and Ground Expenditures	2,494	2,432	2,235	2,488	2,841	12,490	2,494	2,432	2,235	2,488	2,841	12,490	2,494	2,432	2,235	2,488	2,841	12,490
7 Scheduled Debt Repayments (Existing Debt and Leases)	254	361	442	474	637	2,168	254	361	442	474	637	2,168	254	361	442	474	637	2,168
8 New Debt and Leases	—	26	48	62	79	215	—	45	105	164	236	550	—	45	105	164	236	550
9 Dividends	155	172	187	204	216	934	96	96	96	96	96	480	96	96	96	96	96	480
10 Other Cash Requirements	84	99	112	127	146	568	84	99	112	127	146	568	84	99	112	127	146	568
11 Total Uses	2,987	3,090	3,024	3,355	3,919	16,375	2,928	3,033	2,990	3,349	3,956	16,256	2,928	3,033	2,990	3,349	3,956	16,256
12 Additional Funds Required	1,063	919	673	816	1,196	4,667	1,490	2,036	1,962	2,393	3,262	11,143	1,438	1,894	1,709	2,181	2,981	10,203

SOURCE: Derived from material appearing in *Major U.S. Airlines: Economic Review and Financial Outlook 1969–1973*, Air Transport Association of America, June 1969.

TABLE 1.7

Air Carrier Capital Structure Choices, 1969–1973

		Assumes Carriers Will Earn 10.5 Percent ROI (Millions of Dollars)						Assumes Constant Fare Yields, Inflated Unit Costs, Productivity Gains, and Passenger Load Factor Erosion (Millions of Dollars)						Assumes Constant Fare Yields, Inflated Unit Costs, Productivity Gains, and Constant Passenger Load Factor (Millions of Dollars)					
		1969	1970	1971	1972	1973	Total	1969	1970	1971	1972	1973	Total	1969	1970	1971	1972	1973	Total
1	External Capital Required*	809	532	183	280	480	2,284	1,236	1,630	1,415	1,755	2,389	8,425	1,184	1,488	1,162	1,543	2,108	7,485
2	Additions to Equity Through Earnings Retentions**	611	667	710	750	772	3,510	191	(45)	(135)	(337)	(730)	(1,056)	230	76	65	(125)	(449)	(223)
	All External Capital Needed Is Raised Through Selling Debt and Equity so as to Maintain a 1.56 to 1 Debt/Equity																		
3	Debt Additions Supported by Earnings Retentions @ 1.56 to 1 Debt/Equity Ratio	953	1,040	1,108	1,170	1,205	5,476	298	—	—	—	—	298	359	128	101	—	—	588
4	Outside Equity Financing	(133)	(146)	(155)	(164)	(169)	(767)	366	665	635	891	1,377	3,934	322	530	414	678	1,098	3,042
5	Debt Addition Supported by Outside Equity Financing @ 1.56 to 1 Debt/Equity Ratio	(209)	(227)	(243)	(256)	(264)	(1,199)	572	965	780	864	1,021	4,193	503	830	647	865	1,010	3,855
6	Total Outside Capital Raised	809	532	183	280	480	2,284	1,236	1,630	1,415	1,755	2,389	8,425	1,184	1,488	1,162	1,543	2,108	7,485
7	Final Debt/Equity Ratio	1.56	1.56	1.56	1.56	1.56	1.56	1.56	1.56	1.56	1.56	1.56	1.56	1.56	1.56	1.56	1.56	1.56	1.56
	All External Capital Needed Is Raised Through Selling Debt																		
8	Debt Addition Assuming All Outside Capital Needs Are Met with Debt	809	532	183	280	480	2,284	1,236	1,630	1,415	1,755	2,389	8,425	1,184	1,488	1,162	1,543	2,108	7,485
9	Final Debt/Equity Ratio	1.50	1.39	1.22	1.11	1.05	1.05	1.84	2.40	3.00	4.08	7.00	7.00	1.80	2.23	2.53	3.13	4.44	4.44

* This amount is equal to line 12 less lines 7 and 8 of Table 1.6.
** This amount is the sum of line 1 plus line 4 minus line 9 of Table 1.6.

SOURCE: Derived from material appearing in *Major U.S. Airlines: Economic Review and Financial Outlook 1969–1973*, Air Transport Association of America, June 1969.

TABLE 1.8

MAJOR UNITED STATES AIRLINES
IMPACT OF INFLATION AND PRODUCTIVITY ON CASH OPERATING EXPENSES

	Inflation Cost Increase	*Productivity Saving* *(Millions of Dollars)*	*Net Saving in Cash Operating Costs*
1959	69	16	(53)
1960	38	91	53
1961	33	224	191
1962	9	145	136
1963	5	169	164
1964	140	314	174
1965	45	266	221
1966	236	390	154
1967	121	316	195
1968	376	591	215
1969E	372	346	(26)
1970E	884	696	(188)
1971E	1395	1212	(183)
1972E	2030	1584	(446)
1973E	2782	1990	(792)

Internal Sources of Funds—Depreciation and Amortization

Line 2 of Table 1.6 shows depreciation and amortization as the largest internal source of funds.[13] Depreciation and amortization could be calculated exactly for each future year given (1) the carrier's existing stock of equipment, (2) its future equipment acquisition plans, and (3) its depreciation accounting policy for shareholder reports.

Internal Sources of Funds—Deferred Taxes

Deferred taxes, potentially the third most important internal source of airline funds during periods of reasonable earnings, resulted from the difference in depreciation charges for shareholder and tax reporting. For tax purposes the airlines depreciated their aircraft over eight years using the sum-of-the-years' digits method with a 5% residual value. For shareholder reports the life was usually extended to 12 or 14 years; the residual value was raised to 10% or 15%; and the straight-line method of depreciation was employed. Thus, because the air carriers depreciated their equipment more rapidly for tax purposes than they did for

---

[13] Depreciation and amortization are, of course, sources only in the sense that these (and some other) noncash charges against accounting income need to be added to accounting profits after tax to determine the amount of funds provided by operations. Depreciation is tax deductible and, to that extent, has an impact on taxes and hence profit after tax.

shareholder reports, their annual *cash* tax payments were far below the amounts shown in shareholder income reports.

Given the predictability of depreciation (see above), it was possible to state that by the end of 1973 the difference in reporting could give rise potentially to deferred taxes of $1,918 million (Table 1.6, left section, line 3). Assuming a tax rate of 50%, the industry could avail itself of the full amount of the deferral if it had pretax profits of $3,836 million or more to report to its shareholders.

Internal Sources of Funds—The Investment Tax Credit

The investment tax credit[14] represented the smallest source of internally generated airline funds. Capital outlays for equipment amounting to $12.5 billion should have generated investment tax credits (ITCs) equal to $875 million. However, ITCs were available only to the extent that the federal income taxes incurred by the industry were sufficient to allow use of the credit. To take advantage of the entire credit, the airlines would have to have pretax profits of $7,336 million, resulting in a tax liability (as reported to shareholders) of $3,668 million. Deferrals resulting from accelerated depreciation charges would offset $1,918 million of this total, and the remaining $1,750 million would be needed to take advantage of half that amount ($875 million) in ITCs.

If the airlines generated after-tax profits of less than $1,918 million then their tax liability would be less than $1,918 million and some potential tax deferrals could be lost as a source of funds. With after-tax profits of less than $1,918 million the ITCs would, of course, be of no use to the carriers as a source of funds. The projections at the center and right-hand side of Table 1.6 indicate the airlines would *not* be generating sufficient profit to make even partial use of the tax incentives available to them. Consequently, the investment tax credit would at best be an uncertain and unpredictable source of funds, since the cash savings actually realized from the credit would vary directly with airline profits and taxes.

Profit—The Fundamental Determinant
of Both Internal and External Fund Sources

While (in Table 1.6) profit lags well behind depreciation and amortization in total dollar significance under all three sets of assumptions, this source of funds is really the "tail that wags the dog." As previous paragraphs have explained, other items mentioned as internal sources of funds depended on the level of profits. Thus a zero level of pretax profits between 1969 and 1973 would assure a funds flow from depreciation and amortization equal to $5,346 million over the period. If pretax profits increased to $3,836 million over the period, deferred taxes stemming from differences in reporting depreciation would be an additional funds source of $1,918 million. Finally, all $875 million of the investment tax credits

---

[14] For a description of this credit, see J. K. Butters, *Case Problems in Finance*, p. 589.

generated by the industry equipment purchases would be available as a funds source only if industry pretax profits over the period exceeded $7,336 million.

Profits were also critically important because of their impact on the availability of debt financing as a funds source. Each dollar of profit carried over to net worth generated debt capacity in excess of one dollar. Profit, then, was the crucial element in an air carrier's funds flow, yet it was precisely this item which was subject to the greatest degree of uncertainty.

The range of industry profitability separating where the industry was *heading* (middle of Table 1.6 line 1) and where the carrier managers would like to have seen it *aimed* (left side of Table 1.6, line 1) was extraordinarily wide. While the CAB would almost certainly not permit the carriers' financial position to deteriorate to the level shown in the middle section of Table 1.6, in its discussions about fare increases the Board was concerned about the potential costs of excess capacity. Some measure of this "cost" can be seen from a comparison of the middle and right-hand sections of Table 1.6. The $833 million difference[15] in after-tax profits for the five-year period could be attributed wholly to the expected 3.2 percentage point erosion in passenger load factors. This contrast clearly shows the powerful adverse impact on profit which results when carriers "overbuy" equipment; i.e., when the rate of expansion in available seat miles of industry capacity exceeds the rate of traffic growth.

Since profitability was so crucial to an air carrier's financial strength, the following section of this chapter will explore in some detail (1) the determinants of airline profitability, and (2) the inherent instability of airline profits. In order to explain the wide differences in individual carrier profitability, the chapter will temporarily move away from aggregate industry data.

Determinants of Airline Profitability

Before beginning the analysis of airline economics, it is appropriate to define or redefine some industry terminology. The unit of production of an air carrier is called an "available seat mile" (ASM). It represents one passenger seat flown one mile. The airlines use "available seat miles" rather than "passenger miles" flown as a measure of production since air carrier costs are more directly related to the number of *seats* than to the number of *passengers* flown over a given distance. Once an airplane is scheduled on a particular flight, the total cost of that flight varies only slightly with the number of passengers that the plane is carrying. This characteristic of individual flight operation gives rise to the industry view of itself as having an extremely high percentage of fixed costs over all. An industry rule of thumb states that the variable cost of adding an extra passenger to a flight amounts to only 10% of the fare paid by that passenger and that the remaining 90% passes directly through as a contribution to operating profit.

---

[15] This is the difference between the sum of lines 1 and 4 for each section in the table.

While *costs* are tied most closely to available seat miles, the *revenue* generated on a flight is directly related to (1) the number of passengers carried, (2) how far they are flown, and (3) how much these passengers pay per mile of flight. The first two factors are measured in terms of revenue passenger miles (RPMs).

The 1968 operating data for Trans World Airlines (TWA) provide a good illustration of airline economics. In 1968, TWA flew 30,656 million available seat miles (ASMs) on both domestic and international routes. Paying passengers filled 49.65% of the available capacity, thereby generating 15,221 million revenue passenger miles (RPMs). TWA received a total of $788,909,000 for this transportation service in 1968, giving the company an average yield per RPM equal to 5.183¢. The cost to TWA for providing passenger transportation was equal to $757,774,000. If this total cost were broken down according to the rule of thumb mentioned earlier, the fixed and variable components were equal to $678,883,000 and $78,891,000 respectively. In accord with industry practice, short-run fixed costs were considered to be unrelated to the number of passengers flown and were expressed on a "per unit of capacity" basis. TWA's fixed unit cost per available seat mile could thus be computed as 2.215¢ for 1968. TWA's figure for variable costs could be expressed on a per unit basis in terms of revenue passenger miles flown. On a per unit basis these variable costs were equal to .518¢ per revenue passenger mile in 1968 (see Table 1.9).

TABLE 1.9

OPERATING DATA FOR 1968: TRANS WORLD AIRLINES

Available Seat Miles Flown (Millions)	30,656
Revenue Passenger Miles Flown (Millions)	15,221
Passenger Revenue (Thousands of Dollars)	788,909
Total Passenger Costs (Thousands of Dollars)	757,774
Total Fixed Costs (Thousands of Dollars)	678,883
Total Variable Costs (Thousands of Dollars)	78,891
Revenue Yield = Revenue/RPM (Cents)	5.183
Fixed Unit Cost = Fixed Costs/ASM (Cents)	2.215
Variable Unit Cost = Variable Costs/RPM (Cents)	.518
Passenger Load Factor (Percent)	49.65
Breakeven Passenger Load Factor (Percent)	47.48
Operating Profit (Thousands of Dollars)	31,135

Factors Influencing Airline Profits

Given the assumption of a high fixed cost structure in the short run, airline profitability could vary widely in response to relatively small changes in a number of variables. Figure 1.1 gives a simple picture of how TWA's costs, revenue, and operating profits might have varied in 1968 as a function of the carrier's actual passenger load factor. Over a one-year period individual carriers actually had a

FIGURE 1.1

TRANS WORLD AIRLINES 1968 BREAKEVEN CHART

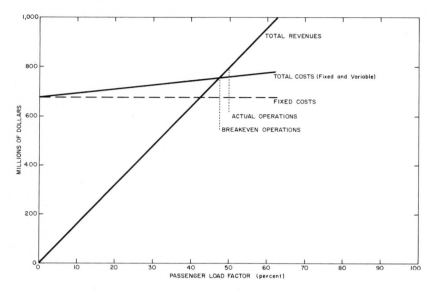

SOURCE: Derived from data in Table 1.9.

good deal more control over what are called "fixed costs" in Table 1.9 than this table suggests. For simplicity in presentation, however, we will assume that a carrier's flight schedule is essentially frozen over 12-month intervals. In reality, the carriers make major schedule changes semiannually, and minor changes at least on a monthly basis.

Equations 1.1 and 1.2 give a mathematical view of the way in which airline profits respond to changes in a number of variables.

EQUATION 1.1

$$\text{Operating Profit} = \text{ASMs [Revenue Yield} - \text{Variable Unit Cost]}$$
$$\times$$
$$\text{[Passenger Load Factor} - \text{Breakeven Passenger Load Factor]}$$

EQUATION 1.2

$$\text{Breakeven Load Factor} = \frac{\text{Fixed Unit Cost}}{\text{Revenue Yield} - \text{Variable Unit Cost}}$$

The first equation shows how operating profits are algebraically related to ASMs, yields, unit costs, and the spread between *actual* and *breakeven*[16] passenger load factors. By using this equation we can show that in 1968, a one percentage point

---

[16] The breakeven passenger load factor is that load factor which a carrier would have to achieve to just cover all of its costs, thus achieving a zero level of profit.

increase in TWA's actual passenger load factor would have raised the carrier's operating profit from $31.1 million to $45.3 million. In a similar fashion, the second equation could be used to show that a 1% decrease in fixed unit costs would reduce the carrier's breakeven passenger load factor from 47.48% to 47.01%. When this piece of information is then used in the first equation, we see that a 1% decrease in TWA's fixed unit costs in 1968 would have raised operating profits from $31.1 million to $37.8 million. If the same procedure outlined above were carried out for a 1% increase in revenue yields, we would find that the carrier's breakeven load factor would have been reduced from 47.48% to 47.02% and that operating profits would have risen accordingly from $31.1 million to $37.8 million.

Actual Passenger Load Factors

Actual passenger load factors for the domestic trunk airlines have varied substantially in recent years because of the inability of the air carriers to phase in new seating capacity in line with the growth in passenger traffic. Columns 4 through 6 in Table 1.10 show that capacity expansions differing sharply from traffic growth could rapidly alter passenger load factors. Capacity expansion is based primarily on decisions taken far in the past. Firm purchase commitments for aircraft typically had to be made 14 to 18 months in advance of actual delivery dates,[17] and this lead time might increase to three or more years for models ordered prior to the start of commercial production.

While capacity was added according to a schedule determined some time in the past, increases in passenger traffic were not nearly so predictable. Although the carriers expended a great deal of time and effort in predicting traffic growth, one industry analyst stated,

> For planning purposes Carrier X used to project traffic growth pretty much by intuition. This approach yielded them consistently terrible results, so they built an elegant model using historical data which tied traffic growth to G.N.P., personal disposable income, corporate profits, and a number of other important variables. While the model "fit" past data very well, it wasn't any better than intuition as a predictive tool, and now Carrier X is back to adjusting the model's predictions by gut feel.

The carriers generally tried to plan capacity additions which were in line with their projections of traffic growth, but they sometimes overbought aircraft for reasons that will be outlined in Chapter 5. Overbuying of aircraft led to reduced load factors which in turn resulted in lower profits. Indeed, industry operating

---

[17] This was the typical pattern of lead times for B-727 and B-707 aircraft during the period from 1967 to 1969. Occasionally one or two aircraft could be purchased on shorter notice if the manufacturer was building planes on a speculative basis, or if some other carrier cancelled an order. During about 80% of the time cycle over which a particular model aircraft was being produced, however, carriers could not anticipate deliveries in less than 14 months from the time of an order.

TABLE 1.10

STATISTICAL FACTS—DOMESTIC OPERATIONS OF THE DOMESTIC TRUNK AIRLINES

1	2	3	4	5	6	7	8	9	10	11	12	13
Year	Available Seat Miles (Millions)	Revenue Passenger Miles (Millions)	Growth in ASMs Over Prior Year (Percent)	Growth in RPMs Over Prior Year (Percent)	Actual Passenger Load Factor (Percent)	Breakeven Passenger Load Factor (Percent)	Percentage Points Above Breakeven Passenger Load Factor	Total Operating Profits (Millions of Dollars)	Return on Investment (Percent)*	Yields (Cents/RPM)	ASMs in Jet Aircraft (Percent)	Industry Debt/Equity Ratio
1939	1,210	654	28.0	42.9	54.1	—	—	5	—	5.07	0	.13
1949	11,118	6,571	11.4	12.5	59.1	—	—	25	5.2	5.75	0	.66
1950	12,385	7,766	11.7	18.6	62.7	—	—	63	11.2	5.54	0	.53
1951	14,671	10,210	18.5	31.9	69.6	—	—	110	13.6	5.59	0	.47
1952	18,068	12,120	23.1	18.7	67.1	—	—	95	13.6	5.54	0	.46
1953	22,114	14,297	22.1	18.0	64.7	—	—	88	11.2	5.43	0	.39
1954	25,623	16,234	15.6	13.5	63.4	56.5	6.9	99	10.4	5.37	0	.42
1955	30,001	19,217	16.8	18.8	64.1	56.6	7.5	123	11.8	5.32	0	.40
1956	33,753	21,643	13.0	12.7	64.1	58.7	5.4	101	9.4	5.28	0	.56
1957	39,838	24,500	18.0	13.0	61.5	59.6	1.9	42	4.8	5.25	0	.76
1958	40,695	24,436	2.1	.0	60.0	56.0	4.0	95	6.5	5.58	5	.88
1959	45,793	28,127	12.8	15.2	61.4	57.5	3.9	105	7.1	5.80	36	1.08
1960	49,154	29,233	7.5	4.0	59.5	58.3	1.2	34	2.8	6.01	56	1.58
1961	52,525	29,535	7.0	1.0	56.2	56.0	.2	(11)	1.5	6.19	72	1.99
1962	59,736	31,828	13.8	9.7	53.3	51.3	2.0	75	4.1	6.35	81	1.98
1963	67,601	36,384	13.2	14.2	53.8	50.7	3.1	129	4.3	6.07	83	1.68
1964	75,242	41,658	11.2	14.4	55.4	48.9	6.5	297	9.6	6.01	87	1.48
1965	88,731	48,987	18.0	17.5	55.2	47.6	7.8	416	11.2	5.94	92	1.15
1966	97,174**	56,802	9.5	16.5	58.5	50.3	8.2	454	9.7	5.69	96	1.28
1967	124,142	70,990	28.0	25.0	57.2	51.3	5.9†	410	7.7	5.50	98	1.33
1968	153,864	81,611	23.9	15.0	53.0	49.5	3.5	320	5.7	5.45	99	1.57
1969	185,832	92,573	20.8	13.4	49.8	47.1	2.7	304	5.1	5.63		1.53
1970	191,972	93,939	3.3	1.5	49.3***	49.6***	(.3)	16	1.1	5.81		1.83

* Return on Investment is defined as net income before interest and after taxes as a percent of net worth plus long-term debt.

** Production problems encountered by the airframe manufacturers caused a large number of aircraft deliveries scheduled for 1966 to be deferred to 1967.

*** Includes Pan American domestic data.

† In 1967 the eleven domestic trunk carriers plus Pan American as a group in the domestic and international markets flew with an actual passenger load factor equal to 56.9% and a breakeven load factor equal to 48.8%, giving these carriers a spread of 8.1 percentage points between their actual and breakeven load factors.

SOURCE: CAB; ATA.

profits were so closely related to passenger load factors that one industry spokes-man speculated that the rich airline returns of the mid-1960s (column 10, Table 1.10) occurred primarily because actual traffic growth was much higher than the carriers had anticipated when they made their equipment plans. "The industry simply didn't have a chance to overbuy equipment quickly enough when it was confronted with larger than anticipated traffic increases."

Breakeven Load Factors

Actual passenger load factors represented only one-half of the airline profit picture. Operating profit depended on the *difference* between the actual load factor and the breakeven load factor. While actual load factors in the mid-1960s were far lower than they were ten years earlier, over the same period industry breakeven load factors dropped at an even faster rate (column 7, Table 1.10), thus widening the differential and expanding industry profits. Since the yields per revenue passenger mile in 1956 were not markedly different from the yields of 1966, it is clear from the definition of breakeven load factors (footnote 16 and Equation 1.2) that the change in breakeven had to be due to a reduction in unit costs. This lowering of unit costs coincided with the industry's changeover from piston-power aircraft to jets that offered dramatically lower operating costs. This fleet changeover process was almost complete by the end of 1967 (column 12, Table 1.10).

During this period, productivity cost savings resulting from the introduction of new equipment far outpaced the rate of cost increases caused by inflation (Table 1.8). These savings might have been (1) added to industry profits, (2) passed on to the consumer in terms of reduced fares, or (3) absorbed in the process of generating lower load factors. In fact, they were realized in the form of lower load factors.

Route Structure as a Factor in Individual Carrier Profitability

To this point the discussion of airline profitability has ignored the relation-ship between a carrier's route structure and its yields, unit costs, and passenger load factors. When this relationship is brought into the discussion, it helps to ex-plain wide differences in profitability among the individual air carriers. (Figure 1.2 shows differences in load factors and return on investment for a sample of carriers.) First, while the industry yield per revenue passenger mile averaged 5.45¢ in 1968, this number merely represented the average of a wide range of actual yields experienced by the carriers on different routes. For instance, yields per RPM were traditionally higher on international flights over the Pacific than they were on flights to Western Europe. In addition, because of special fare discounting, routes which catered mainly to vacation rather than business traffic generally produced lower yields. Lower yields, of course, raised a carrier's breakeven load factor (as shown in Equation 1.1). Thus a carrier's "mix" of routes with varying yields per revenue passenger mile could substantially influence its breakeven load factor.

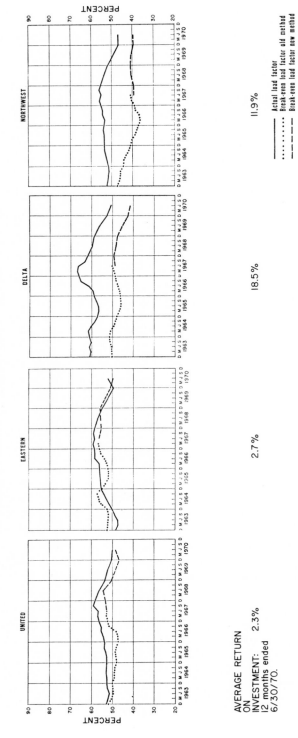

FIGURE 1.2

Trends in Actual and Breakeven Passenger Load Factors: by Selected Carrier Groups
Scheduled Service of Certificated Route Air Carriers

AVERAGE RETURN
ON
INVESTMENT: 2.3%   2.7%   18.5%   11.9%
12 months ended
6/30/70.

Source: Air Carrier Analytical Charts and Supplemental Carrier Statistics, CAB, March 1970.

Second, some carriers faced very little competition from other carriers on many of their routes. Where a carrier had a "monopoly" or a market share of greater than 80% on a route, it was under less pressure to expand seating capacity as passenger traffic grew. For this reason, a carrier would almost always achieve substantially higher passenger load factors on a "monopoly" route than it would on a competitive route, and would usually spend significantly less per RPM generated on advertising. The "mix" of competitive versus monopoly routes served by a carrier (Table 1.11), could thus importantly influence both its actual and break-even passenger load factors (Figure 1.2).

TABLE 1.11

MIX OF TRAFFIC CARRIED IN MONOPOLY VERSUS HIGHLY COMPETITIVE MARKETS
SELECTED TRUNK CARRIERS
1967

Carrier's Market Share Position on Routes	Percentage of the Carrier's Total Revenue Passenger Miles Flown on Routes in Which the Carrier Held Market Shares Within the Intervals Indicated in the Left Scale			
	United	*Eastern*	*Delta*	*Northwest*
100% (Total Monopoly)	20.5%	10.5%	14.6%	10.2%
80% to 100%	33.5	30.4	45.2	46.4
60% to 100%	53.8	47.1	57.9	63.3
40% to 100%	71.5	81.1	89.1	76.3
20% to 100%	96.2	95.3	95.7	97.2
0% to 100%	100.0	100.0	100.0	100.0

SOURCE: Competition Among Domestic Air Carriers, Volume VIII-5, 1967, Civil Aeronautics Board.

Finally, the fare structure (which had evolved as a result of CAB rate decisions over the years) tended to favor the carriers which were heavily committed to serving nonstop, long haul routes. Over short distances, the cost of providing air transportation was probably higher than most consumers would be willing to pay for air service. To encourage the provision of short distance air transport at low rates, the CAB had permitted a fare structure in which profit on long hauls was supposed to "subsidize" a carrier's unprofitable short hauls. Figure 1.3 depicts the average "cost" of service (including a profit) and the average yield per revenue passenger mile, with both of these factors plotted against the length of the route flown. The exhibit indicates that a carrier had to have a route structure which allowed it to fly each passenger an average of 1,400 miles in order to earn a 10% return on investment if the planes were to fly with a 50% passenger load factor at 1967 fares. Clearly then, through its influence on unit costs, the mix of long versus short haul routes could have an important impact on a carrier's breakeven load factor.

FIGURE 1.3

Typical Carrier
Yields Versus Cost of Service
for Flights of Various Lengths
1967

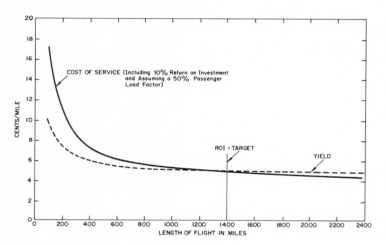

Source: Private Carrier Data.

Managing Corporate Liabilities:
The Industry's External Financing Sources

The asset management function cannot be carried on in a vacuum. An intelligent plan for the use of funds ought to be accompanied by a parallel plan which maps out sources of funds. Liabilities management is thus an essential corollary to asset management. For air transport companies, capital availability is often the constraining factor which limits corporate expansion. Since this is true, managing corporate liabilities becomes a crucial management task.

Long-Term Debt, the Major External Source of Funds

The projections of funds sources and uses in Table 1.6 show that without a fare increase or some other unexpected and fortuitous event the twelve major airlines could expect a cumulative internal cash deficit of somewhere between $10 billion and $11 billion during the period 1969–1973 (line 12, Table 1.6). Whatever its ultimate size, this cash shortage would have to be met with outside financing, and the principal source of the financing would almost certainly have been some form of long-term debt. The carriers should have had little trouble rolling over the more than $2 billion in debt scheduled for repayment from 1969 through 1973, and assuming reasonable profitability some additional debt should have become available as the airlines expanded their equity base through earnings retentions.

The amount of new debt which the carriers would be able to take on in the future was naturally a matter of crucial significance. In this regard, the carriers were in a tug-of-war with industry lenders in determining a proper debt to equity ratio for companies in the air transport business. The principal lenders to the airline industry had in the past given the carriers wide latitude in their debt to equity ratios. At one point during the dark days of the early 1960s when airline profits all but disappeared, for a period of two years the lenders allowed the carriers to reach debt to equity ratios nearing two to one (Table 1.12). Lenders

TABLE 1.12

DOMESTIC TRUNK CARRIERS: HISTORICAL MEASURES OF INDUSTRY DEBT BURDEN

Year	Long-Term Debt (Millions of Dollars)	Equity (Millions of Dollars)	Debt/ Equity	Interest on Long-Term Debt (Millions of Dollars)	Cash Flow* (Millions of Dollars)	Long-Term Debt/ Cash Flow	Earnings before Interest & Taxes (Millions of Dollars)	Earnings before Interest & Taxes/ Interest (Times)
1951	134	288	.47	6	104	1.3	115	19.0
..	.	.	.	.	.	.	.	.
1955	199	504	.40	8	187	1.1	128	16.0
1956	324	575	.56	11	194	1.7	111	10.0
1957	469	638	.76	18	210	2.3	55	3.0
1958	589	687	.88	27	230	2.6	99	3.7
1959	805	743	1.08	35	291	2.8	109	3.1
1960	1,069	739	1.58	47	272	3.9	57	1.2
1961	1,409	717	1.99	69	275	5.1	−10	−.2
1962	1,450	731	1.98	80	373	3.9	115	1.4
1963	1,330	795	1.68	78	428	3.1	173	2.2
1964	1,436	970	1.48	77	541	2.7	371	4.8
1965	1,597	1,386	1.15	81	676	2.4	535	6.6
1966	2,278	1,779	1.28	93	734	3.1	574	6.2
1967	2,989	2,255	1.33	105	943	3.2	576	5.5
1968	3,768	2,408	1.56	154	909	4.2	474	3.1
1969	3,755	2,611	1.44	189	973	3.9	442	2.3
1970	4,280	2,485	1.72	198	731	5.9	79	.4

* Cash flow includes the sum of profit after taxes, depreciation and amortization, and deferred taxes.

SOURCE: U.S. Civil Aeronautics Board, *Air Carrier Financial Statistics.*

were not comfortable with airline debt at these levels, however, and most of these men looked for a long-term average even lower than the 1.56 to 1 level reached in 1968.

The Financing Problem Assuming Dismal Earnings Projections

If the carriers were to maintain the 1.56 to 1 debt to equity ratio realized in 1968, and the industry failed to gain a fare increase, then the external equity financing required to meet the industry's cash shortfall might amount to $3.9 billion as shown in the middle section of line 4, Table 1.7. The total debt which these internal (line 2) and external (line 4) equity additions could support would amount to $4.5 billion as shown on lines 3 and 5 of Table 1.7, leaving carrier managers with a total capital raising burden equal to $8.4 billion. If the carriers hoped to meet their external capital needs without resorting to any new equity additions, then due to the depressed condition of the industry, the debt to equity ratio would, as indicated in line 9 of Table 1.7, rise to the outlandish level of 7 to 1.

Clearly the CAB would never leave the industry in such a precarious position; at least $2 billion would have to be added to the industry's pretax profit over the period just to bring the return on investment into the 4%–5% range. This sum would lower the industry's external equity capital need by about $1.5 billion, leaving a total of $2.4 billion to be raised assuming a 1.56 to 1 debt to equity ratio. Even with this large increment to profit, however, the sums of external capital required were still staggering.

Current Constraints on Borrowing Capacity

If the carriers were able to earn at least a 4%–5% return on investment and if lenders had permitted the airlines to raise their debt to equity ratio well above 1.56 to 1, the industry's external capital needs possibly could have been raised principally from debt sources. The industry's lenders seemed to feel, however, that the volatility of airline earnings in relation to the industry's capital investment did not justify higher debt to equity ratios. Indeed, the airline debt to equity ratio of 1.56 to 1 already looked quite high in terms of the volatility of the industry's past profit performance. Other regulated industries had shown a far more secure and consistent pattern of returns (Figure 1.4).

In addition, aggregate industry totals masked the fact that some carriers (especially the larger ones) had debt/equity ratios which substantially exceeded 1.56 to 1 (Table 1.13), especially if long-term leases were capitalized as debt.

Concentration of Airline Financing Sources

A lack of enthusiasm among lenders for higher debt to equity ratios was not, however, the item of immediate and major concern for airline financial officers. These men were more concerned with the problem of simply finding lenders to advance the funds required to *sustain* the existing 1.56 to 1 debt to equity ratio as the airline equity base increased. Their problem stemmed from the fact that in the past almost all airline debt had been placed privately with insurance compa-

FIGURE 1.4

DEBT TO EQUITY RATIOS AND RETURN ON INVESTMENT
FOR SELECTED INDUSTRIES

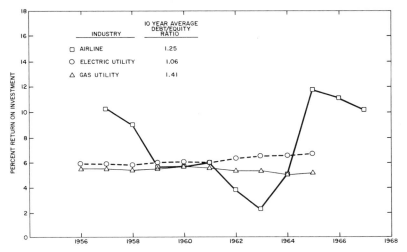

nies and banks. In 1968 these institutions owned, respectively, 37% and 27% of all domestic trunk airline debt (Table 1.14). In addition, almost all of the debt held by these institutions was concentrated in a very few insurance companies and banks that maintained departments of financial officers and staff analysts with a specific expertise in airline lending. In 1968, three major insurance companies owned 60% of the total airline debt purchased by the life insurance industry. These same insurance companies held only 35% of total life insurance company financial assets. Similarly, three commercial banks held 47% of all airline debt in the hands of banking institutions. These same three banks held only 15% of total commercial bank financial assets.

As long as total airline debt remained below one or two billion dollars, a few financial institutions could, on a private placement basis, provide all of the debt capital needed by the industry. By 1968, however, airline debt had grown to the point where large noteholders were unwilling or unable to participate in new loan commitments solely because of the amount of total airline debt they already held. In the future, this problem promised to become acute.

Growth Rate of Debt Holdings by Individuals and Institutions

By 1968, the debt capital requirements of the airlines industry were expanding so rapidly that air carrier financial managers had to begin to consider the impact of their collective debt desires on the United States capital markets. Total airline debt was not, in the late 1960s, large with respect to all corporate debt outstand-

TABLE 1.13

Domestic Trunk Carriers
Long-Term Debt and Debt Equivalents Versus Equity
(*December 31, 1968*)

	Long-Term Debt/Equity	Percentage of Aircraft Fleet on Long-Term Lease
American	1.80	14.2
Braniff	2.56	8.3
Continental	2.83	1.9
Delta	.93	1.2
Eastern	2.66	31.2
National	.75	1.9
Northeast	6.54	80.6
Northwest	.52	0
Trans World	1.67	16.2
United	1.43	18.7
Western	1.96	0

Source: U.S. Civil Aeronautics Board, *Air Carrier Financial Statistics;* U.S. Civil Aeronautics Board, Docket #21866-2, Notice of Proposed Rulemaking, September 10, 1970, Appendix A, p. 1.

ing. As shown in Table 1.15 the outstanding total value of the debt securities issued by United States nonfinancial corporations totaled $135.6 billion in 1968 versus $3.8 billion for the airlines alone.

However, airline debt was growing more rapidly than total corporate debt, and there were some indications that corporate bonds in general were becoming less attractive to their traditional purchasers than alternative investments.

According to Table 1.15, the corporate debt of nonfinancial corporations had grown at a compound rate of 7.3 annually over the 9-year period 1959–1968. Airline debt, by comparison, had grown at an annual rate exceeding 18%. During the same period, life insurance companies, the principal purchasers of airline debt securities, were willing to expand their holdings of corporate bonds at the far slower rate of 4.8%. Indeed, the trend of the data in Table 1.16 indicates that almost all of the sectors supplying debt capital to corporations, with the exception of state and local governments' retirement funds, were expanding their corporate bond portfolios at a much slower rate than their total financial assets were growing. Private pension plans, for example, nearly tripled their financial assets between 1959 and 1968, but they less than doubled their bond holdings over the same period. Households doubled their financial assets, yet their total corporate bond holdings held constant until 1965. Even with the doubling in long-term interest rates which occurred between 1965 and 1970, of all the significant bond purchasing financial sectors, only households[18] were expanding their bond holdings at a rate substantially more rapid than their growth in total financial

---

[18] Sidney Homer, "Stocks versus Bonds: A Comparison of Supply and Demand Factors," *The Institutional Investor,* August 1968.

TABLE 1.14

Summary of Airline Indebtedness
(As of December 31, 1968, in Millions of Dollars)

Carrier and Carrier Groups	Total	Insurance Companies	Banks	Airline Suppliers	Other Identified	Other Unidentified
Domestic Trunkline:						
American	695.7	349.4	.6	69.5	105.8	170.2
Eastern	638.2	213.5	167.5	39.2	76.7	141.3
Trans World	592.1	299.5	104.9	—	93.8	93.9
United	815.3	347.3	73.1	20.0	256.4	118.6
Other	1,175.2	244.8	699.8	79.8	66.2	102.7
Total	3,916.5	1,454.5	1,045.9	190.5	598.9	626.7
International and Territorial:						
Pan American	673.1	258.9	143.0	0	114.0	157.3

Insurance Firms Financing Airlines
(As of December 31, 1968, in Millions of Dollars)

	Total Loans No.*	Amount	AA	EA	TW	UA	PA	BN	CO	DL	NA	NE	NW	WA	Others
Metropolitan Life	4	515.6	192.2	—	66.2	166.7	90.5	—	—	—	—	—	—	—	0
Prudential	9	366.7	93.8	55.0	2.5	81.7	60.0	—	—	21.0	—	—	11.6	37.9	3.2
Equitable Life Assurance	6	221.8	32.3	103.0	66.2	15.0	—	—	—	—	—	—	—	—	5.3
Aetna Life	13	162.8	—	—	45.0	10.0	10.0	—	15.4	—	—	3.0	1.7	—	77.7
John Hancock Mutual Life	5	93.8	30.5	—	46.2	12.0	2.5	—	4.8	4.2	—	—	—	—	2.6
Connecticut General Life	11	67.6	—	7.0	12.7	4.6	14.5	6.6	—	4.5	—	—	2.3	—	10.9
Mutual Life of New York	3	59.6	—	—	—	35.1	—	20.0	7.0	—	—	—	—	—	0
Travelers	7	53.8	—	—	20.9	—	9.0	10.0	—	—	—	1.0	1.9	—	4.0
Northwestern Mutual Life	5	51.4	—	5.0	15.0	—	15.1	10.4	7.0	—	—	—	5.8	—	0
New England Mutual Life	9	39.6	—	3.0	7.5	5.0	7.9	15.4	—	—	—	2.0	1.6	—	0
Other*		216.4	.6	40.5	17.3	17.2	49.3	—	24.7	2.8	—	4.0	6.0	7.1	32.1
Total		1,849.1	349.4	213.5	299.5	347.3	258.9	67.5	58.9	32.5	0	10.0	31.0	45.0	135.8

Banks Engaged in Financing Carriers
(As of December 31, 1968, in Millions of Dollars)

	Total Loans No.*	Amount	AA	EA	TW	UA	PA	BN	CO	DL	NA	NE	NW	WA	Others
Chase Manhattan	18	362.7	—	46.0	—	3.4	12.2	14.7	91.7	11.6	15.0	11.6	—	110.5	183.1
Bank of America	14	287.5	—	1.0	—	3.4	6.8	—	—	—	—	—	132.0	—	139.2
Bankers Trust	6	167.6	—	8.0	—	3.3	10.8	9.5	—	28.1	25.0	—	—	—	4.0
First National City	10	153.0	—	27.7	39.1	10.4	12.2	14.7	—	8.3	25.0	—	—	—	34.9
Morgan Guaranty	6	84.9	—	6.7	—	3.3	19.2	—	—	—	—	—	—	—	8.3
Chemical Bank of New York	6	74.2	—	14.6	—	3.3	6.8	—	—	—	—	—	—	—	9.8
Manufacturers Hanover	8	61.0	—	6.1	3.8	5.2	10.8	14.7	—	28.1	—	—	—	—	3.2
Continental Ill. National	8	52.9	—	5.1	—	1.0	6.8	9.5	—	13.2	15.0	—	—	—	9.3
United California	6	31.6	—	—	—	—	—	—	—	11.6	15.0	—	—	—	.6
Irving Trust	3	30.0	—	6.4	—	—	3.4	—	—	—	5.0	—	—	—	8.6
Other		424.7	.6	45.9	62.0	36.5	54.3	16.4	—	64.4	—	—	—	—	139.6
Total		1,730.1	.6	167.5	104.9	73.1	143.0	89.0	91.7	165.0	100.0	11.6	132.0	110.5	540.6

*Treating all indebtedness of a carrier as a single issue.

NOTE: Totals may not add due to rounding.
SOURCE: U.S. Civil Aeronautics Board, Annual Report, 1969, pp. 102–112.

TABLE 1.15

VALUE OF CORPORATE BONDS OUTSTANDING
(*Billions of Dollars*)

	1959	1960	1961	1962	1963	1964	1965	1966	1967	1968	1969	1970
All Nonfinancial Corporations	71.9	75.3	80.0	84.5	88.4	92.4	97.8	108.0	122.7	135.6	147.6	167.9
Domestic Trunk Air Carriers	.8	1.1	1.4	1.5	1.3	1.4	1.6	2.3	3.0	3.8	3.8	4.3

SOURCE: Flow of Funds Accounts 1959–1970, Board of Governors of the Federal Reserve System, May 4, 1971; U.S. Civil Aeronautics Board, Air Carrier Financial Statistics.

assets. Given the alternative investment opportunities in other financial asset types, long-term fixed income investments in corporate bonds were evidently losing their attractiveness to the traditional suppliers of this type of capital.

Lease and Convertible Debt Financing

As alternatives to straight debt and common equity, the air carriers had also made extensive use of two somewhat more complex financing instruments: investment tax credit (ITC) leases and convertible debentures. By the end of 1968 air carriers were financing equipment worth $1 billion via ITC leases, and had about $1 billion in convertible debt outstanding.

The ITC leases, though not appearing on the carriers' balance sheets,[19] involved long-term financial obligations having nearly the same financial burden as term loans secured by flight equipment. Commercial banks and wealthy individuals, the latter often contacted via investment bankers, acted as principals in most ITC lease financing. The principals themselves typically supplied roughly 20% of the capital involved in an ITC lease transaction. The remainder of the purchase price was usually borrowed (normally with the guarantee of the carrier-lessee) from insurance companies, pension funds, or the public via the sale of loan certificates which were similar to railroad equipment trust certificates.

As a financing vehicle, ITC leases became so popular with cash-short airline financial officers that in 1969 . . . "about half the trunks' new aircraft acquisitions . . . were obtained by lease." [20]

ITC leases were equally popular with banks which frequently acted as owner-lessors. A full-payout lease involving the purchase of $100 million in aircraft equipment would generate an immediate tax savings of $7 million for a prospective bank-owner (as a result of the 7% investment tax credit). Since the investment required to generate this $7 million boost in after-tax profits was only $20 million as explained above, bankers did not require much additional encourage-

[19] The amounts of yearly lease obligations were footnoted, but the amount of financing provided by the lease was not shown as a liability. Of course, the value of the leased flight equipment was also absent from the asset side of the carriers' balance sheets.

[20] U.S. Civil Aeronautics Board, Docket #21866-2, Notice of Proposed Rulemaking, September 10, 1970, p. 3.

TABLE 1.16

SECTOR STATEMENTS OF FINANCIAL ASSETS:
VALUE OF CORPORATE BONDS AND STOCKS OUTSTANDING
(Billions of Dollars)

Year-end Outstanding	1959	1960	1961	1962	1963	1964	1965	1966	1967	1968	1969	1970
LIFE INSURANCE COMPANIES												
Total Financial Assets	110.1	115.0	122.8	129.2	136.9	144.9	154.1	161.8	173.0	182.8	190.2	199.0
Corporate Bonds	46.5	48.2	50.7	53.2	56.0	58.3	61.1	63.5	67.3	71.2	72.7	74.2
Corporate Shares	4.6	5.0	6.3	6.3	7.1	7.9	9.1	8.8	11.8	13.2	13.1	14.5
STATE AND LOCAL GOVERNMENT RETIREMENT FUNDS												
Total Financial Assets	17.3	19.6	22.0	24.5	26.9	29.7	33.1	37.1	41.5	46.1	50.8	57.9
Corporate Bonds	5.5	6.7	8.5	10.4	12.3	14.2	16.3	18.9	22.3	24.8	27.8	31.8
Corporate Shares	.3	.4	.6	.8	1.0	1.3	1.6	2.1	2.8	4.1	5.8	8.0
PRIVATE PENSION FUNDS												
Total Financial Assets	34.1	38.2	46.3	47.3	55.4	63.9	72.6	73.8	88.1	100.1	101.2	107.2
Corporate Bonds	14.1	15.7	16.9	18.1	19.6	21.2	22.7	24.6	25.5	26.2	26.8	29.2
Corporate Shares	14.5	16.5	22.9	21.9	27.7	33.5	39.7	38.5	51.1	61.4	61.6	64.3
HOUSEHOLDS, PERSONAL TRUSTS, AND NONPROFIT ORGANIZATIONS												
Total Financial Assets	935.0	957.1	1,100.4	1,074.2	1,201.6	1,331.4	1,469.6	1,446.1	1,679.4	1,880.8	1,840.0	1,886.9
Corporate Bonds	9.4	9.8	10.4	9.7	9.2	9.3	10.6	12.3	17.1	22.6	27.9	39.7
Investment Co. Shares	15.8	17.0	22.9	21.3	25.2	27.2	35.2	34.8	44.7	52.7	48.3	47.6
Other Corp. Shares	385.0	377.2	476.4	414.2	486.8	560.2	629.7	559.1	706.2	818.5	724.7	699.4
OTHER INSURANCE COMPANIES												
Total Financial Assets	27.1	28.2	31.6	32.6	35.3	38.1	39.8	40.0	44.1	48.4	49.0	51.8
Corporate Bonds	1.6	1.7	1.7	2.1	2.0	2.4	3.0	3.6	4.3	5.5	6.3	7.4
Corporate Shares	9.1	9.4	11.8	11.1	13.0	14.7	15.3	13.8	16.1	18.1	16.8	16.9
OPEN-END INVESTMENT COMPANIES												
Total Financial Assets	15.8	17.0	22.9	21.3	25.2	27.2	35.2	34.8	44.7	52.7	48.3	47.6
Corporate Bonds	1.1	1.2	1.6	1.6	1.8	2.1	2.6	2.9	3.0	3.4	3.6	4.3
Corporate Shares	13.9	14.8	20.3	18.3	22.1	23.7	30.9	28.9	39.2	46.1	40.9	39.7
MUTUAL SAVINGS BANKS												
Total Financial Assets	38.9	40.6	42.8	46.1	49.7	54.2	58.2	61.0	66.4	71.2	74.2	79.0
Corporate Bonds	3.6	3.8	3.6	3.5	3.2	3.1	2.9	3.2	5.3	6.6	6.9	8.3
Corporate Shares	.8	.8	.9	1.0	1.2	1.3	1.4	1.5	1.7	1.9	2.2	2.5
COMMERCIAL BANKS												
Total Financial Assets	217.0	226.0	243.2	264.0	283.5	307.0	337.6	356.6	397.4	441.4	461.3	499.3
Corporate Bonds	1.2	1.0	.9	.8	.8	.9	.8	.9	1.6	1.9	1.9	2.5
Bank Loans N.E.C.	57.9	61.4	64.8	71.1	78.8	87.6	104.2	113.3	120.8	136.5	154.9	156.9

SOURCE: Flow of Funds Accounts, 1959–1970, Board of Governors of the Federal Reserve System, May 4, 1971.

ment over and above this 33% first-year return on equity to whet their interest in such financings.

Convertible debt was a hybrid security having characteristics of both straight debt and common equity. Like any debt security, a convertible debenture required the issuer to pay interest and to repay principal, though these obligations were typically subordinated to the claims of any straight debt holders. In addition, a convertible debenture gave its holder the right to convert his security into a prespecified number of shares of common stock of the issuing company. The exchange of the convertible security for common stock, of course, ended the issuer's obligation to pay interest and sinking funds; the book value of the converted bonds was shifted to the carrier's common equity accounts.

Since the option on common stock provided an element of value to a convertible debenture, such securities could be issued carrying lower coupons than straight debt securities having the same par value. On the other hand, a convertible debenture typically provided greater current income and safety than the purchase of a comparable dollar amount of its issuer's common stock. Thus, convertible bonds could be sold at a premium over the value of the common stock that would be received upon conversion. As a result, raising $100 million of capital via convertible debenture would involve the potential issuance of a fewer number of common shares than would raising $100 million via sale of common stock for cash and, during the period prior to conversion, would involve lower interest (and typically, lower sinking funds) than $100 million of straight debt.

Convertible securities were held by both individual and institutional investors, although some of the speculative appeal to individuals had been dampened by the October 1967 imposition of margin requirements on the purchase of these securities. Institutional investors constrained by law or policy to invest primarily in debt securities (e.g., life insurance companies and many pension funds) often purchased convertibles as a means of increasing their total returns above those typically available on straight debt securities. Other institutions purchased convertibles as a means of participating in the possible growth of companies whose common stock was viewed as somewhat too risky or as having too little current dividend yield. Thus, a number of sectors of the United States economy were potential markets for additional convertible debenture financing by airlines. The enthusiasm of investors for any particular issue depended critically, however, on their view of the growth prospects of the underlying common stock. For this reason, the availability of convertible debenture financing was influenced by many of the equity market factors discussed in the following sections.

Equity Financing—Constraints on the Issuance of Common Stock

While the airlines faced problems in the debt capital markets, airline executives did not view the equity market situation as significantly more attractive. Common stock prices of the major airlines had declined rapidly since early in 1967. By March of 1968, stock prices had fallen to 60% of the highs reached a year earlier

(Figure 1.5). Since a substantial number of shareholders at that date had undoubtedly suffered significant losses in their airline stock holdings, some carrier managers believed that these shareholders would oppose the sale of additional equity on the grounds that it might dilute or delay the opportunity for share price recovery.

FIGURE 1.5

PRICE PERFORMANCE OF ONE STABLE AND ONE VOLATILE AIRLINE COMMON STOCK
VERSUS
DOW JONES INDUSTRIAL AVERAGE, 1967–1971

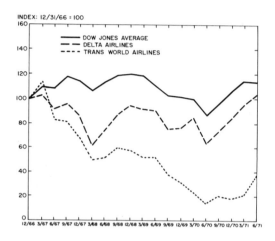

SOURCE: Bank & Quotation Record.

The terms of some airlines' outstanding convertible debt further complicated matters. Many of the carriers had issued relatively large amounts of convertible debt in late 1966 and early 1967 when stock prices were far higher. Anti-dilution provisions in these convertible securities called for increases in the number of shares issued upon conversion in the event of subsequent stock sales at prices below the levels prevailing in late 1966 and early 1967.

A number of factors contributed to the decline in air carrier common stock values. First, airline profit margins, which tended to swing in wide cycles, turned down sharply in early 1967 after reaching a peak in 1966. Second, most industry analysts expected a downturn of some duration, as this had been the industry pattern historically. A mid-1967 government economic feasibility study on the supersonic transport highlighted this pattern.

A decline in the ratio of earnings to revenues is expected between now and 1971 due to heavy initial purchase and interest costs for new aircraft. An upward swing should follow between 1971 and 1974 as costs taper and Boeing 747 operating efficiency improves. Another decline in 1975–1977 period is forecast due to the introduction of the . . . supersonic transport.[21]

Third, declines in earnings per share caused by this downturn were likely to be amplified by the need for new equity capital and the resultant increase in the number of shares outstanding.

Institutional Equity Holders

The 1965–1971 period saw major swings in the relative holdings of airline equity by individual and institutional investors. Some of the major carriers had more than 25% of their common stock held by mutual funds and "performance" investors in 1966. By 1967, mutual funds had substantially changed their earnings and stock price forecasts for air transport companies and had changed from major buyers to major sellers of airline securities (Table 1.17). They did not return as significant buyers until the fourth quarter of 1970. As reported in *Fortune* magazine in March 1968, "Among the big institutional investors where only two years ago these stocks were in high repute, the word now is, the airlines are dead." [22]

The vice president of finance of TWA commented on the changed expectations as follows:

> If on the other hand, our profits are squeezed so that airline equities come unglued as they have in the last four to six months, the ability to do our job will be affected. Once airline common stocks are no longer attractive as growth situations, their holding is shifted to a different type of investor who looks for yield, which in turn puts dividend pressure on the industry.[23]

Other industry observers were extremely wary of institutional investors. Comments made toward the end of 1968 could be summarized as follows:

> You can't get a strong upward move in airline equities unless the funds begin moving many millions of dollars into accumulating blocks of airline stock. But institutional stock purchases cut both ways. When fund managers start to move away from an industry, it doesn't take them long to really knock the bottom out of equity values in that industry (Figure 1.5 and Table 1.17). The funds began dumping airlines when the carriers' profits started to soften late in 1966. They've been net sellers in every quarter since that time. Some funds are beginning to nibble at buying the airline now, however, since many analysts see a strong upturn in industry profits around 1971.
> This "in and out" trading every couple of years by the funds causes two problems. First, it may tend to exaggerate market price changes in airline equities at

[21] Booz, Allen and Hamilton, *Supersonic Transport Financial Planning Study,* May 1967.
[22] C. J. Murphy, "The Airlines' Turbulent New Economics," *Fortune,* March 1968, p. 117.
[23] J. J. Kerley and C. H. Brunie, "Industry Report, The Airlines," *The Institutional Investor,* March 1967.

TABLE 1.17

NET SALES OF AIRLINE STOCKS BY MUTUAL FUNDS

1966 — Net Shares Sold

	1st Quarter	2nd Quarter	3rd Quarter	4th Quarter
American	116,100	255,900	62,800	(23,900)
Braniff	300	33,000	—	(15,300)
Continental	—	(13,000)	(84,900)	(142,000)
Delta	(70,700)	(52,700)	(57,700)	4,600
Eastern	23,000	(179,300)	73,400	124,500
National	(44,600)	—	21,700	(122,500)
Northeast				
Northwest	(106,300)	5,800	(14,700)	(36,600)
Pan American	(197,300)	(61,500)	(394,100)	277,000
Trans World	(15,200)	(1,035,000)	98,100	(164,200)
United	(30,500)	(112,900)	110,050	179,000
Western	(145,000)	163,200	(39,700)	125,700
Total	(470,200)	(996,700)	563,150	206,300

1967 — Net Shares Sold

	1st Quarter	2nd Quarter	3rd Quarter	4th Quarter
American	(192,900)	(26,800)	349,400	539,200
Braniff	50,500	—	—	(3,900)
Continental	(71,500)	(46,700)	303,500	416,000
Delta	216,800	106,900	47,900	48,000
Eastern	(235,600)	33,800	(437,700)	364,400
National	210,900	87,500	—	5,100
Northeast				
Northwest	190,500	194,500	265,700	—
Pan American	133,300	35,500	138,600	141,500
Trans World	156,000	237,000	288,300	—
United	141,000	54,500	34,300	82,600
Western	165,800	144,100	1,200	241,300
Total	151,200	423,100	988,800	1,834,200

1968 — Net Shares Sold

	1st Quarter	2nd Quarter	3rd Quarter	4th Quarter
American	334,000	309,300	28,300	(187,100)
Braniff	—	—	—	—
Continental	55,000	140,000	—	(175,000)
Delta	75,000	74,400	141,000	(136,000)
Eastern	127,700	(384,000)	158,100	780,000
National	—	(38,200)	(72,000)	253,700
Northeast				
Northwest	172,100	53,200	—	—
Pan American	204,000	107,500	(70,000)	3,350
Trans World	56,500	24,000	16,800	(65,800)
United	115,700	90,000	57,400	(32,700)
Western	38,800	58,000	—	25,000
Total	1,178,800	254,200	259,600	465,450

1969 — Net Shares Sold

	1st Quarter	2nd Quarter	3rd Quarter	4th Quarter
American	(190,500)	212,400	(43,000)	195,100
Braniff	—	—	—	—
Continental	10,700	—	—	—
Delta	(114,000)	31,000	20,400	(15,000)
Eastern	17,500	(175,000)	—	—
National	(21,400)	49,000	31,500	50,200
Northeast				
Northwest	9,600	162,000	(275,300)	147,600
Pan American	(34,500)	500,000	53,300	470,000
Trans World	(279,000)	192,000	(167,500)	36,000
United	96,000	83,600	460,500	103,600
Western	—	(69,000)	—	—
Total	(505,600)	986,000	79,900	987,500

1970 — Net Shares Sold

	1st Quarter	2nd Quarter	3rd Quarter	4th Quarter
American	572,900	(238,500)	(343,500)	(140,100)
Braniff	(67,300)	500	—	—
Continental	—	—	—	(236,000)
Delta	43,800	40,600	(183,200)	(264,800)
Eastern	(292,000)	(278,900)	—	(60,500)
National	(195,000)	—	—	—
Northeast				
Northwest	(76,400)	100,200	486,000	(305,000)
Pan American	—	(215,000)	—	(54,300)
Trans World	(325,000)	(160,000)	—	—
United	—	125,900	—	(360,700)
Western	—	—	—	—
Total	(339,000)	(625,200)	(40,700)	(1,421,400)

1971 — Net Shares Sold

	1st Quarter	2nd Quarter
American	(330,400)	(726,000)
Braniff	—	(629,000)
Continental	(234,800)	(84,800)
Delta	(185,500)	(337,200)
Eastern	(225,200)	(419,700)
National	(250,600)	(146,200)
Northeast		
Northwest	(230,900)	(511,000)
Pan American	(451,400)	(778,000)
Trans World	(301,500)	(201,100)
United	(499,700)	(660,100)
Western	—	—
Total	(2,710,000)	(4,493,100)

SOURCE: *Commercial and Financial Chronicle.*

both the top and bottom of the industry's earning cycle. Second, "in and out" traders rarely develop any allegiance to management. The mutual funds are under an enormous amount of short-term performance pressure, and if somebody comes along who will buy a block of stock that they've accumulated at a few points above the market, out it goes. With this type of situation, if some conglomerate wants to make a grab for a carrier, the block holdings of the funds make the carriers sitting ducks for take-overs. Some carrier managers might well find themselves in the position of having weathered a profit downturn caused by the purchase of lots of new equipment and then, just as the new equipment is about to pay off in higher profits, somebody else ends up running the business and reaping the rewards.

Competitive Gains Via Good Market Timing

The intent of this chapter was primarily to present industry background material and to set the necessary foundation upon which to build an understanding (in later chapters) of the fight for competitive advantage. A slight diversion into the area of competitive advantage might be useful at the close of the material on equity financing, however, since expertise on market timing in issuing equity is clearly one avenue along which a competitive advantage might be built. One only needs to look at the timing of the equity issues of Pan American World Airways over the years (Figure 1.6) to see the potential for real benefits in raising

FIGURE 1.6

PRICE ACTION OF PAN AMERICAN WORLD AIRWAYS
COMMON STOCK, 1956–1971

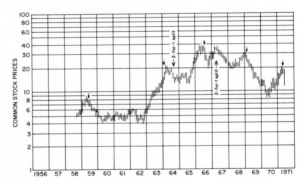

NOTE: ↓ represents the date of equity or convertible debenture offerings.
SOURCE: The Value Line Investment Survey.

capital "on the cheap." In early 1969, for instance, the management of Pan American turned an abortive takeover attempt by two conglomerates into a sizable competitive plus by issuing $175 million in convertible debt at an extremely attractive conversion ratio. The takeover attempts, while short-lived, drove the price of Pan American's common stock to a considerable premium (at a time when the common stock prices of the other carriers were sinking steadily—Figure 1.5) which it was unable to sustain after the attempt was thwarted. Thanks to the conglomerates and its sagacious market timing, Pan American was able to raise an extremely large chunk of capital with far less dilution (i.e., more cheaply) than any of its competitors.

As a double bonus, Pan American was also able to time the announcement of the filing of its registration statement for this offering so as to precede by about 48 hours the sale date of a $150 million TWA convertible debenture issue which had been filed some weeks earlier. The timing of Pan American's announcement almost certainly added to TWA's interest cost or reduced the conversion price from that which might have been realized had Pan American withheld its registration for a few days. As TWA's chief competitor, Pan American thus not only enjoyed a comparatively lower cost for the capital it raised as a result of the unusual price action of its stock, but may have been able to increase this cost advantage even further by the timing of its announcement. Clearly, the fight for competitive advantage in air transportation can take many rather colorful forms.

SUMMARY

The material presented in Chapter 1 is geared primarily toward developing industry level appreciation for the problems and prospects of the domestic trunk carriers with particular reference to the 1970s. The chapter examines market structure, projected growth in demand, equipment acquisition plans, expected profitability, and external financing needs and sources. From that broad analysis comes the conclusion that the industry can anticipate very serious profitability and financing problems all through the early 1970s. While the chapter adequately *outlines* these problems, it makes no attempt to establish their *cause*. This task will be reserved for later chapters.

PART II

The Airline Competition Study

CHAPTER 2

A Relative Profitability Model
of Air Carriers

AN INVESTIGATION OF COMPETITIVE ACTIVITY in an industry must build upon a clear understanding of the key profitability variables in that industry. Chapter 2 aims at identifying those factors in air transportation upon which a meaningful competitive advantage might actually be built. The chapter will specifically focus on the relative profitability[1] of various carriers, since ultimately a competitive advantage ought to be reflected in this performance measure.

Relative Profitability

A careful analysis of the relative profitability of the individual firms operating in an industry can often help to isolate those variables which are crucial both to the short-run profitability and the long-run success of the individual corporate participants. In air transportation, much has been written qualitatively (but little work has been done quantitatively)[2] which relates a carrier's relative profitability to factors that, with some effort, can be defined and measured quantitatively.

---

[1] For purposes of this study, the relative profitability of a specific carrier for a specific year is defined as that carrier's percent share of total industry operating profit (before interest, taxes, and extraordinary items) divided by that carrier's share of total industry operating revenue.

[2] Some notable exceptions include Robert J. Gordon, "Airline Costs and Managerial Efficiency" in *Transportation Economics*, National Bureau of Economic Research, 1965, and Mahlon R. Straszheim, *The International Airline Industry*, The Brookings Institution, 1969.

TABLE 2.1

COMPARATIVE PROFITABILITY INDEX, DOMESTIC OPERATIONS,
DOMESTIC TRUNK CARRIERS, 1955–1966
(*RELPRO Index*)

	1955	1956	1957	1958	1959	1960	1961*	1962	1963	1964	1965	1966
American	1.31	1.46	1.79	1.31	1.06	2.62	−11.65	1.28	1.74	1.08	.92	1.03
Braniff	.86	.87	2.21	1.71	1.31	1.95	−12.46	2.32	1.30	1.10	.93	1.17
Continental	.49	.75	.95	.54	1.36	4.69	−19.78	2.27	1.79	1.40	1.52	1.87
Delta	1.12	1.10	1.67	1.23	.83	3.17	−22.11	4.70	2.80	1.51	1.51	1.93
Eastern	1.15	1.36	1.07	.68	.71	−1.00	24.46	−2.01	−1.87	.12	.54	.32
National	1.36	1.89	1.32	.78	−.12	−4.65	1.71	4.12	1.62	1.57	1.75	1.60
Northeast	.09	−.56	−8.35	−2.14	−2.91	−7.08	40.82	−3.74	−4.80	−.35	−.05	.05
Northwest	.82	.54	0.	.87	.75	1.04	−3.89	2.45	2.11	1.94	2.12	2.05
Trans World	.56	−.24	−.81	.32	1.55	−.15	22.02	−.74	.97	1.14	.81	.58
United	.82	1.01	1.21	1.60	.96	1.18	−3.53	.79	.88	.68	.77	.55
Western	1.24	1.06	3.73	.61	2.98	4.10	−6.03	2.82	3.51	2.04	1.38	1.64
Industry	1.00	1.00	1.00	1.00	1.00	1.00	1.00	1.00	1.00	1.00	1.00	1.00

Definition of RELPRO Index: $\dfrac{\text{(carrier's operating profit/industry's** operating profit)}}{\text{(carrier's operating revenue/industry's** operating revenue)}}$

* In 1961 the industry suffered a small operating loss. The fact that a loss was incurred means that carriers operating profitably that year show a negative relative profitability index.
** The Industry is defined as the 11 domestic trunk carriers in operation as of 12/31/66.

SOURCE: *Handbook of Airline Statistics*; Part IV, 1961 and 1967.

As shown in Table 2.1, the relative profitability of the 11 domestic trunk carriers varied widely in any single year. For many individual trunks, relative profitability varied almost as sharply over time. Any number of hypotheses might be offered to account for the wide variability in carrier relative profitability. In the late 1960s airline managers and writers were "explaining" the high profitability of Northwest Airlines in terms of its (1) high percentage of monopoly traffic, (2) long distance which the average passenger flew when traveling with Northwest, and (3) the caliber of the carrier's management. In contrast, Northeast Airlines' relatively poor profitability was "explained" in terms of its (1) highly seasonal traffic pattern, (2) the "thinness" (in terms of the number of passengers traveling per day) of many of the carrier's routes, and (3) the relatively short distance traveled by the average passenger flying with Northeast.

The goal of this chapter will be to relate (via regression techniques) the relative profitability of the domestic operations of the 11 domestic trunk carriers to specifically defined and quantitatively measurable variables, and thus to develop a crude relative profitability model of the firm. The relationship will be established for the period from 1955 through 1966. While cost, time, and data availability considerations limit refinement in variable measurement, we will discover that even crudely defined and measured variables yield significant results.

THE VARIABLES DEFINED QUALITATIVELY

The specific variables which are often mentioned [3] by airline executives in terms of their impact on carrier relative profitability include:

---

[3] Cherington, for instance, mentioned many of these variables 13 years ago in his work entitled *Airline Price Policy*, p. 52.

(1) The degree of *competition* on the carrier's routes.
(2) The distribution of *haul lengths* on the carrier's routes.
(3) The *density* distribution of passenger traffic on the carrier's routes.
(4) The *seasonality* of traffic flows on the carrier's routes.
(5) The *yields* (by haul length segments) received by the carrier.
(6) The intensity (in hours per day) of productive aircraft *utilization*.
(7) The *quality* (or passenger appeal) of the carrier's *equipment*.
(8) The carrier's *capacity aggressiveness* in trying to seize market share.
(9) The overall *quality* of carrier *management*.

Each of these variables affects relative profitability through its influence on costs and/or revenues as outlined in the following pages.

Competition

In serving a city-pair monopoly[4] market a carrier management might be able to schedule fewer flight frequencies than would be possible in a competitive situation thus achieving higher load factors. The carrier might also tend to cut back on passenger services in monopoly markets in order to reduce costs.

In the reverse of the above situation, a carrier serving many city-pairs with competition from three or more carriers might have a significant portion of its total RPMs, generated in markets where the carrier enjoyed a 30% or less market share. One might expect a high proportion of such competition to reduce a carrier's relative profitability through load factor erosion as shown in Figure 2.1.[5]

Passenger Haul

The distribution of a carrier's passenger haul lengths is important since, in general, there is a substantial cost involved (not reflected fully in the airline fare structure) in simply ticketing, boarding, and unloading a passenger and his baggage regardless of the distance he travels. Short haul traffic was thus thought to operate normally at a loss with internal subsidy coming from highly profitable long haul traffic.

Traffic Density

The density distribution of a carrier's city-pair traffic (particularly as related to aircraft size) should also be important to relative profitability. For instance, if the number of passengers traveling between a city-pair on an average day is less than 100 in each direction, it would be difficult to achieve a breakeven load factor

---

[4] For purposes of this study, "monopoly traffic" is traffic between city-pairs in which the carrier in question has an 80% or better market share.

[5] Further support for the "typicalness" of the data in Figure 2.1 can be found in U.S. Civil Aeronautics Board, Board Order #71-4-54, April 12, 1971, Appendix F, p. 15.

FIGURE 2.1

LOAD FACTORS VERSUS DEGREE OF COMPETITION IN CITY-PAIR MARKETS OF
VARYING INTERCITY DISTANCE: TYPICAL DOMESTIC TRUNK CARRIER—1967

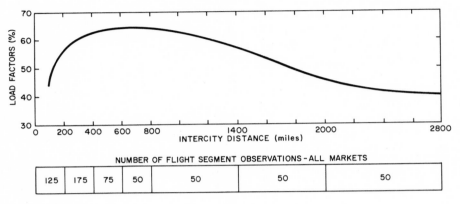

NUMBER OF FLIGHT SEGMENT OBSERVATIONS - ALL MARKETS

125	175	75	50	50	50	50

LOAD FACTORS

60%	64%	66%	78%	72%	70%	- -	MONOPOLY MARKETS
48	64	60	66	62	54	50%	2 CARRIER MARKETS
38	48	54	54	42	46	40	3 OR MORE CARRIER MARKETS
44	60	60	64	60	50	42	AVERAGE OF ALL MARKETS

Source: Private Carrier Data

SOURCE: Private Carrier Data.

(using 100-passenger aircraft) with a minimal frequency pattern of only two
round trips per day. City-pairs with limited traffic exchange are costly to service,
and such routes could be expected to penalize a carrier's relative profitability.

Seasonality

Seasonality of traffic is another important characteristic of a carrier's route structure. Actually, seasonality is only one of three important peak-to-valley traffic demand measures. The airlines also have to contend with (1) time-of-day peaks and
(2) day-of-week peaks (Figure 2.2). While these latter two peaking problems certainly add to airline costs, they are common to all carriers. Intercarrier compari-
sons might not yield very widely differing results along these two dimensions. Substantial differences in seasonality are apparent, however, in an intercarrier comparison. A high degree of seasonality in passenger traffic would work through
increased costs to reduce a carrier's relative profitability. Seasonal operations

FIGURE 2.2

PEAK-TO-VALLEY TRAFFIC VARIATION

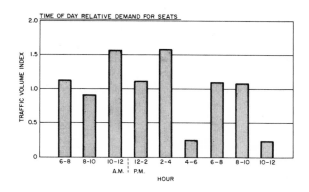

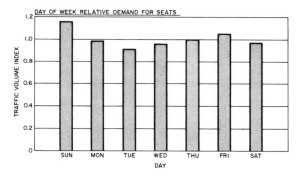

SOURCE: Private Carrier Data.

would increase costs, since many excess airline personnel cannot be laid off in slack
periods because of high retraining costs.

Yield

A carrier's yield curve would influence its profitability primarily through revenues. If a carrier could charge more than the industry average for a trip of a
given length, the carrier's relative profitability ought to be favorably affected.

Utilization

A carrier's aircraft utilization policy ought to have a clear impact on relative
profitability, since a significant portion of a carrier's total costs is fixed over a one-
year period. These fixed costs would include, at the minimum, depreciation and
hull insurance which account for more than 10% of total operating costs. Spread-

ing these fixed costs over a larger base would presumably enhance relative profitability.

Equipment Quality

Equipment quality would presumably affect carrier relative profitability through both revenues and costs. If a carrier could achieve an equipment advantage on a competitive route, presumably this equipment would attract more passengers and operate with a higher passenger load factor, thus enhancing the carrier's relative profitability. On the cost side of the equation, new equipment has historically operated at lower ASM unit costs than the equipment it has replaced.

Capacity Aggressiveness

The aggressiveness of a carrier in building market share by purchasing more aircraft than necessary to simply retain market share might also have an effect on a carrier's year-to-year relative profitability. Intuitively, one would expect some lag in consumer response to a carrier's added capacity on a route. For this reason, the immediate impact of capacity aggressiveness would probably be to reduce a carrier's relative profitability. Over the longer term, however, it might substantially increase the carrier's relative profitability.

Management Quality

Finally, the quality of carrier management (along dimensions other than utilization policy, equipment quality, and capacity aggressiveness) ought to have an impact on a carrier's relative profitability.

QUANTIFYING THE VARIABLES

The process of transforming qualitative factors which have intuitive attraction into explicitly defined quantifiable variables is a task which must be approached in the spirit of balancing intellectual integrity against data availability and ease of collection. The next section of this chapter will take up each variable (in the order presented previously) and define it first rather ideally and then with an eye toward data availability.

Interrelationship of the Variables

The relative profitability implications of three of the variables mentioned earlier are somewhat interrelated. For example, from the previous discussion one might predict that a monopoly operation in a city-pair market would be quite profitable. Such a prediction would probably be in error if the total trip length in the city-pair market was less than 300 miles. The prediction would probably also be in error even if the trip length were 2,500 miles, if only five passengers per day made such a trip. Ideally, then, an elaboration of these variables ought to take this interrelationship into account.

To that end, one might arbitrarily cut each of the three original variables (competition, haul length, and density) into three segments, and end up with a 27-element matrix with the percentage of a carrier's total RPMs flown during a given year "pigeonholed" as shown in Figure 2.3, and explained below:

(1) **Total** traffic for a given carrier would be broken into origin and destination city-pairs for the carrier in question. These city-pairs would then be sorted and arranged in order of competitiveness. All city-pairs in which the carrier in question held a market share of 80% through 100% would be placed in one category. All city-pairs in which the carrier held a market share ranging from 30% up to (but not including) 80% would be placed in a second category. All city-pairs in which the carrier held a market share ranging from .1% up to (but not including) 30% would be placed in the third category.

(2) The city-pairs (over which the carrier in question operated) in each of the three categories mentioned above would then be sorted according to three additional tests related to the length of the passenger haul. First, all city-pairs with intercity distances less than or equal to 600 miles would be arranged in one category. Second, all city-pairs with intercity distances ranging from 601 to 1,200 miles would be arranged in a second category. Finally, all city-pairs with intercity distances of over 1,200 miles would be arranged in a third category. At the conclusion of this step all city-pairs flown by the carriers in question would have been allocated within a 3 x 3 matrix.

(3) The city-pairs in each of the nine categories would then be further sorted according to three additional tests related to the density of traffic traveling between them. These densities would be adjusted by the average aircraft size in use in the industry during the particular year in question. The cuts would be made at one full plane load/day, more than one but two or less plane loads/day, and more than two plane loads/day.

The resulting $3 \times 3 \times 3$ matrix (as shown in Figure 2.3) would thus show the percent of total RPMs flown by each carrier (and the "industry" comprised of these carriers) categorized by (1) market share, (2) length of haul, and (3) city-pair traffic density (adjusted for changing aircraft sizes). The sum of the percent RPMs in all 27 categories would, of course, equal 100.

The percentage figure appearing in each position of the matrix could then be compared to the industry average for the position that year in order to calculate an index value. These index values would thus form an idealized "profile" of the carrier's route structure over time.

FIGURE 2.3

ROUTE STRUCTURE PROFILE

HYPOTHETICAL PERCENTAGE OF A TYPICAL CARRIER'S TOTAL RPMs FLOWN IN A SPECIFIC YEAR CHARACTERIZED BY (1) COMPETITIVENESS, (2) LENGTH OF HAUL, (3) TRAFFIC DENSITY

———— INCREASING RELATIVE PROFITABILITY ————▶

		X≤600 MILES			600<X≤1200 MILES			X>1200 MILES		
		Y≤2	2<Y≤4	Y>4	Y≤2	2<Y≤4	Y>4	Y≤2	2<Y≤4	Y>4
CARRIER's % MARKET SHARE IN CITY PAIRS	100-80	5.1%	3.8%	1.2%	5.1%	6.7%	6.8%	5.2%	3.5%	1.2%
	79-31	4.3%	5.2%	3.6%	1.2%	2.5%	3.7%	2.0%	2.0%	2.0%
	30-.1	1.2%	3.2%	5.1%	1.3%	8.1%	5.0%	4.0%	4.0%	3.0%

Y = (ONE WAY PASSENGERS/DAY)/(AVERAGE SEATS/AIRCRAFT)
X = LENGTH OF HAUL (MILES)

(Right axis: INCREASING RELATIVE PROFITABILITY ↑)

SOURCE: Hypothetical example.

Competition

Unfortunately, a lack of data in a form suitable for computer analysis prior to 1962 makes the above idealized profile operationally unattainable. Instead, the problem of data availability forces us to use far grosser indices which ignore the interdependency issue entirely. The degree of competition indices that we shall actually use in the study are defined below.

COMP80 will equal a ratio, the numerator of which is the percentage of total RPMs flown by the carrier in city-pairs where the carrier controls between 80% and 100% of the market. The denominator of the ratio will equal the comparable factor calculated for the entire industry, i.e., all 11 trunks. Thus, if American Airlines in 1965 generated 24.1% of its total RPMs in city-pair markets where it carried 80% to 100% of the traffic (compared to the industry average of 33.5% for such traffic), its COMP80 index would equal 24.1/33.5 or .72 for the year 1965 (Table 2.2).

Behind this definition lies the assumption that if one carrier accounts for 80% or more of the traffic in a city-pair market, that market is a monopoly due to the fact that no other carriers are certified, or they are certified with restrictions making it impossible for them to compete effectively.

COMP30 is defined in a similar manner, except that it refers to traffic generated in city-pairs where the carrier controls between .1% and 30% of the total market.

Behind this definition lies the assumption that if a carrier accounts for less than

TABLE 2.2

COMPARATIVE SHARE INDEX OF TOTAL CARRIER RPMs FLOWN IN MONOPOLY*
MARKETS, DOMESTIC OPERATIONS, DOMESTIC TRUNK CARRIERS, 1955–1966
(*COMP80 Index*)

	1955	1956	1957	1958	1959	1960	1961	1962	1963	1964	1965	1966
American	.95	.89	.85	.81	.79	.84	.90	.90	.76	.77	.72	.66
Braniff	1.51	1.45	1.44	1.48	1.72	1.62	1.63	1.68	1.70	1.66	1.76	1.73
Continental	1.81	1.93	1.83	1.59	1.23	1.03	1.16	1.04	.92	.93	.96	.98
Delta	1.30	1.30	1.42	1.38	1.58	1.22	1.16	1.24	1.24	1.37	1.35	1.42
Eastern	1.14	1.11	1.19	1.14	.95	1.03	.88	.66	.78	.89	.91	.88
National	.42	.47	.53	.62	.63	.75	.73	1.10	1.07	.95	1.07	1.11
Northeast	1.88	1.94	1.34	.65	.73	.59	.41	.39	.42	.53	.54	.48
Northwest	1.15	.91	1.04	1.01	1.12	1.16	.74	1.09	1.50	1.50	1.47	1.42
Trans World	.91	.87	.90	.81	.93	.90	.79	.81	.69	.67	.80	.72
United	.86	1.00	.84	1.03	1.00	1.04	1.22	1.15	1.23	1.15	1.01	1.07
Western	1.00	1.09	1.18	1.18	1.43	1.40	1.45	1.35	1.36	1.33	1.46	1.54
Industry	1.00	1.00	1.00	1.00	1.00	1.00	1.00	1.00	1.00	1.00	1.00	1.00

Actual percentage of total industry RPMs flown in city-pair markets where the dominant carrier held an 80% or higher market share:

| 48.6 | 46.8 | 42.2 | 41.6 | 34.0 | 34.7 | 35.3 | 34.5 | 34.5 | 33.0 | 33.5 | 31.4 |

$$\text{Definition of COMP80 Index:} \frac{\text{Percentage of the carrier's RPMs which were flown in city-pair markets where the carrier held an 80\% or higher market share}}{\text{Percentage of industry RPMs which were flown in city-pair markets where the dominant carrier held an 80\% or higher market share}}$$

* A monopoly market is defined as a city-pair in which one carrier controls an 80% or higher RPM share.

SOURCE: *Competition Among Domestic Air Carriers*, Volume 4, 1955–1958; Table 6, 1959–1966.

30% of the traffic in a city-pair market, that market almost certainly has more than two carriers certified to serve it, or the carrier in question suffers from a certificate limitation in that market making it impossible for the carrier to compete effectively. The basis for this assumption should become clear in Chapter 5.

Passenger Haul

The haul length variable, HWLRAT, is defined as the average trip length (airport-to-airport mileage) per passenger on the carrier's routes for the year in question.

Again, using American as an example, if the carrier had an average haul length of 834 miles in 1965 compared to an average haul length of 701 miles for the industry, the carrier's HWLRAT index for the year 1965 would be 834/701 or 1.19 (Table 2.3).

Traffic Density

Data availability forces the definition of the density factor away from the number of plane loads per day exchanged between two city-pairs to a measure of market concentration. For purposes of the study, the density variable, DENS10, is defined as a ratio. The numerator of the ratio equals the percentage of total passengers carried between the carrier's top 10 city-pairs during a given year. The denominator of the ratio is the comparable value for the entire industry.

TABLE 2.3

Comparative Average Haul Length Index, Domestic Operations,
Domestic Trunk Carriers, 1955–1966
(*HWLRAT* Index)

	1955	1956	1957	1958	1959	1960	1961	1962	1963	1964	1965	1966
American	1.06	1.08	1.10	1.10	1.16	1.20	1.18	1.17	1.23	1.23	1.19	1.17
Braniff	.67	.70	.71	.71	.70	.73	.72	.71	.71	.71	.70	.72
Continental	.66	.63	.72	.80	.96	1.03	1.02	.98	1.04	1.09	1.06	1.10
Delta	.81	.83	.82	.82	.81	.85	.91	.95	.93	.91	.93	.94
Eastern	.91	.89	.92	.89	.86	.82	.78	.75	.72	.72	.76	.75
National	1.27	1.21	1.09	1.03	1.00	.98	1.04	1.09	1.17	1.15	1.12	1.11
Northeast	.36	.35	.53	.69	.66	.61	.69	.70	.69	.61	.58	.64
Northwest	1.19	1.15	1.13	1.15	1.21	1.12	1.07	1.04	.96	.94	.90	.90
Trans World	1.36	1.37	1.33	1.35	1.41	1.40	1.38	1.35	1.38	1.43	1.37	1.36
United	1.23	1.20	1.22	1.18	1.10	1.10	1.05	1.01	1.03	1.03	1.05	1.06
Western	.85	.86	.83	.86	.87	.88	.89	.85	.79	.76	.77	.79
Industry	1.00	1.00	1.00	1.00	1.00	1.00	1.00	1.00	1.00	1.00	1.00	1.00

Actual length of industry's average passenger haul (miles):

	557	576	608	618	632	649	661	681	682	688	701	716

Definition of HWLRAT Index: $\dfrac{\text{Length of carrier's average passenger haul}}{\text{Length of industry's average passenger haul}}$

Source: *Handbook of Airline Statistics:* Part III, 1961 and 1967.

Seasonality

Ideally, in measuring seasonality of demand, one would like to capture both peak-to-valley differences and some aspect of variation about the mean or average monthly traffic. While the data for such an analysis are available, time and cost considerations force the use of a grosser but still valuable index of seasonality. For purposes of this study, SEASON is defined as a ratio. For each carrier, the maximum RPMs generated in one of the four months—February, June, August, and November—is divided by the minimum RPMs generated in another of these same months to arrive at the numerator in the ratio. The same procedure is then followed on total industry data to get the denominator of the ratio.

Yield

Yields (passenger revenue per revenue passenger mile) vary widely among the carriers. This difference is attributable to (1) historic anomalies in fare construction, (2) differences in the mix of first class, coach, and discount traffic achieved by the carriers, and a host of other factors. Ideally, in constructing a yield index one would like to compare a carrier's yield in different mileage blocks (for instance, on trips between 0 and 200 miles, 200 to 400 miles, etc.) to similar values for the industry at large. The indices in each mileage block could then be weighted (by the carrier's percentage of total traffic flown in each mileage block) to arrive at a single number. If this number were 1.000 it would indicate that the carrier received exactly the same revenue that the average carrier would have received in flying over the same routes. So far as I can determine, data on yields, by carrier and by mileage block, do not exist in any form prior to 1965. The definition of YIELDS for purposes of this study thus simply represents the carrier's average passenger revenue per revenue passenger mile divided by the similar value for the industry. Given the nature of fare construction, this index is probably as much an index of haul lengths as it is of yields. Of the "data availability" compromises made in this study, this is probably the most serious.

Utilization

Ideally, an index of the relative intensity of aircraft utilization for each carrier should contain a weighting by the productivity potential of the aircraft in the carrier's fleet. Thus, idle time on large 4-engine jets would weigh more heavily in the index than idle time on piston aircraft still assigned to service. In practice, this weighting does not occur in statistics reported by the CAB. The utilization figures reported are simply the ratio of total revenue aircraft hours flown during the average day divided by the average number of aircraft in the carrier's fleet. All aircraft are thus weighted equally in the calculation. For purposes of this study, the index of utilization (called UTILIZ) was defined as a ratio. The numerator of the ratio was equal to the average number of revenue hours flown by the average aircraft each day. The denominator of the ratio was the comparable value for the industry as a group.

Equipment Quality

Equipment quality is difficult to quantify with a single variable over an extended period of time. Certainly during the transition from piston powered aircraft to jets one might quantify this variable in terms of the percentage of jet RPMs generated by each carrier versus the percentage of jet RPMs generated for the industry in each year to arrive at a quality index called PJETAD. This transition was nearly complete by 1963, however, so some other basis of comparison would be needed for later dates. The faster and more efficient fanjet aircraft produced by Boeing and McDonnell Douglas represented a significant equipment quality advance when they were introduced in the early 1960s. A second equipment quality index (labelled FJETAD) for the early to mid-1960s might thus be developed in the form of a ratio. The numerator of this ratio equals the number of RPMs generated by the carrier in fanjet aircraft divided by the number of RPMs generated by the carrier in all aircraft. The denominator of the ratio represents comparable data for the total industry.

Capacity Aggressiveness

Equipment capacity aggressiveness would be an extremely difficult variable to quantify. One could easily measure the ratio of a carrier's percentage increase in equipment capacity each year to that of the industry, but this might measure the impact of new route awards more than it would capacity aggressiveness. A partial solution to the problem might be to look only at city-pairs where no new competitors have been added between 1955 and 1966. One could measure the carrier's annual percentage increase in capacity on such routes and then contrast this with the percentage capacity increases on these routes made by competing carriers. This approach neglects, however, the carrier's relative aggressiveness in penetrating new markets, and in defending old markets where new competition has been certified. The approach also lacks operational usefulness since such data are not readily available.

Management Quality

Finally, general management quality is a variable which also ought to have an impact on carrier relative profitability. The measure of this effectiveness might have to be left as a residual factor, i.e., *some portion* of the carrier's relative profitability index that remains to be explained after all other measurable variables have been taken into account might be attributed to the general management factor.

Categorization of Variables

All of the variables mentioned in the study to this point can be categorized by degree of management control and subjective judgment on definitional and/or data quality. This has been done in Table 2.4. First, it is clear that degree of competition (as related to the number of active competitors certified in various

TABLE 2.4

CATEGORIZATION OF VARIABLES USED IN
RELATIVE PROFITABILITY STUDY

Factor	Computer Symbol	Controlling Agent	Subjective Evaluation of Definition and Data Used in Study				
			Good	Fair	Poor	Not Measured	
Degree of Competition	COMP80	CAB	x				⎫
	COMP30	CAB	x				Route
Haul Length	HWLRAT	CAB		x			structure
Density of Traffic	DENS10	CAB		x			variables
Seasonality	SEASON	CAB		x			⎭
Yields	YIELDS	CAB			x		⎫ Fare structure variable ⎭
Utilization of Equipment	UTILIZ	Mgmt.		x			⎫
Equipment Quality	PJETAD	Mgmt.		x			Equipment
	FJETAD	Mgmt.		x			policy
Capacity Aggressiveness	—	Mgmt.				x	variables
Management Quality	—	Mgmt.				x	

city-pair markets), traffic density, haul length, and seasonality variables are all closely related to a carrier's route structure. As such, they are far less responsive to management desires than to CAB fiat. This same statement can be made regarding yields. Only five of the eleven variables mentioned in this study are clearly under management control. These are equipment quality (2 variables are used to define this in the study), equipment utilization, capacity aggressiveness, and general management effectiveness. As mentioned earlier in the text, two of the eleven variables deemed important in the study could not be measured; their impact must be relegated to the residual category. In addition, the measure used for one of the variables, YIELDS, was subjectively assumed to be a poor approximation of reality.

Firm Effects

As candidates for inclusion in an equation geared toward explaining differences in individual firm profitability, the quantifiable variables already outlined have some obvious intuitive appeal. Other important profitability factors have undoubtedly been missed in this selection of variables, however, and some of these might be picked up by the inclusion of an additional "dummy variable" for each firm. This variable would carry a value of 1.0 each year for the firm associated with this variable, and a value of zero each year for all of the other firms in the industry. By using the technique of introducing dummy variables into the regression equation, any previously unidentified, constant, and persistent factor influencing an individual carrier's profitability during the period 1955–1966 should be picked up and highlighted by the dummy variable designed to characterize that carrier's "firm effect" in the regression equation. The existence of strong firm effects would not result in the *direct* identification of additional variables which might be important in defining a firm's relative profitability. If strong firm effects were observed, however, we might try to link these effects to more explicitly defined variables which might then be categorized as management or CAB controlled. As we shall see later, firm effects show some measure of statistical significance within the Little 7 subset of carriers, but these firm effects do not seem to increase the explanatory power of the regression equation enough to require such treatment.

RESULTS OF THE REGRESSION MODEL

Regression runs made with the definitions and data[6] described previously yield some significant results. If we eliminate data

(1) where the industry operated at a loss or very near breakeven (1960 and 1961), and
(2) where the industry suffered a major work stoppage (in 1966 the operations of 5 trunk carriers were suspended for 43 days),

---

[6] These data are smoothed through the use of two-year moving averages for all of the variables.

then the variables which are defined and measured in this study explain 72% of the total relative profitability for the domestic operations of the 11 domestic trunk carriers in the period 1955–1966 (Table 2.5, line 11). If the regression is run with

TABLE 2.5

FRACTION OF CARRIER RELATIVE PROFITABILITY EXPLAINED
BY CAB AND/OR MANAGEMENT CONTROLLED VARIABLES

Source of R^2	Cumu-lative R^2	Addition to R^2 Due to Variables Added	Degrees of Freedom	Mean Square	Com-puted F	$F_{.05}$	$F_{.01}$
Big 4 Carriers							
1 CAB controlled variables	.84	.84	6	.14000	28.00	2.55	3.76
2 Management controlled variables	.87	.03	3	.01000	2.00	3.05	4.82
3 Firm effect variables	.89	.02	4	.00500	1.00	2.82	4.31
4 Unexplained	1.00	.11	22	.00500			
Total	1.00	1.00	35				
Little 7 Carriers							
5 CAB controlled variables	.58	.58	6	.09666	16.47	2.30	3.22
6 Management controlled variables	.61	.03	3	.01000	1.70	2.81	4.24
7 Firm effect variables	.73	.12	7	.01714	2.92	2.22	3.05
8 Unexplained	1.00	.27	46	.00587			
Total	1.00	1.00	62				
11 Domestic Trunk Carriers							
9 CAB controlled variables	.56	.56	6	.09333	26.00	2.21	3.04
10 Management controlled variables	.60	.04	3	.01333	3.71	2.72	4.04
11 Firm effect variables	.72	.12	11	.01091	3.04	1.91	2.48
12 Unexplained	1.00	.28	78	.00359			
Total	1.00	1.00	98				

the industry divided (as the CAB does for reporting purposes) into the Big 4 and Little 7 carriers, the percentage of total relative profitability explained by the resulting equations for the two groups rises to 89% and 73% for each group, respectively (Table 2.5, lines 3 and 7).

If, for each of the three industry groupings, we rerun the regression equation three times *first* using only those variables under *CAB* control (see Table 2.6 for one example), then adding in those variables under management control, and finally adding in the "firm effect" variables the explanatory power of the regression equation changes as shown in Table 2.5. This procedure allows us to partition the variance of relative profitability into four major component parts; one relating to CAB controlled variables, the second relating to management controlled variables, the third relating to "firm effect" variables, and the fourth relating to unexplained variance or "noise." By computing three ratios, each of which

TABLE 2.6

RELATIVE PROFITABILITY REGRESSION EQUATION: DOMESTIC OPERATIONS,
BIG 4 TRUNK CARRIERS, 1955–1966

Dependent Variable . . .
RELPRO

Independent Variable	Estimated Coefficient	Standard Error	T-Statistic
C	−25.9275	3.67247	−7.1
HWLRAT	6.11454	0.638471	9.6
COMP80	4.06200	0.797810	5.1
COMP30	−0.962030	0.233363	−4.1
YIELDS	16.5457	3.47792	4.8
SEASON	−0.301786	0.744567	−0.41
DENS10	1.25782	0.788347	1.6

R-Squared = 0.84.
Number of Observations = 36.

measures successive levels of explained variance against unexplained variance, we can make use of the F distribution to determine whether each component set of variables added to increase the overall level of explained variance is statistically significant within each carrier grouping.[7]

This allows us to state, in terms of probabilities, our degree of confidence in the hypothesis that a relationship between relative profitability and that set of variables added to the regression equation actually exists, and is not due simply to chance.

The appropriate calculations, the results of which appear in Table 2.5, lead us to the following conclusions.

(1) Within all three carrier groupings, the existence of a relationship between relative profitability and the CAB controlled variables defined in the regression equation is overwhelmingly clear.

(2) Within the Big 4 carrier grouping we cannot say that any relation is clearly indicated between relative profitability and either (a) the management controlled variables defined in the regression equation, or (b) the "firm effect" variables.[8]

(3) Within the Little 7 carrier grouping we cannot say that any relation is clearly indicated between relative profitability and the management controlled variables defined in the regression equation. We can, however, state with a probability of

---

[7] See for example, Chi-Yuan Lin and William L. White, "Four Procedures for Testing Linear Hypotheses," *Industrial Management Review*, Fall 1968, pp. 13–30.

[8] The "firm effect" variables outlined earlier might be perceived at least partially as a measure of management quality. Unfortunately, in each of the regression runs shown in lines 3, 7, and 11 of Table 2.5, the standard error term is so large in relation to the estimated coefficient for each carrier's "firm effect" as to render statistically insignificant the calculated differences between the carrier coefficients.

98% that a relationship does exist between relative profitability and "firm effects." [8,9]

Overall, and perhaps most importantly, the regression analysis suggests that *the CAB exercises greater control over the relative profitability of the carriers than do the carrier management groups themselves.* As Malcolm A. MacIntyre, former President of Eastern Airlines, has written:[10]

> The regulatory agencies are indeed judges, but they are also umpires, and in many areas such as rates, products, and routes, they are *executives.* [Emphasis mine.]

Indeed it would appear that in matters of profitability the CAB represents each carrier's "first string" management team; the second string group (the ones with shareholder responsibility) get to play only when the outcome of this game is essentially decided.

Management Controlled Variables

Table 2.5 suggests that the defined and measured management controlled variables appear to have a tenuous impact in determining a carrier's relative profitability. Capacity aggressiveness and management quality, if measured, would undoubtedly have added to the explanatory power of the regression model, but some of the remaining unexplained difference between the index of determination for any of the equations and 1.0 would clearly be reserved for such factors as differences in accounting practice between carriers (Table 2.7) and the "grossness" of all the variables actually included in the equations.

The interfirm variation in management quality in the airline industry would be a particularly fascinating topic for investigation, *first* because I suspect that if some satisfactory measure[11] of this factor were developed, the intercarrier spread might not be very wide when compared to the spread in relative profitability, and *second* because even if the management quality spread were found to be quite wide, it is by no means clear that this factor would have much influence on long-run relative profitability. The latter somewhat disturbing conclusion comes from the analysis of this chapter combined with material which will be presented in Chapter 6.

---

[9] The unexpected appearance of some statistical significance in the management variables when the Big 4 and Little 7 groups are combined might be explained as follows. Within the Big 4 and Little 7 subgroupings, individual values of some management variable such as jet penetration might not vary much around the mean value of that variable within each of the two subgroups. The mean values for these two subgroups might be quite different, however, leading to the appearance of significance for management variables in the aggregated data which might be quite misleading. If, for example, airframe manufacturers reserved their early delivery positions on new jet aircraft for the larger carriers so as to assure receipt of these most important orders, the ability of the smaller carriers to move into an early parity position in terms of jet penetration with the Big 4 carriers would be quite limited.

[10] Malcolm A. MacIntyre, *Competitive Private Enterprise Under Government Regulation*, p. 55.

TABLE 2.7

MAJOR UNITED STATES AIR CARRIERS

(Reported and Fully Adjusted Calendar 1965 Earnings Per Share)

	AMR	BNF	CAL	DAL	EAL	NAL	NWA	PN	TWA	UAL	WAL
Actual EPS Reported	$4.40	$1.60	$3.77	$4.35	$7.04	$4.51	$5.00	$3.28	$5.74	$3.35	$2.83
Special Adjustments					(3.38)					(.34)	
Capital Gains/Share	(.01)	(.07)	(.51)	(.01)	(.04)	(.06)	(.11)	(.04)	(.08)	(.01)	(.20)
Dilution from Pref., Deb., Warrants, Options	(.45)	—	(.17)	—	(.54)	(.09)	—	(.42)	(1.17)	(.41)	(.08)
Earnings after Special Gains and Dilution	$3.94	$1.53	$3.09	$4.36	$3.08	$4.36	$4.89	$2.82	$4.49	$2.59	$2.55
Overhaul Reserve Prov.	—	.01	.46	.08	.20	(.17)	—	—	—	—	.06
Jet Depreciation	.07	.07	.28	.30	.01	.25	.14	.02	.50	(.05)	.35
Devel. & Preoperating Cost Amortized	.09	.01	.28	—	.72	.03	.06	.16	.04	.04	—
Investment Tax Credit	(.49)	(.25)	(.16)	(.20)	—	(.10)	(.15)	(.45)	(.73)	(.32)	(.14)
Capitalized Interest	(.13)	(.03)	(.06)	(.09)	(.12)	—	(.07)	(.06)	(.06)	(.09)	(.01)
Asjusted EPS	$3.48	$1.34	$3.89	$4.45	$3.89	$4.37	$4.87	$2.49	$4.24	$2.17	$2.81

Evidence bearing on the first point raised in the preceding paragraph relates to the unusual degree of personnel mobility even at the highest management levels in competing air transportation firms. As shown in Table 2.8, in the seven-year period from 1962 through 1969, 15 managers ranging from full vice presidents to chief executive officers have moved from one carrier to another. American Airlines (a relatively high return carrier for the Big 4) has clearly been the industry's managerial training ground while Eastern and TWA (both relatively sick carriers) have clearly been outside management "users." While no specific documentation can be offered, it has been suggested that general employee mobility in lower echelon jobs within the industry is substantially higher. With this degree of employee mobility it is hard to imagine that any carrier has achieved a significant long-term managerially based competitive advantage. If my impression is correct, a substantial fraction of the relatively high inflow of outside managers into sick carriers may do little more than provide a vent for the frustrations of directors and/or chief executive officers of such companies.

In summary, then, one factor emerges with some force from the analysis presented in this chapter. The impact on relative profitability (as measured by the index of determination) of the variables controlled by airline management looks small by comparison with the impact of the variables controlled by the CAB.

---

[11] As indicated in footnote 8, the most obvious candidate for this measure, firm effects, is not adequate to the task.

TABLE 2.8

TOP MANAGEMENT INTERCHANGES AMONG THE MAJOR UNITED STATES AIR CARRIERS

(Full Vice Presidents or Higher from 1962–1969 with Date of Change)

Management Suppliers	Management Users												Supplier Totals
	American	Braniff	Continental	Delta	Eastern	National	Northeast	Northwest	Pan American	TWA	United	Western	
American					1963 D. D. Taylor		1966 F. C. Wiser		1964 W. Player	1969 M. A. Brenner			4
Braniff													0
Continental		1965 H. L. Lawrence											1
Delta					1962 T. Cole								1
Eastern	1963 J. O. Jarrard									1968 M. T. Hopkins			2
National													0
Northeast										1968 F. C. Wiser			1
Northwest													0
Pan American													0
TWA					1968 T. B. McFadden					1967 B. Cooke			2
United					1963 F. D. Hall					1968 W. J. Smith			2
Western	1967 T. S. Schrader		1967 D. P. Renda										2
User Totals	2	1	1	0	4	0	1	0	1	5	0	0	15

SOURCE: *Moody's Transportation Manual, 1962–1970.*

CHAPTER 3

The Fight for Competitive Advantage—Fares

As INDICATED IN CHAPTER 2, while fare structure and route structure were extremely important to an individual carrier's relative profitability, statutory power over these factors resided with the CAB. Although the carriers might expect to exercise little competitive power independently in these areas, since they are so obviously significant to profitability it is important to understand how the carriers and the CAB interact in these areas.

The CAB (first under the Civil Aeronautics Act of 1938 and later under its slightly modified revision called the Federal Aviation Act of 1958) has been charged by the United States Congress with regulating commercial United States air transportation. The guidelines given to the Board in accomplishing its function are general and brief. While the entire Act runs slightly over 100 pages, the sections relating specifically to the Board's jurisdiction over routes and fares include only 6 and 4 pages, respectively. Procedural matters consume the bulk of the space devoted to route jurisdiction. The establishment of guidelines for deciding which carrier (or carriers) shall fly between specific city-pairs at any point in time is accomplished in a single paragraph.[1]

Sec. 401. (d) The Board shall issue a certificate authorizing the whole or any part of the transportation covered by the application if it finds that the applicant is fit,

---

[1] U.S. Senate, Committee on Interstate and Foreign Commerce, "Federal Aviation Act of 1958," U.S. Government Printing Office, 1959, p. 28.

willing, and able to perform such transportation properly, and to conform to the provisions of this Act and the rules, regulations, and requirements of the Board hereunder, and that such transportation is required by the public convenience and necessity; otherwise such application shall be denied.

On the question of fares, the CAB's jurisdiction can be quite complete. Individual carriers may initiate fare changes whenever they desire, but the CAB (as alternatives to accepting the changes) has the right to (1) disallow the changes; (2) establish maximum and minimum fare(s) between the city-pair(s) in question; or (3) exactly prescribe specific fare(s) for the city-pair(s) in question. The policy guidelines given to the Board in the fare area are again contained in a single paragraph.[2]

RULE OF RATE MAKING

Sec. 1002. (e) In exercising and performing its powers and duties with respect to the determination of rates for the carriage of persons or property, the Board shall take into consideration, among other factors—

(1) The effect of such rates upon the movement of traffic;
(2) The need in the public interest of adequate and efficient transportation of persons and property by air carriers at the lowest cost consistent with the furnishing of such service;
(3) Such standards respecting the character and quality of service to be rendered by air carriers as may be prescribed by or pursuant to law;
(4) The inherent advantages of transportation by aircraft; and
(5) The need of each air carrier for revenue sufficient to enable such air carrier, under honest, economical, and efficient management to provide adequate and efficient air carrier service.

CONGRESSIONAL DECLARATION OF AIR POLICY

While very general guidance specifically pertaining to route and fare policy is provided in the subsections of the Act mentioned previously, the Act also contains a general expression of Congressional intent by which all CAB decisions are to be guided.[3]

Sec. 102. In the exercise and performance of its powers and duties under this Act, the Board shall consider the following, among other things, as being in the public interest, and in accordance with the public convenience and necessity:

[2] *Ibid.*, pp. 77–78.
[3] *Ibid.*, p. 5.

(a) The encouragement and development of an air-transportation system properly adapted to the present and future needs of the foreign and domestic commerce of the United States, of the Postal Service, and the national defense;

(b) The regulation of air transportation in such manner as to recognize and preserve the inherent advantages of, assure the highest degree of safety in, and foster sound economic conditions in, such transportation, and to improve the relations between, and coordinate transportation by air carriers;

(c) The promotion of adequate, economical, and efficient service by air carriers at reasonable charges, without unjust discriminations, undue preferences or advantages, or unfair or destructive competitive practices;

(d) Competition to the extent necessary to assure the sound development of an air-transportation system properly adapted to the needs of the foreign and domestic commerce of the United States, of the Postal Service, and of the national defense;

(e) The promotion of safety in air commerce; and

(f) The promotion, encouragement, and development of civil aeronautics.

Clearly the policy guidelines are stated at a level substantially removed from operational usefulness in determining which carrier(s) should fly between Cincinnati, Ohio, and New York City, and what the coach fare ought to be for the trip.

It is a rather simple exercise to formulate a number of "what if . . . ?" questions to demonstrate internal inconsistency among the various policy goals. "Taken literally, it (the Declaration of Policy) requires an impossibility by suggesting the simultaneous maximization of things that probably cannot be simultaneously maximized." [4] On the other hand, it allows the Board wide flexibility in decision making. "In most cases the Board has sufficiently broad discretion that any one of a wide variety of results is either legally justifiable or at least not subject to meaningful judicial review." [5]

The Civil Aeronautics Act of 1938 sheds little light on actual CAB operating policies regarding fare levels or changes. It might be useful, therefore, to examine how and what CAB policies have evolved and how they have influenced competitive relationships among the domestic trunk air carriers.

Fare Structure

Historically, probably the most significant policy decision made by the CAB relates to the question of fare structure. Fare structure has always been at least as controversial a subject among carriers and regulators as the question of fare level. The controversy is firmly rooted in very fundamental economic relationships: (1) the cost of providing air service for trips of various lengths; and (2) the demand (at various fare levels) for such transportation over the same trip lengths.

Air carrier managers quite reasonably maintain that the value element of speed becomes magnified as a trip length increases. For a very short flight (say of 200

[4] Richard E. Caves, *Air Transport and Its Regulators*, p. 127.
[5] William K. Jones, "Licensing of Domestic Air Transportation, Part II," p. 91.

miles) the benefits of air transportation often are not high enough to induce many
intercity travelers to pay a fare substantially higher than car, bus, or train rates for
the privilege of flying. This leads to an unfortunate situation for air carriers since,
as the left half of Figure 3.1 indicates, short haul costs are such that there may in

FIGURE 3.1

PROFIT POTENTIAL OF SHORT VERSUS LONG HAUL MARKETS

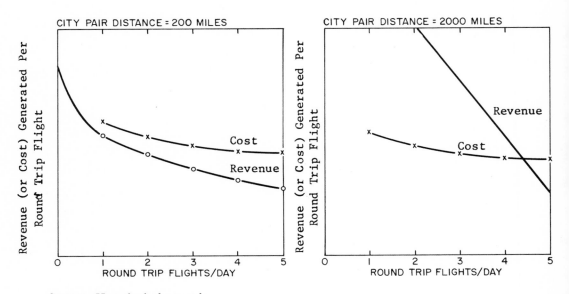

SOURCE: Hypothetical example.

fact be *no* fare level which equates revenues and costs[6] for short haul air travel. If
carriers were to employ full cost pricing for travel over all trip lengths, short haul
markets might be either abandoned or left undeveloped.

The economics of long haul air transportation are neatly reversed when compared with the short haul example. On longer trips the value of speed is so great
that many passengers would pay a substantial premium for air service in preference to competitive modes, and probably travel more frequently than they would
if air service were not available. As the right half of Figure 3.1 indicates, on long
haul routes monopoly profits might be achieved (with some reduction in demand)
if fares were lifted above the full cost equilibrium level indicated.

If Figure 3.1 reasonably depicts the economics of air transportation, then in a
relatively free market one would expect to find a well-developed long haul air
transport system coupled with near-total absence of short haul service. From a

---

[6] "Costs" here is simply equal to fully allocated average unit cost (including a profit) for the
quantity of air travel specified.

public policy point of view, this development pattern for air transport was deemed unacceptable back as far as 1938. In its place evolved the concept of internal cross subsidy. Higher than free market equilibrium point fares would be allowed in long haul markets ("value-of-service" as opposed to "cost" based pricing), and the excess profit earned there by the carriers would be used internally to subsidize below cost fares in short haul markets which these carriers were required to serve, thus making short haul air service economically possible. Where total revenue from all of a carrier's operations was insufficient to cover all costs (including a reasonable profit) the government made up the difference via direct subsidy.

While fare structure has always been a relatively important issue for the domestic trunk air carriers, in terms of short-run profitability this concern with structure increased dramatically in the mid-1950 period. Prior to the early 1950s the domestic trunk carriers relied heavily upon direct subsidy from the United States government to underwrite the cost of loss operations (Table 3.1). The long haul-short haul internal cross-subsidization issue was hardly crucial when the government absorbed the noninternally subsidized losses. Indeed, it was advantageous in this early period for short haul carriers to argue *against* fare increases in short haul markets. Low fares helped to build their traffic and market share. Whenever pressure built up in Congress regarding the absolute level of subsidy payments, the short haul carriers could and did argue that fare increases aimed at reducing total subsidy should be concentrated in long haul markets where the "value of service" (and implicitly the willingness of passengers to pay increased fares) was higher.

The Impact of Subsidy Reduction

The rules of the game changed substantially in the early 1950s, however, as Local Service carriers began to take over many of the trunks' thinly traveled short haul routes. At that point it became clear that subsidy payments to the trunks were about to be eliminated (Table 3.1).

With the elimination of direct subsidy, one might expect the spread in relative profitability between various trunk carriers to widen dramatically unless the carriers were well balanced in terms of both degrees of competition and haul lengths over their routes (Tables 2.2 and 2.3.). If these factors were not balanced, then carriers with high profit potential (i.e., more than the average fraction of long haul routes and less than average competition on such routes) might be expected to drive down the profitability of those long haul routes on which they faced competition in order to build their market shares. The resulting excess capacity and low profitability on such long haul routes would then defeat the whole concept of internal cross subsidization. If such behavior were occurring we would expect to find load factors declining with (a) increasing length of haul, and (b) increasing degree of competition. This is, of course, exactly what was observed in Chapter 2 (Figure 2.1).

TABLE 3.1

DIRECT GOVERNMENT SUBSIDY PAYMENTS TO UNITED STATES AIR CARRIERS
AND THE PERCENTAGE OF THIS SUBSIDY TO TOTAL PASSENGER REVENUES, 1939–1970

Year	Subsidy to Domestic Trunk Carriers	Subsidy as a Percentage of Passenger Revenue	Subsidy to Local Service Carriers	Subsidy as a Percentage of Passenger Revenue
	(Millions of Dollars)	*(Percent)*	*(Millions of Dollars)*	*(Percent)*
1939	12.3	35.7	—	—
1940	13.8	26.2	—	—
1941	13.9	20.1	—	—
1942	13.9	18.8	—	—
1943	5.0*	5.8	—	—
1944	2.0*	1.7	—	—
1945	2.3*	1.4	—	—
1946	4.1	1.5	1.1	366.6
1947	9.1	3.0	3.7	160.9
1948	21.6	6.4	9.4	200.0
1949	26.2	6.9	12.4	167.6
1950	26.7	6.2	15.0	145.6
1951	16.5	2.9	17.3	106.1
1952	6.6	1.0	19.0	96.0
1953	3.5	.5	21.9	94.0
1954	3.8	.4	24.3	85.6
1955	2.8	.3	22.6	67.5
1956	1.8	.2	24.6	61.2
1957	1.6	.1	28.6	60.3
1958	2.3	.2	32.7	57.9
1959	1.2	.1	36.5	49.9
1960	0	0	51.5	59.7
1961	0	0	56.3	54.3
1962	0	0	64.7	51.6
1963	0	0	67.6	47.2
1964	2.6**	.1	65.5	38.7
1965	3.5**	.1	62.3	30.6
1966	3.2**	.1	60.1	22.7
1967	2.5**	.1	55.1	17.6
1968	1.3**	0	36.2	8.7
1969	—	0	36.2	6.9
1970	—	0	41.0	6.5

* W. W. II caused a surge in air traffic which could not be met with new aircraft deliveries. As a result, load factors and profitability soared, abnormally reducing subsidy needs.
** Certain local service markets on Northeast's routes were still subsidized.

SOURCE: U.S. Civil Aeronautics Board, *Subsidy for United States Certificated Air Carriers.*

Emergence of Competitive Advantage

With the elimination of direct subsidy, it became possible for individual trunk carrier managements to think realistically in terms of achieving a future competitive advantage over rivals which could not be nullified by direct government subsidy payments. So long as haul length imbalances existed among the carriers, and fares were not clearly related to cost, a relative profit advantage might be achieved by tinkering with the structure of industry fares. This relative profit advantage could either be *displayed* in terms of a relatively high level of current earnings or *buried* via investment for higher future returns in market share gains captured at the expense of less astute and/or financially depressed competitors.

In practice, fare structure competition has taken two forms which, for convenience, will be labeled (1) The Cross-Subsidization Issue and (2) the "My Fare vs. the Average Industry Fare Issue."

The Cross-Subsidization Issue

The short haul carriers never deceived themselves regarding their chances of changing the industry's fare structure quickly through general industry agreement.[7] Neither could they envisage persuading the CAB to increase short haul fares selectively when the trunks, as a group, were earning satisfactory profits.[8] The only way to effect change, therefore, was to wait for periods of industry-wide profit pressure and try to load the bulk of the extra revenue from any fare increase which the CAB might permit into short haul markets. As the CAB took the factor of "need" into account in reviewing fare proposals, the short haul carriers often got some small structural change when fares were increased, but not enough to cause the long haul carriers to balk at accepting the form of the general increase due to slippage in their *relative* profit advantage.

In every discussion of fares from the mid-1950s to the present, the short haul domestic trunk carriers have argued strongly for concentrating general fare level increases most heavily in short haul markets. The long haul carriers, with equal vigor, have resisted the trend to "cost" (as opposed to "value of service") based

---

[7] In a recent example, Mohawk Airlines (a local service carrier) received permission from the CAB to initiate discussions among the trunk and local service carriers relating to the division of fares where both types of carriers were involved in carrying a passenger during a single trip. Sensing that they had a good deal to lose, but nothing to gain from any redivisioning of fares, the long haul carriers all thanked Mohawk for the invitation, and expressed their regrets at being unable to attend.

[8] The CAB was well aware of this problem as the staff's fare study will attest. "A carrier whose earnings are substantially in excess of those of other carriers is not going to voluntarily sacrifice its profits. Consequently, the only fare revision that would have any chance of unanimous acceptance would be one that equalized the profit potential of all carriers at a level close to that of the most profitable carrier. In view of the present level of earnings of the more profitable carriers, this is obviously an impractical solution." U.S. Civil Aeronautics Board, *A Study of the Domestic Passenger Air Fare Structure,* January 1968, p. 177.

pricing. As might be expected, the long haul carriers with the fewest short haul routes championed the concept of cross-subsidization most aggressively.

The "My Fare Versus the Average Industry Fare" Issue

A competitive advantage might also be gained along a second dimension in the pricing area if a carrier were able to charge fares that were higher than the industry average for given haul lengths. Equation 1.2, for instance, shows how a carrier's breakeven load factor responds to changes in fares (revenue yield). For breakeven load factors in the range of 40% to 60%, a 1% increase in fares (according to this equation) will decrease the breakeven load factor by about .5 percentage points. Each percentage point in the spread between actual and breakeven load factors represents about 1.5 percentage points in ROI (Table 1.10). When one considers this fact along with the degree of variance actually existing in fares for similar haul lengths prior to 1969 (Figure 3.2), it is clear that this approach to fare strategy could have (and indeed may have) offered a significant competitive impact.

Since the fare area seems to represent rich territory for establishing a competitive advantage, it might be worthwhile to review the formal process by which fares for a carrier in specific city-pairs are established.

According to the Civil Aeronautics Act of 1938 and its revision, a carrier's fares are established between specific city-pairs on the following basis:

(1) On a newly authorized route, the carrier can initially set whatever fare it desires.
(2) On existing routes a carrier may at any time file fare changes with the CAB which can cover any or all of its city-pair markets. The CAB has the right to disallow the change if it finds that the new fares are unlawful.
(3) The CAB can prescribe a carrier's fare for any city-pair market in terms of either an exact amount or within maximum and/or minimum limits if it finds that the fare changed by the carrier in such market is unlawful.

The Formal Versus the Informal Process of Changing Fares

From the Act alone it is almost impossible to tell how much fare flexibility is available to management. Points (1) and (2) above might lead one to expect that the carriers enjoy great latitude in pricing. On the other hand, points (2) and (3) might lead one to expect that the CAB controls fares completely.

In practice (1) competition, (2) widely differing product mixes, (3) narrow profit margins coupled with a perceived short-run demand inelasticity, and (4) the CAB's greater concern with the level of *industry* rather than *individual carrier* profits, combine to remove almost all fare flexibility from carrier management.

Competition

In competitive markets, carrier managers generally believe that fare differentials cannot be maintained without serious dislocation of market shares. For this rea-

FIGURE 3.2

FREQUENCY DISTRIBUTION OF VARIATIONS OF JET DAY COACH FARES AS OF SEPTEMBER 1966
FROM AVERAGE JET DAY COACH FARES AT EQUAL HAUL LENGTHS

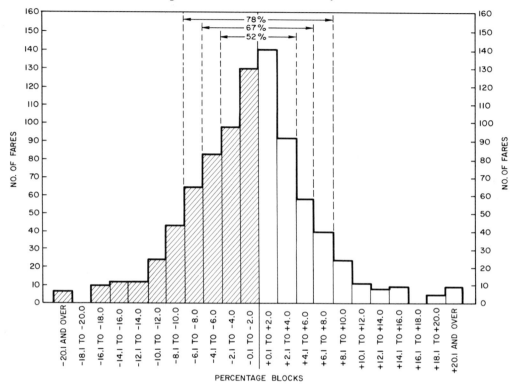

SOURCE: U.S. Civil Aeronautics Board, *A Study of the Domestic Passenger Air Fare Structure,* January 1968, p. 103.

son, agreement[9] must be reached on any fare change in a competitive market if the fare is to be *increased,* but any one carrier reducing fares in such markets can effectively force other carriers to match the reduction. The airlines thus suffer a pricing inflexibility common to oligopoly producers of all nondifferentiable products.

The Product Mix

In addition to this problem, however, reaching agreement on basic price changes is made even more difficult for air transport companies than cigarette companies, for example, due to the widely differing product mixes of the carriers. While a 5% across-the-board price increase will have the same revenue impact on each

---

[9] Agreement here is not meant to imply any illegal collusive action on the part of the carriers.

cigarette manufacturer as a 15¢/carton increase,[10] a 5% across-the-board fare increase has a very different revenue impact on each carrier than a $2.50 per ticket increase, even though either proposal might change industry revenue by a similar amount.

Narrow Profit Margins

The thinness of pretax profit margins coupled with a perceived short-run demand inelasticity in air transportation adds a third dimension to the fare change problem. The carriers estimate that traffic losses and downgrading from first class to coach service resulting from fare increases take away only 10% of the extra revenue which would be generated from fare increases if demand were totally inelastic.[11] This fact and the fact that industry operating profit margins rarely exceed 10% in the best of years (or 5% in years when general fare increases are under consideration) combine to yield an enormous profit payoff to the carrier that can accomplish the adoption of a fare revision formula which gives it a significantly higher revenue increase than the industry average.

CAB Concern Over Industry Profits

Traditionally the CAB's "first order" concern has been with industry (rather than individual carrier) ROIs.

> The public interest is defined as the maximization of industry-wide profits without placing any carrier in jeopardy. Politically, this definition would seem to be required, for industry-wide profit is the most obvious, although hardly the most reliable, index for determining whether the agency is doing a good job.[12]

The carriers thus view the fare change process as a "zero sum" game with a fixed but "CAB defined" increment to total industry profit up for grabs. This view further bolsters the tendency for each carrier to submit and hold out for a self-serving fare proposal. If one carrier feels that it needs a 5% increase in fares in order to attain a satisfactory profit level, but fears that the CAB will probably allow only a 3% increase in average industry fares, then there is only one way for the carrier to achieve its goal. That is through an unequal allocation of the additional revenue.

The Carriers' Lack of Influence in Fare Structure Changes

The need to achieve general industry agreement coupled with (1) the high payoff from getting a self-serving plan accepted; (2) the lack of any "obvious" split

---

[10] This assumes a base carton price of $3.00.

[11] U.S. Civil Aeronautics Board, "Report on Meetings Between the Civil Aeronautics Board and the Domestic Trunk Carriers on Domestic Passenger Fares," February 6, 1969, p. 9.

[12] Alan H. Silberman, "Price Discrimination and the Regulation of Air Transportation," p. 223.

which might carry a "moralistic or legalistic force toward realization";[13] (3) each industry participant being fully aware[14] of the revenue implications of all rival proposals; and (4) the existence of an outside arbiter which can be relied upon to coerce eventual agreement, conspire to remove almost all fare flexibility from the carriers individually or as a group (Figure 3.3). This is a significant phenomenon, and it will be explored briefly in the remainder of this chapter.[15]

The Informal and Formal Fare Change Process

In practice there have been seven general fare level changes since the early 1950s. The effective date of these changes, as well as the size and structural implications of each change, are shown in Table 3.2 and Figure 3.4.

TABLE 3.2

HISTORY OF GENERAL INDUSTRY FARE CHANGES, 1949–1969

Date of General Industry Fare Change	Form of General Industry Fare Change	Derived* Value of New Jet Day Coach Average Fare		Average Increase in Overall Fare Level
		(Terminal Charge)	(Line Haul Charge in Cents/Mile)	
April 1952	$1.00 per ticket increase	$3.7990	5.0345	3.5%
February 1958	$1.00 per ticket + 4% across the board	4.9510	5.2359	6.6
October 1958	Remove discount of 5% on round trip ticket sales + other discount changes	5.1243	5.4192	3.5
July 1960	$1.00 per ticket + 2.5% across the board	6.2524	5.5547	5.0
February 1962	3% across-the-board increase	6.4400	5.7213	3.0
February 1969	Table 3.7	N.A.	N.A.	4.3
October 1969	Fares conform to a fixed formula based on a fixed terminal charge and a line haul charge which declines with increasing distance	9.0000	¢ miles	6.3
			6.0 0–500	
			5.6 501–1000	
			5.2 1001–1500	
			5.0 1501–2000	
			4.8 2000 + over	

* These fares are derived by calculating backward (using the structure of the general fare increases as a guide) from the average industry fare curve at September 1966.

SOURCE: U.S. Civil Aeronautics Board, *A Study of the Domestic Passenger Air Fare Structure*, January 1968; Handbook of Airline Statistics, 1967 Edition.

Most fare level and structure changes since 1952 have followed a similar pattern. Before a change becomes effective, domestic trunk earnings have to have declined

---

[13] S. Siegel and L. E. Fouraker, *Bargaining and Group Decision Making*, p. 54.

[14] This complete awareness is a recent industry phenomenon, and it probably has substantially *increased* the problem of getting general agreement on any proposal. For instance, see Kenneth J. Arrow, "The Organization of Economic Activity: Issues Pertinent to the Choice of Market Versus Nonmarket Allocation," in *The Analysis and Evaluation of Public Expenditures: The PPB System*, Joint Economic Committee, Congress of the United States, Washington, 1969, pp. 52–53; or James T. Bonnen, "The Absence of Knowledge of Distributional Impact: An Obstacle to Effective Public Program Analysis and Decisions," in the above volume, p. 424.

[15] The chapter will then provide an in-depth look at the process by which fare structure changes were accomplished in the 1968–1969 period. It will present an elaboration of the process presented in Figure 3.3.

FIGURE 3.3

THE PROCESS OF CONFLICT RESOLUTION OVER FARE INCREASES
DOMESTIC TRUNK CARRIERS, 1952–1969

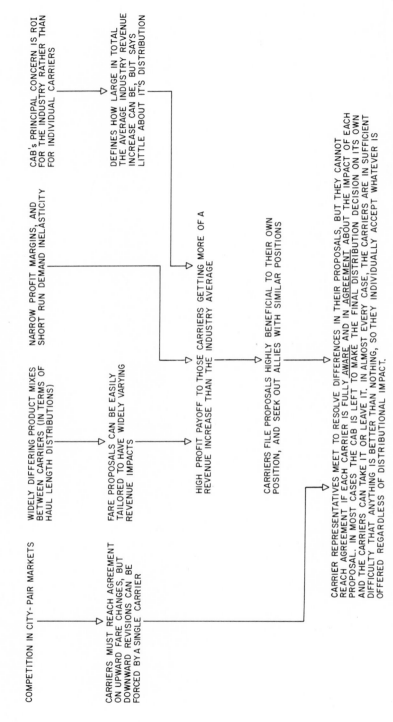

FIGURE 3.4

STRUCTURAL CHANGES IN AVERAGE INDUSTRY FARES, 1952–1969

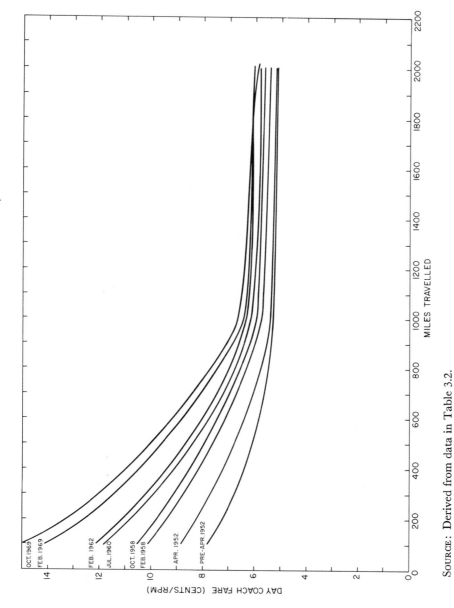

SOURCE: Derived from data in Table 3.2.

fairly seriously to an ROI of about 5% or lower.[16] Preparatory gestures are usually made long in advance of an earnings crisis, however, since the carriers anticipate a substantial regulatory lag. After the first sign that a downturn is in progress (generally after one or two quarters of declining profit margins), carrier managers[17] begin talking in the press about the incredible volume of equipment that has to be financed over the following two to five years, and how it cannot be accomplished if earnings are not adequate. Commercial bankers, investment bankers, air frame, and engine manufacturers then begin making speeches about the need for a healthy air transportation industry and the role of profit in sustaining the industry's health.

After this initial public airing of the problem, the CAB (in the form of a member's speech to some obscure group) will often suggest that load factor control in the form of capacity purchase and schedule restraint, rather than fare increases, is the answer to the industry's profit problems.

At this point the Air Transport Association (ATA) will often make some type of presentation to the Board pointing out the problems of financing new equipment and emphasizing the restraint which the carriers have exercised in their equipment buying plans. The ATA is forbidden from discussing fares with the CAB, so the presentation must deal with this issue by implication.

Shortly after the ATA presentations, top management groups from the individual carriers may arrange nonpublic meetings with the Board and/or the staff for individual appeals. Following these meetings and carrier "sizeups" of the probability of getting any favorable fare action from the CAB, some carrier will file a fare change with an effective date from 30 to 90 days in the future. Other carriers then make their own filings (the proposals usually differ in terms of the overall *amount* as well as the *distribution* of increased revenue).

At this point in the scenario the CAB will usually suspend all of the proposals, and if the Board is favorably inclined to grant some increase it will often arrange a fare meeting with the airline presidents and/or their tariff staffs. These meetings are nonpublic and antitrust immunity is in force for the duration of the discussion. The carriers make known to the Board members their feelings about the merits of all the proposals in one or two all-day meetings. Generally, there is *substantial* agreement between carriers that an increase is needed, less agreement as to the *size* of the increase, and complete disagreement as to how any increase should be allocated (i.e., fare structure changes).

This lack of consensus effectively leads the CAB to choose both the size and the distribution of revenue increases, via a Board statement to the carriers regarding the specific changes they might be inclined to accept.

---

[16] In the fall of 1970 the CAB was, for the first time in history, unwilling to grant a general fare increase in spite of a decline in trunkline earnings far below the 5% level. The reasons for this apparent change in policy will be discussed in Chapter 6.

[17] The carrier managers that speak out first on the need for fare increases are generally those in the deepest difficulty. In the early phases of a downturn the more prosperous industry participants often try to take advantage of the situation to build market share. They thus hold back until the overall deterioration gets serious enough so that they too feel the pinch.

The carriers then have the option of either filing the changes suggested by the CAB or not. Since each carrier is always better off (in terms of total profit) *with* the change than *without* it, they all usually accept whatever relief is available regardless of its distribution.[18] A model of the conflict resolution process followed in arriving at fare changes for the trunk carriers is presented in Figure 3.3.

Clausewitz once observed that "Theory is instituted that each person in succession may not have to go through the same labour of clearing the ground and toiling through his subject, but may find the thing in order, and light admitted on it." [19] As little has been written previously about the process of changing the structure of airline fares, the remainder of this chapter must, of necessity, retain some elements of "ground clearing and toiling." It is needed, however, to lend empirical support to the somewhat surprising conclusions regarding fare changes described in Figure 3.3.

CONFLICT RESOLUTION IN FARE LEVEL AND STRUCTURE CHANGES, 1967–1969

The groundwork for the two general fare increases which the CAB approved in 1969 was being laid as early as the first quarter of 1967 when domestic trunk operating profit margins took a downturn (in relation to the comparable quarter in the prior year) for the first time in five years[20] (Figure 3.5). This downturn was seen as a clear signal by some mutual funds that the heyday in airline stocks was over.[21] While some investors were still responding favorably to rising *per share* airline earnings in early 1967, the funds started dumping airline equities as soon as they saw the first-quarter 1967 operating results indicating that profitability had begun to decline (Figure 3.5, Table 3.3).

Three factors contributed to a reluctance on the part of carriers to press the CAB immediately for general fare relief early in 1967. *First,* the industry's return on investment, while declining, was still quite good. The air carriers long ago gave up trying to convince the CAB of the need for adjustment until (1) returns were well below the allowed level of 10.5% and (2) the long-term nature of a downtrend in earnings was clearly established. *Second,* the carriers were afraid to

---

[18] Prior to 1952, the structure of the domestic fare curve was relatively simple. In 1943, for instance, fares were constructed by applying a fixed rate per passenger mile to the airport-to-airport mileage between local points. The coach "fare curve" for various passenger haul lengths was thus quite close to a horizontal line at 4¢ per passenger mile. When subsidy for most of the trunks was effectively discontinued in 1952, however, the issue of internal cross subsidization became crucial. Since 1952, the short haul carriers have, with substantial CAB support, moved the curve steadily in the direction of full cost pricing for trips of all distances (Figure 3.4).

[19] Carl von Clausewitz, *On War*, p. 191.

[20] Margins actually were down in the third quarter of 1966, but this was due to an industry-wide strike.

[21] Some funds had sold airline stocks heavily at an earlier date, but this was probably due to the severe strike which occurred in the third quarter of 1966. Five of the trunk carriers, including three of the Big 4, suspended operations for 43 days because of the strike.

TABLE 3.3

4-Quarter Moving Average Return* on Investment Data
Domestic Trunk Carriers, Domestic Operations, 1966–1970
(Percent)

Year/Quarter	American	Braniff	Continental	Delta	Eastern	National	Northeast	Northwest	Trans World	United	Western	Industry
1966/2	10.3	20.0	21.4	27.5	10.3	21.6	−30.6	21.1	11.5	11.3	14.9	13.7
/3**	11.6	21.4	20.4	31.7	6.1	17.0	8.2	16.6	7.4	7.0	17.2	11.9
/4	11.1	16.0	21.8	29.9	6.0	16.3	3.7	16.6	7.7	7.5	16.7	11.6
1967/1	10.8	13.1	21.7	28.4	5.7	16.3	4.1	16.1	16.1	5.8	6.8	10.8
/2	10.2	9.3	19.4	27.0	5.2	14.4	−2.2	14.8	4.2	7.1	14.9	9.9
/3	9.0	4.7	16.5	21.6	8.2	18.7	−11.0	16.8	5.8	10.7	12.1	10.4
/4	7.9	2.2	14.5	20.0	6.5	17.9	−15.5	15.0	4.5	9.2	8.9	8.9
1968/1	7.2	2.1	12.4	18.4	5.0	16.1	−5.8	14.1	11.2	2.9	8.3	7.9
/2	6.7	2.7	9.6	17.8	3.8	15.7	.8	13.0	2.8	7.2	11.5	7.3
/3	6.3	3.8	7.7	17.4	2.6	14.4	.2	12.0	2.7	5.8	9.7	6.5
/4	6.0	5.3	5.7	16.0	.8	13.6	1.1	11.3	1.7	5.0	7.3	5.7
1969/1	4.6	6.1	5.3	15.3	.7	11.8	−.7	9.4	1.7	6.0	4.4	5.3
/2	4.5	6.9	4.6	14.5	1.0	12.0	−7.0	8.9	.5	6.2	2.4	5.1
/3	5.1	6.8	4.5	14.2	1.0	11.6	−21.3	7.9	.6	6.6	−.7	5.2
/4	6.6	6.2	4.7	14.2	3.0	10.0	−66.9	9.0	1.5	6.0	−.2	5.1
1970/1	7.6	5.0	4.5	14.4	4.1	8.4	−82.5	12.2	−.7	5.6	.0	5.1
/2	6.3	3.7	5.1	14.5	4.6	4.1	−92.3	—	−2.8	3.6	−.5	4.1
/3	3.7	1.2	5.4	14.4	4.5	.9	−110.0	—	−4.2	1.8	3.1	2.9
/4	−1.2	1.8	5.4	13.3	3.7	−.5	−57.1	8.0	−8.3	−1.1	4.0	1.1

* Includes investment tax credits.
** Eastern, National, Northwest, Trans World, and United suffered a 43-day strike in this quarter.

Source: U.S. Civil Aeronautics Board, Air Carrier Financial Statistics.

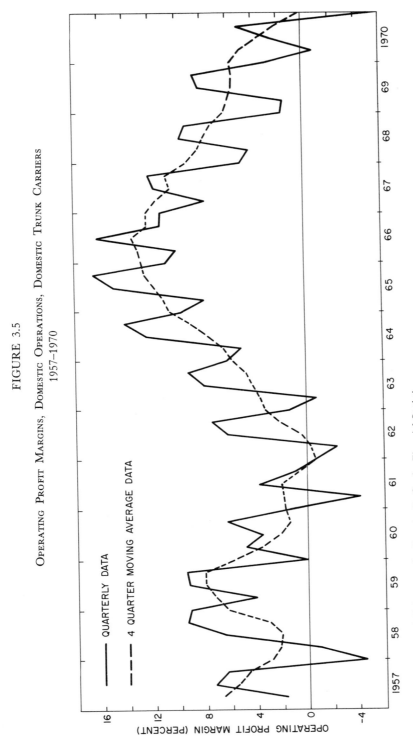

FIGURE 3.5

OPERATING PROFIT MARGINS, DOMESTIC OPERATIONS, DOMESTIC TRUNK CARRIERS
1957–1970

SOURCE: U.S. Civil Aeronautics Board, *Air Carrier Financial Statistics.*

speak out individually regarding fare increases for fear of injuring their positions in key route cases pending before the CAB, such as the Transpacific case.[22] *Third,* many of the carriers were taking advantage of their last chance to get off an equity offering at attractive prices, and were, therefore, reluctant to advertise any deterioration in the industry's profit picture.[23]

A Revenue Increase From a Limited Fare Change

The first publicly visible activity on the fare front was delayed until November 1967, when the industry mounted a two-pronged attack on the problem. *First,* two of the three transcontinental carriers (TWA and United) decided to test the CAB's resolve on holding the fare line with a proposal designed to slow the growing popularity of discount fares by reducing the time periods when they could be used. While neither basic fare levels nor the fare structure would be changed by this proposal, it did promise to generate some improvement in revenue and profit, especially for the long haul carriers where the use of discount fares was most prevalent.[24] The proposal was well structured for the environmental situation since it (1) provided the carriers with increased revenue, but (2) offered low public visibility to the increase out of deference to the CAB's potential exposure to criticism for allowing an increase. The other trunk carriers quickly followed the United-TWA lead on this proposal.

While awaiting the CAB's response on the discount reduction proposal, the industry launched the second part of its effort to raise fares. On November 28, 1967, the ATA, at the collective and nearly unanimous[25] request of the domestic trunk carriers, made a lengthy (41 pages and 30 slides) and well-reasoned presentation before the Board and the CAB staff. The proposal outlined the difficulty which

---

[22] *Wall Street Journal,* September 14, 1967.

[23] During the first half of 1967 an enormous volume of new airline equity financing was undertaken:

Airline	Type of Offering	Amount	Date Filed/Sold	
American	4 1/4% convertible debenture	$167,400,000	June/July	1967
Continental	3 1/2% convertible debenture	$ 35,000,000	April/May	1967
Eastern	475,000 common shares	$ 42,800,000	February/February	1967
TWA	4% convertible debenture	$100,000,000	February/March	1967
United	4 1/4% convertible debenture	$130,800,000	June/July	1967
		$476,000,000		

[24] TWA estimated that Discover America discount fares reduced coach yields by 7% over the carrier's domestic system, but that the erosion reached 31% transcontinentally. TWA estimated that on its system the availability of Discover America discounts generated $16.7 million in revenue from passengers who would not have flown without the discount, but that it lost through diversion $20.0 million in revenue from passengers who would have flown even if the discount were not available. *Aviation Daily,* November 15, 1967, p. 80.

[25] Only Continental Airlines, a very high return carrier (Table 3.3), refused to participate in the study, perhaps in the hope of impressing the CAB with its lack of interest in a fare increase.

the carriers would have in fulfilling their equipment purchase commitments if the industry's profit position was allowed to continue deteriorating.

The CAB's response to the ATA presentation was reasonably favorable. Some two weeks later, the Board permitted much of United's plan (to reduce discount traffic) to go into effect for the entire industry.

A Second Limited Fare Change

Shortly after the partial victory on the Discover America discount proposal, the industry again tested the water via a unanimous proposal (first suggested by American in November) to round upward to the nearest even dollar all fares for trip distances of less than 750 miles, while fares on those trips of more than 750 miles would be rounded down to the nearest even dollar. The proposal was justified in terms of its cost saving through simplification of ticket writing, tariff filings, etc., but curiously enough the revenue decrease occasioned by fare reductions was more than offset by the increases, and the industry enjoyed a revenue boost of nearly *$10 million* based on 1967 ticket sales.[26]

The next major move in the fare situation came in a speech made by CAB member John Adams to the New York Society of Security Analysts on January 12, 1968. Mr. Adams, speaking for himself and not the Board,[27] suggested in the meeting that cost increases, if not the result of overcapacity, might be offset through fare increases. He went even further to suggest that revenue boosts might come in the form of a rise in first class fares and/or an increase in the taper for short vs. long haul fares rather than a straight across-the-board increase.[28]

On January 18, 1968, the CAB accepted the carrier's fare rounding proposal and praised the plan since it would "simplify ticketing and reservations procedures and should generally benefit the public." [29] While this proposal actually changed both the level and structure of fares somewhat, it was, again, far less visible to the public than a straight increase and was thus more easily accepted by the CAB.

The CAB's Suggestion for Future Fare Changes

Late in January 1968, the Rates Division of the CAB's Bureau of Economics issued the results of a two-year study[30] of the structure of domestic passenger air fares.[31] The 260-page volume was obviously well planned and well documented. In accord with the usual custom, it was issued as a staff study without the Board's

---

[26] *Aviation Daily*, January 19, 1968, p. 99.

[27] This distinction appears to be official religion for members of regulatory bodies.

[28] *Wall Street Journal*, January 15, 1968.

[29] *Aviation Daily*, January 19, 1968, p. 99.

[30] The document was entitled *A Study of the Domestic Passenger Air Fare Structure*.

[31] A major portion of the man-hours devoted to the study were spent in analyzing airline costs by equipment type and segment length. This material was incorporated in the study, thus giving it a far broader scope than its title implies.

imprimatur. Nonetheless, the scope of the undertaking (in comparison to the man-hours available for such general studies at the CAB) indicated that the Board was extremely interested in the result. The two findings and conclusions with greatest significance to the carriers are reproduced below:

(1) The fare structure has a moderate taper. Fares per mile vary inversely with distance, but *a greater taper appears warranted.* (Emphasis mine.)
(2) The fare structure consists of several well defined patterns and relationships with a limited number of wide variations and departures from the pattern. *Some of these variations can and should be modified.*[32] (Emphasis mine.)

In this latter case the staff went so far as to suggest that all fares falling more than 8% away from the average industry fare curve (Figure 3.2) should be adjusted so that they fall no more than 4% away from the curve.

With the publication of this document, the carriers were put on notice that the next time the Board was in a position to twist the carriers' arms (i.e., the next time that the general level of fares was altered), structural changes could be anticipated. Changes along the first dimension (fare taper) would enhance the relative profit potential of the short haul carriers at the expense of long haul carriers. Changes along the second dimension (narrowing the variance of fares around the fare curve) would

(1) Enhance the relative profit potential of East-West carriers at the expense of North-South carriers.
(2) Increase the relative profit potential of carriers operating in the Northeast.
(3) Increase the relative profit potential of carriers operating with a high percentage of traffic on competitive routes at the expense of monopoly carriers.
(4) Increase the relative profit potential of short haul carriers at the expense of long haul carriers.
(5) Increase the relative profit potential of carriers operating in heavily traveled markets at the expense of carriers operating in thinly traveled markets (Table 3.4).

While profit margins (as well as absolute profits by this date) continued to sag in early 1968, the carriers were individually preoccupied with assessing the impact on future profitability of various suggested changes in the fare structure study. In a very real sense, the rules of the game changed with the publication of the CAB study. Traditionally acceptable options such as across-the-board percentage fare increases appeared to be foreclosed. Each carrier had to work within a new general framework and try to mold it to his advantage. No carrier was in a hurry to establish a position before fully comprehending the new environment.

While the carriers individually were relatively silent for many months after the publication of the CAB fare study, the ATA was still actively promoting the financial plight of the carriers. In June of 1968, the ATA made a second presenta-

---

[32] U.S. Civil Aeronautics Board, *A Study of the Domestic Passenger Air Fare Structure*, January 1968, p. 5.

TABLE 3.4

CATEGORIZATION OF CITY-PAIR MARKETS IN WHICH FARES
VARY FROM THE INDUSTRY AVERAGE FOR EQUIVALENT HAUL LENGTHS
SEPTEMBER 1966

Jet Day Coach Fares
with More Than 6 Percent Variation from the Computed Fare
By Direction Characteristic

Direction	Markets with Variations More Than			Markets	Variations Greater Than 6 Percent as Percent of Total
	±6%	+6%	−6%		
East-West	61	21	40	300	20%
North-South	59	51	8	275	21
Total Direction	120	72	48	575	21%

By Area Characteristic

Area					
Northeast	80	10	70	137	58%
Southeast	23	11	12	70	33
North Central	21	3	18	31	68
South Central	27	9	18	42	64
Northwest	7	4	3	18	39
Southwest	12	4	8	22	55
Total Area	170	41	129	320	53%

By Competitive Status

Competitive Status					
Noncompetitive	133	78	55	461	29%
Competitive	157	35	122	434	36
Total	290	113	177	895	33%

By Mileage Block

Mileage Block					
0–399 Miles	169	43	126	298	57%
400–799 Miles	81	41	40	238	31
800–1,199 Miles	23	18	5	152	15
1,200–1,799 Miles	11	7	4	100	11
1,800 Miles and Over	6	4	2	107	6
Total	290	113	177	895	33%

By Market Density

Market Density					
Heavy	28	1	27	53	53%
Medium	100	22	78	295	34
Light	162	90	72	547	29
Total	290	113	177	895	33%

SOURCE: U.S. Civil Aeronautics Board, *A Study of the Domestic Passenger Air Fare Structure*, January 1968.

tion to the CAB members and staff. In this meeting Dr. George James, Vice President for Economics of the ATA, outlined the impact of the continued profit deterioration on the carriers' equipment plans and tried to answer a question raised by Board member Adams' speech of January 12, 1968, regarding load factor control. This presentation was longer and more comprehensive than that of November 1967; it ran to 42 pages with 41 slides.

Route Considerations Hinder the Presentation of Fare Proposals

Progress in the Transpacific route case in mid-1968 was adding to individual carrier reluctance to file for new general fare increases. Most of the carriers seeking routes in the Pacific had argued for 25% to 40% reductions in fares in Pacific markets. A carrier proposing such large decreases overseas and then asking for increases domestically would be in a somewhat awkward position. While this consideration might not be of great concern in most route cases, in terms of its potential for long-term reallocation of profits the Transpacific decision promised to be probably the most important route proceeding in history. The routes involved were long haul, high fare, high growth, and without any doubt the most profitable of all major markets (Table 3.5). All of the trunk carriers had made application for

TABLE 3.5

PROFIT SIGNIFICANCE OF TRANSPACIFIC OPERATIONS

	11 Domestic Trunks and Pan American			Pacific Operations of Northwest and Pan American		
	Total Operating Revenues All Air Operations (Millions of Dollars)	Growth in Operating Revenues (Percent)	Total Operating Profit All Air Operations (Millions of Dollars)	Total Operating Revenues Pacific Air Operations (Millions of Dollars)	Growth in Operating Revenues (Percent)	Total Operating Profit Pacific Air Operations (Millions of Dollars)
1964	3,747		437	247		59
1965	4,380	16.9	618	297	20.0	83
1966	5,030	14.8	702	431	45.0	128
1967	6,114	21.5	686	526	22.0	137
1968	6,906	13.0	536	549	4.4	107

	1964	1965	1966	1967	1968
Operating Profit Pacific Operations (NW + Pan Am) / Operating Profit Total Operations (All U.S. Carriers)	.14	.13	.18	.20	.20
Operating Profit Pacific Operations (Pan Am) / Operating Profit Total Operations (Pan Am)	.55	.53	.58	.72	.90
Operating Profit Pacific Operations (NW) / Operating Profit Total Operations (NW)	.46	.46	.54	.52	.51

SOURCE: Derived from data in U.S. Civil Aeronautics Board, *Air Carrier Financial Statistics*.

Pacific routes, and most of the carriers felt that the final decision would be rendered by the end of 1968 [33] before the President (who had to approve the final decision) left office. Thus, the carriers were individually willing to suffer profit losses for a few additional months rather than endanger their positions. "But as soon as the Pacific case is decided, the lid will be off," [34] one carrier manager reported.

---

[33] *Aviation Daily*, April 15, 1968, p. 219.
[34] *Wall Street Journal*, November 6, 1968, p. 34.

A Back Door Fare Increase Proposal Fails

Late in July 1968, the president of TWA asked the Board for permission to hold industry-wide talks on the problem of air congestion. "The exploration of all possible solutions should be authorized," said Tillinghast, and include "the possibility of rescheduling or eliminating schedules during congested traffic periods and the *use of fare differentials between peak and low volume periods.*" [35] (Emphasis mine.)

The CAB quickly approved the discussions relating to congestion at New York, Chicago, Los Angeles, and Washington, but one Board member, John G. Adams, warned, "I dislike the possibility of an overall percentage fare increase which could come out of this tactic . . . rather than from a rate proceeding." [36] Adams clearly felt that the carriers were attempting to use a back door to gain a general fare increase without forcing any one carrier to bear the onus of individually proposing such a change.

True to Adams' anticipation, in late September 1968, 9 of the 11 domestic trunks "asked for permission to discuss fares between all U.S. points and between U.S. points and Canadian points" in an effort to solve the congestion [sic] problem. [37] In early October this request was denied.

The Fare Maneuvering Begins in Earnest

Some time shortly after Labor Day (the exact date was a closely guarded secret) the CAB sent its decision on the Transpacific case to the White House for approval. Evidently confident that the final die was already cast, on October 1, 1968, Braniff filed a proposal to reduce all of its fares 5% and simultaneously increase the price of each ticket by $3.00. The revenue impact of the proposal was estimated [38] to be a 4.5% increase for Braniff vs. a 1.6% increase for the entire industry.

Early one evening in November 1968, CAB chairman John H. Crooker met privately in New York with the presidents of Pan American, TWA, Eastern, and American along with a number of private investors. [39] Evidently no specific fare proposals were discussed, but the conversations focused on general financial problems. Shortly thereafter, CAB member John G. Adams reiterated (in a speech before the New Orleans Chamber of Commerce) the same comments he had made the previous January to the New York Society of Security Analysts.

On December 6, 1968, officials of TWA met privately with the CAB staff and Board members to propose a fare change which would increase TWA's domestic revenues by 5.31% vs. 5.76% for the domestic trunk industry. On December 9, 1968, the top officers of United and Eastern made separate private proposals which

---

[35] *Aviation Daily,* July 25, 1968, p. 133.

[36] *Aviation Daily,* July 30, 1968, p. 156.

[37] *Aviation Daily,* September 23, 1968, p. 110.

[38] *Trans World Airlines, Domestic Passenger Air Fares, The Time and Course for Change,* December 6, 1969, slide 30.

[39] *Aviation Daily,* November 8, 1968, p. 40; *Aviation Daily,* November 12, 1968, p. 47.

would increase their revenues by 5.73% and 6.6% respectively versus increases of 4.47% and 5.2% for the domestic trunk industry respectively. On December 17, 1968, Northeast Airlines filed a fare proposal quite similar to that suggested by Eastern. As the proposals suggested by the various trunks were mutually exclusive, the Board agreed (at the suggestion of United's President George Keck) to hold a closed door meeting with industry executives on January 13, 1969, to arrive at an acceptable solution to the fare dilemma.

The Airline Presidents Meet to Discuss Fares

At this meeting the CAB chairman, John H. Crooker, stated that, "After analysis, the Board has concluded that none of the proposals could be approved, in toto, and that all should be suspended." [40] The chairman then went on to state that the use of a specific mathematical formula relating fares to a fixed terminal charge plus a varying per mile rate "would assist in moving the fare structure in the right direction in terms of taper and . . . would also produce internal consistency within the fare structure." [41] Both of these aims were in complete accord with the conclusions of the January 1968 CAB staff study on fares. Chairman Crooker then went on to state that the current financial picture of the carriers called for some immediate interim relief but that over the longer term the . . .

> sense of the Board favored further staff effort toward the development of a cost-oriented formula which would replace the present fare norms as a guideline in evaluating proposed fares. In this connection he outlined one possible approach which will be subjected to detailed analysis in the months ahead. This approach would assign differing cost elements according to whether the service in question was between points categorized as a village, city, metropolis, major hub, or any combination of these. The assignable cost per mile to reflect distance flown would decline as distance increases, rather than remain as a constant factor.[42]

The Board's Proposal Vis-à-Vis a General Fare Increase in February 1969

In terms of immediate interim fare relief, the chairman "enumerated" the following fare adjustments that the Board, or a majority of the Board, would be inclined to permit:[43]

(1) Imposition of a seven-day minimum stay and seven-day advance ticket pickup requirement on Discover America fares.
(2) Decrease the youth fare discount from 50% to 33⅓%, with provision for a firm reservation.

[40] U.S. Civil Aeronautics Board, "Report on Meeting Between the Civil Aeronautics Board and the Domestic Trunk Carriers on Domestic Passenger Fares," February 6, 1969, p. 1.
[41] *Ibid.*, p. 4.
[42] *Ibid.*, p. 5.
[43] *Ibid.*, p. 6.

(3) Increase by $1.00 the jet coach fares in markets up to 1,100 miles.
(4) Increase by $2.00 all jet first class fares, with additional increases ranging from $1.00 to $8.00 in east-west markets above 800 miles where first class fares are presently at depressed levels.

The chairman pointed out that the Board was not insisting on the above specific adjustments in promotional fares. However, the potential revenue benefit made available by these adjustments—estimated at approximately $37 million for the domestic trunkline industry based on 1967 traffic—would be borne in mind in future assessment of the industry's financial condition. Fares for other classes of service, such as those provided with propeller equipment and night coach, could be adjusted to maintain existing relationships with jet fares. In addition, it was indicated that a majority of the Board was inclined at this point in time to permit a surcharge of $1.00 on fares to/from New York/Newark, Washington/Baltimore, and Chicago in markets up to 750 miles—estimated to amount to $23.4 million in additional revenue for the trunklines.

The Board, at the carriers' request, then distributed a chart (Table 3.6) which purported to represent the absolute and percentage revenue increase to be enjoyed by each carrier. The total package promised to give the trunk carriers $162.8 million in additional revenue (before an assumed 10% dilution as referenced in footnote 11, or about a 4% total increase in revenues. Northeast, a "need" carrier, was promised the largest percentage revenue increase (5.7%) while National, a highly profitable carrier, was to receive only a 2.9% increase. "To provide the carriers with some time to evaluate these estimates, it was decided to recess until Thursday, January 16th." [44]

From Tables 3.6, 3.3 and Figure 3.4 it was clear that, as might have been anticipated from the January 1968 CAB staff report, the short haul and/or "need" carriers had won the day. In the short two-day recess about all any carrier could ever hope to accomplish in terms of revenue reallocation was a slight shift. The Board had specified a top limit to the size of the increase (about $160 million) and had framed a general allocation pattern.

When the meeting reconvened, TWA's president stated that the youth fare alteration proposed by the Board would not only fail to yield the $22.0 million revenue increase advertised, but would in fact result in a net revenue *reduction* due to diversion of existing full fare youth travel to a guaranteed seat at a lower fare. TWA proposed to eliminate the youth fare change and substitute three other revenue-producing alterations which would have a particularly favorable impact on its revenue position.

After considerable discussion involving the TWA and other carrier proposals, the CAB members adjourned to reassess their positions, and returned at 2:00 p.m. to state that, "A majority would be disposed to permit the following specific adjustments": [45]

[44] *Ibid.*, p. 10.
[45] *Ibid.*, p. 15.

TABLE 3.6

ESTIMATED EFFECT OF FARE INCREASE ON TOTAL 1967 PASSENGER REVENUES

(Amounts in Millions)

	First Class Fares*		Coach Fares**		Hub Charges***		Subtotal for Normal Fares		Youth Fares†		Discover America††		Combined Totals	
	Amount	Percent	Amount	Percent	Amount	Percent	Amount	Percent	Amount	Percent	Amount	Percent	Amount	Percent
American	$ 9.8	1.38%	$ 8.4	1.18%	$ 5.2	.73%	$ 23.4	3.29%	$ 6.0	.84%	$ 3.1	.44%	$ 32.5	4.57%
Eastern	4.5	.85	11.8	2.23	5.2	.99	21.5	4.07	4.6	.83	1.2	.23	22.7	4.30
TWA	7.0	1.27	5.2	.94	2.9	.52	15.1	2.73	—	—	2.6	.47	22.3	4.03
United	13.0	1.49	11.5	1.32	5.1	.58	29.6	3.39	7.1	.82	3.8	.44	40.5	4.65
Big Four	34.3	1.29	36.9	1.39	18.4	.69	89.6	3.37	17.7	.66	10.7	.40	118.0	4.43
Braniff	1.5	1.00	3.2	2.13	.2	.13	4.9	3.26	—	—	.3	.20	5.2	3.46
Continental	.8	.75	1.4	1.31	—	—	2.2	2.06	1.0	.93	.4	.37	3.6	3.36
Delta	3.0	.83	5.5	1.53	1.3	.36	9.8	2.72	—	—	1.1	.30	10.9	3.02
National	1.4	.72	2.6	1.32	.8	.41	4.8	2.45	—	—	.8	.41	5.6	2.86
Northeast	.8	1.12	1.6	2.24	.9	1.26	3.3	4.62	.6	.84	.2	.27	4.1	5.73
Northwest	1.8	.87	3.3	1.58	1.8	.87	6.9	3.32	1.5	.72	.8	.39	9.2	4.43
Western	1.5	1.02	2.9	1.99	—	—	4.4	3.01	1.1	.75	.7	.48	6.2	4.24
Little Seven	10.8	.87	20.5	1.65	5.0	.41	36.3	2.93	4.2	.34	4.3	.34	44.8	3.61
Total Trunks	45.1	1.16	57.4	1.47	23.4	.60	125.9	3.23	21.9	.56	15.0	.38	162.8	4.17
Total Locals	27.1	8.63	1.5	.48	4.3	1.37	32.9	10.48	—	—	—	—	32.9	10.48
Totals	$72.2	1.71%	$58.9	1.39%	$27.7	.66%	$158.8	3.76%	$21.9	.52%	$15.0	.36%	$195.7	4.64%

* Increase of $2.00 in all first class fares up to 800 miles, plus increases on certain east-west tickets of 800 miles or more another $1.00 to $8.00 depending on distance.
** Increase of $1.00 in coach fares up to 1,100 miles; thereafter no increase.
*** Add $1.00 to each first class and coach fare involving New York/Newark, Washington/Baltimore, and Chicago in markets up to 750 miles.
† Cut discount from 50% to 33 1/3% and provide reservation.
†† Apply seven-day minimum stay and seven-day advance pickup rules.

SOURCE: U.S. Civil Aeronautics Board, "Report on Meeting Between the Civil Aeronautics Board and the Domestic Trunk Carriers on Passenger Fares," February 6, 1969, Attachment C.

The Board's Final Proposal Vis-à-Vis a General Fare Increase in February 1969

(1) *First class fares*—an increase of $3.00 one way across the board, and additional increases of from $1.00 to $7.00 depending on distance in east-west first class fares in certain specific markets of 800 miles or more in which fares have been depressed below industry norms. This is estimated to produce an additional $15 million in first class revenues for the trunkline industry over the formula suggested at the Monday meeting.

(2) *Coach fares*—an increase of $2.00 in one way markets up to 500 miles, and an increase of $1.00 one way in markets from 500 to 1,800 miles, with no increase above 1,800 miles. This is estimated to produce an additional $35 million in domestic trunkline coach revenues over that suggested at the Monday meeting.

(3) *Discover America fares*—the carriers would be permitted to establish a seven-day minimum stay requirement, and a seven-day minimum advance ticket pickup requirement.

Noticeably absent from the Board's new suggestions were the youth fare change and the hub surcharge. In their place was substituted an additional $1.00 per ticket increase in short haul fares. The Board's removal of the surcharge for congested hub airports (the third element of Table 3.6) was explained "in view of the size of the [other permitted] increases." [46] In addition, the Board announced that it was "sympathetic with the objective of eliminating clear inequities (above or below the norm) which may exist in the present fare structure, and will do its best to permit corrections as appropriate." [47] This was a clear signal that in the next round of fare discussions the second topic recommended in the CAB staff study would be addressed. Indeed, the formula presented at the close of the earlier meeting emphasized this point even more strongly.

Table 3.7 shows how the carriers' "end point" positions changed over the course of the two meetings in both percentage and dollar revenue increments. Clearly an enormous amount of money was redistributed between the carriers in a very short period of time. While the analogy to the division of Europe after World War II is a little too grand, to the carriers the reallocation process looked like a crapshoot of sobering proportions.

After the meeting the president of Continental Airlines made some threats about not going along with the fare increase,[48] but by January 24, 1968, all of the carriers had filed for changes to be effective February 20, 1968, along the lines suggested by the CAB.

Most of the carriers had complained that the February 20 fare increase was too small. In fact, on February 14, the president of United stated that the carrier would "move within the next three to six months for another increase in passenger fares." [49]

---

[46] *Ibid.*, p. 16.

[47] *Ibid.*, p. 17.

[48] The other carriers could have filed for the increases on all routes *except* those over which Continental competed. Continental's route structure might have been small enough so that the other carriers could go ahead on most of the changes without complete unanimity.

[49] *Aviation Daily*, February 24, 1969, p. 278.

TABLE 3.7

ESTIMATED EFFECT OF FARE INCREASE ON TOTAL 1967 PASSENGER REVENUES
AND ON TOTAL 1969 ESTIMATED PASSENGER REVENUES

(Amounts in Millions)

	First Class Fares*		Coach Fares**		Subtotal		Discover America***		Combined Totals (1967)		Estimate for Year 1969	
	Amount	Percent	Amount	Percent	Amount	Percent	Amount	Percent	Amount	Percent	Amount	Percent†
American	$12.3	1.73%	$13.6	1.91%	$25.9	3.64%	$ 3.1	.44%	$29.0	4.08%	$33.6	
Eastern	6.8	1.29	17.9	3.39	24.7	4.68	1.2	.23	25.9	4.91	30.0	
TWA	8.6	1.55	8.8	1.59	17.4	3.14	2.6	.47	20.0	3.61	23.1	
United	16.2	1.86	18.3	2.10	34.5	3.96	3.8	.44	38.3	4.40	44.3	
Big Four	43.9	1.65	58.6	2.20	102.5	3.85	10.7	.40	113.2	4.25	131.0	
Braniff	2.3	1.53	5.2	3.46	7.5	4.99	.3	.20	7.8	5.19	9.0	
Continental	1.2	1.12	2.3	2.15	3.5	3.27	.4	.37	3.9	3.64	4.5	
Delta	4.6	1.28	8.8	2.44	13.4	3.72	1.1	.30	14.5	4.02	16.8	
National	2.1	1.07	3.9	1.99	6.0	3.06	.8	.41	6.8	3.47	7.9	
Northeast	1.1	1.54	2.8	3.92	3.9	5.46	.2	.27	4.1	5.73	4.7	
Northwest	2.7	1.30	5.9	2.84	8.6	4.14	.8	.39	9.4	4.53	10.9	
Western	2.2	1.50	5.0	3.42	7.2	4.92	.7	.48	7.9	5.40	9.1	
Little Seven	16.2	1.31	33.9	2.74	50.1	4.05	4.3	.34	54.4	4.39	62.9	
Total Trunks	60.1	1.54	92.5	2.37	152.6	3.91	15.0	.38	167.6	4.29	193.9	3.8%
Total Locals††	34.0	11.79	5.5	1.91	39.5	13.70	—		39.5	13.70		
Totals	$94.1	2.24%	$98.0	2.34%	$192.1	4.58%	$15.0	.36%	$207.1	4.94%		

* Increase of $3.00 in all first class fares, plus increases on certain east-west tickets of 800 miles or more or another $1.00 to $7.00, depending on distance.

** Increase of $2.00 on tickets up to 500 miles; $1.00 on tickets between 500 and 1,800 miles, no change over 1,800 miles.

*** Apply 7-day minimum stay and 7-day advance pickup rules.

† Percent computed for total trunks only, since estimated revenues for 1969 had not been forecast by individual trunkline carrier. No forecast had been made for the local service carriers.

†† Excluding Trans-Texas, since we have been informed that this carrier may establish standard class fares in lieu of existing first class and coach services.

SOURCE: U.S. Civil Aeronautics Board, "Report on Meeting Between the Civil Aeronautics Board and the Domestic Trunk Carriers on Domestic Passenger Fares," February 6, 1969, Attachment E.

Adjusting Fares to the Average Industry Fare Curve

On March 17, 1969, TWA's president met with the CAB staff and Board members to propose adjusting all fares which fell outside ±4% of the average industry fare curve to within these boundaries. The Board had previously indicated its willingness to entertain changes which would narrow the variance of fares around the industry fare curve, and the staff had argued for a somewhat similar adjustment in its January 1968 fare study.

While the east-west long haul carriers would benefit more than other carriers from the suggested change (Tables 3.4 and 3.8), no carrier would in fact suffer a

TABLE 3.8

REVENUE IMPACT CAUSED BY ADJUSTING FARES
AT ALL HAUL LENGTHS TO WITHIN ±4%
OF THE AVERAGE INDUSTRY FARE CURVE

	Absolute Revenue Increase	Relative* Revenue Increase	Rank Ordering of Revenue Impact
American	1.07%	1.25	3
Braniff	.64	.74	7
Continental	.00	.00	11
Delta	.34	.40	8
Eastern	.83	.97	6
National	.29	.34	9
Northeast	.23	.27	10
Northwest	1.67	1.94	1
TWA	1.12	1.30	2
United	.86	1.00	5
Western	.94	1.09	4
Industry	.86	1.00	

* The relative revenue increase for each carrier equals its absolute percentage increase divided by the industry's absolute percentage revenue increase.

SOURCE: Private Carrier Data.

revenue reduction. This peculiar impact was a result of the fact that in deriving the average industry fare curve, no weights (in terms of the number of passengers involved) were applied to the fares between various city-pairs. The New York-San Francisco fare thus had the same significance in determining the industry fare curve as the Billings-Tampa fare even though 460,000 passengers per year were involved in the former city-pair versus 120 passengers per year for the latter.

To most of the carriers the whole concept of narrowing fare variances looked like another back-door increase opportunity. The allocation of this increase was, however, highly uneven.[50] In addition, the boundary levels chosen (i.e., 4%, 6%,

[50] None of the carriers proposing the change indicated their estimate of the revenue increase distribution.

or 8%) as the starting and end points for the variance contraction could change the revenue impact (both in total and in its distribution) rather substantially. There was, therefore (even more than in the case of the American rounding proposal of the prior year), a potential bonus available to the carrier which set the pattern.[51]

On April 2, 1969, United followed the TWA lead and filed for the ± 4% change. Braniff did the same on April 4. On April 23, 1969, American filed for the ± 4% change. In each case, while staying with the ± 4% limit in selecting those fares subject to change, Braniff, United, and American added slightly different conditions to the manner in which these fares would be altered which, presumably, favored them in the overall revenue allocation.

Some Congressmen Begin to Exert Pressure

On April 23, 1969, Representative John E. Moss (D. California) presented the CAB with a complaint filed along with 19 other Representatives (mostly from California) against the ± 4% fare proposals submitted by the carriers. The complaint included an extraordinarily detailed (148 footnotes) history of CAB rate making,[52] and proposed a concept of basing fares on revenue hours of flight for specific aircraft rather than on passenger miles. The document was clearly aimed at game larger than the ± 4% fare proposal, but this tariff filing provided a convenient opportunity for some Congressmen to make known to the CAB their objection to further fare increases.

Shortly after the carriers had filed for the ± 4% adjustment, managers of the largest carriers announced that they would soon ask the Board for general fare increases ranging from 3% to 5%.

On May 11, 1969, the CAB suspended the ± 4% filings proposed by the carriers. A majority of the Board concurred in warning that

> The basic solution to the industry's present financial situation would appear to lie in exercising restraint in ordering new flight equipment and in the use of available capacity, rather than in increasing its price to the public. While the Board said it was not opposed to eliminating wide variations in fares for equal travel distances, it felt that the proposed revisions were premature. It said it's currently developing a cost-oriented formula that may be used as a guide for revising fare inconsistencies.[53]

In its suspension order, the Board took considerable care in indicating that the carriers had gone on record (in answer to Congressman Moss' complaint) that they did not find the formula approach to rate making illegal.

---

[51] In the process of analyzing the competitive impact of various combinations of starting and end-point positions, at least one carrier generated enough printout from a time-share console to fill a file drawer!

[52] *U.S. Congressional Record*, House of Representatives, April 23, 1969.

[53] *Wall Street Journal*, May 12, 1969, p. 8.

. . . the carriers assert . . . that to the extent the complaint [of Congressman Moss] attacks the method used to construct the proposed fares, it ignores its own earlier statement that under the statutory standards of just and reasonable fares it is the *result reached* and not the *method employed,* which is controlling. . . .[54] (Emphasis mine.)

After this turndown, a few carriers felt that they had been "sucked-in" to a position on formulas, and that some of the CAB's members had a well-developed strategy regarding the pattern of industry fares that would ultimately emerge. These carriers saw themselves as "puppets on a string" who, at any one time, were being shown only a small portion of the total picture which would ultimately unfold before them.

The CAB Presents Its Fare Formula Proposals

On May 29, 1969, the CAB made good on its promise to develop a cost-oriented formula to remove fare inconsistencies. On that date the executive director of the CAB sent the carriers a staff document entitled "Domestic Fare Structure—Analysis of Various Fare Formula Hypotheses." This document proposed to make all fares completely consistent over equal distances, since they would be computed mechanically according to one of the six simple formulas suggested for industry-wide discussion.[55]

While a change in the direction of consistency was highly advantageous to the east-west transcontinental carriers, the six formulas also carried changes which were detrimental to these carriers' interests. In the January 1968 fare study, the CAB staff argued that fares substantially in excess of costs in the long haul markets were generating uneconomic volumes of service. This fact, according to the study, explained the low load factors experienced on long haul routes (Figure 2.1). The six formulas proposed by the staff in the May 29, 1969, letter thus suggested that fares be constructed with a fixed terminal charge and a line haul charge that *declined* with increasing distance instead of remaining constant as it did in the industry day coach fare formula. This approach would solve the excessive service problem in the long haul markets, it was hoped, by actually lowering these fares and thus making these markets less attractive for market share assaults.

The long haul east-west carriers were thus tossed a bone which coincidentally rapped them on the nose. Long haul north-south carriers such as National were on the wrong side of the fence on both proposed changes.

The CAB staff prepared two exhibits which showed the revenue change for individual carriers resulting from adoption of each of the six formulas (labeled A to F). These exhibits did not hint at the size of any overall revenue increase which the Board might permit, but when all of the formulas were adjusted to achieve an

---

[54] U.S. Civil Aeronautics Board, *Board Order #69-5-28,* May 8, 1969, p. 2.

[55] The first of these six formulas was the one presented at the end of the fare meetings of January 1968.

increase in the 5% range,[56] the six formulas carried widely differing results for the domestic trunk carriers. The left-hand side of each column in Table 3.9 shows the relative increase (measured in relation to the industry average) which each carrier would receive under each formula proposed. For instance, if the CAB allowed an overall industry increase amounting to 5% under Formula A (column 1), American Airlines would receive a revenue increase of about 5.6% (1.12 × 5%) versus an increase of about 1.4% (.28 × 5%) for National. The right-hand side of each column in Table 3.9 also shows a rank ordering of the relative increases for each carrier, as well as a "best position" (column 7) representing the most favorable possible outcome in all of the formula choices for the carrier in question. The "best position" column clearly indicates that National, Continental and Delta would probably find the entire concept of "formulas" to be extremely unattractive.

In his letter of May 29, 1969, Executive Director Keifer invited the carriers to express their views on the fare formulas "as well as any other alternatives you believe should be considered." [57] The Board scheduled a meeting in July for an exchange of views on the topic.

Tinkering with Proposals to Achieve a Competitive Advantage

On June 12, 1969, Northeast Airlines filed for a fare increase which was patterned after the basic structure proposed by the CAB staff in Formulas A to D. The line haul charges in Northeast's proposal were raised substantially over the CAB's figures, however, and the "cut-point" for reducing these charges was raised from 500-mile to 600-mile intervals. Because Northeast generated a large fraction of its total revenue passenger miles in markets of between 1,000 and 1,200 miles, this seemingly minor change promised to generate almost $3 million of extra revenue from Northeast's New York-Miami traffic alone.

On June 16, 1969, TWA's new president, F. C. Wiser, met with the CAB staff and Board to present a fare proposal which was at considerable variance from fixed formula pricing. The presentation had clearly been planned for an environment different from that posed by the CAB's May 29 document. As a result, TWA quickly scuttled its own plan.

On June 25, 1969, the ATA met with the CAB staff and Board members to present its third and most elaborate presentation regarding the deterioration of the airline financial picture. The documentation for this proposal ran to 50 pages with 44 exhibits.

Between July 8 and July 16, six carriers made informal fare proposals to the CAB in answer to Mr. Keifer's May 29 request. The nature and relative revenue impact of these proposals are summarized in Table 3.9.

---

[56] All the formulas suggested by the CAB were adjusted in Table 3.9 via across-the-board percentage increases to arrive at a 6.63% average increase, the amount finally allowed by the CAB.

[57] U.S. Civil Aeronautics Board, "Letter to Airline Presidents," May 29, 1969.

TABLE 3.9

ESTIMATED RELATIVE REVENUE IMPACT OF FARE PROPOSALS SUGGESTED BY VARIOUS CARRIERS AND THE CAB FOR AIRLINE PRESIDENTS' MEETING OF JULY 21, 1969

	1		2		3		4		5		6		7		8		9		10		11	12	
	CAB A		CAB B		CAB C		CAB D		CAB E		CAB F		Carrier's Best Position Among All 6 Formulas		Carrier's Best Position Without Formulas E and F		TWA Position		American Position		Continental Position	Eastern Position	
American	1.12	5	1.15	5	1.10	5	1.12	5	1.24	4	1.22	2	1.24	2	1.15	5	.97	8	1.14	3	1.00	1.04	5
Braniff	1.38	2	1.41	2	1.37	2	1.30	2	1.84	1	1.03	4	1.84	1	1.41	2	1.16	1	1.37	2	1.00	1.09	4
Continental	.75	8	.73	9	.74	9	.68	10	.44	10	.66	8	.74	8	.75	8	1.03	7	.70	9	1.00	.85	8
Delta	.73	9	.71	10	.75	8	.71	9	.68	8	.65	9	.75	8	.75	8	1.04	6	.87	7	1.00	.84	9
Eastern	1.21	4	1.19	4	1.29	3	1.19	4	1.24	5	.87	7	1.29	3	1.29	3	1.10	3	1.09	4	1.00	.99	6
National	.28	11	.23	11	.31	11	.32	11	-.03	11	.38	11	.38	11	.32	11	.92	10	.54	11	1.00	.53	11
Northeast	.87	7	.81	7	1.06	6	.95	7	.68	7	.62	10	1.06	6	1.06	6	1.06	4	.69	10	1.00	.74	10
Northwest	1.50	1	1.50	1	1.50	1	1.44	1	1.42	2	1.25	1	1.50	1	1.50	1	1.05	5	1.39	1	1.00	1.21	1
TWA	.75	10	.76	8	.72	10	.81	8	.55	9	1.04	5	1.04	5	.81	8	.87	11	.80	8	1.00	.99	7
United	1.04	6	1.08	6	1.02	7	1.06	6	1.23	3	1.17	3	1.23	3	1.08	6	.94	9	1.04	6	1.00	1.11	2
Western	1.36	3	1.29	3	1.28	4	1.23	3	.82	6	.97	6	1.36	3	1.36	3	1.13	2	1.07	5	1.00	1.09	3
Industry Average Relative Impact	1.00		1.00		1.00		1.00		1.00		1.00		1.00		1.00		1.00		1.00		1.00	1.00	

Specific Fare Proposal Changes (CAB)

Coach Fares	CAB A Proposal	CAB B Proposal	CAB C Proposal	CAB D Proposal	CAB E Proposal	CAB F Proposal
Line Haul Rates						
-499 miles	5.8¢	5.8¢	5.6¢	5.20¢	} 4.24¢	} 5.29¢
500–999 miles	5.4	5.4	5.3	4.95		
1,000–1,499 miles	5.0	5.0	5.0	4.70		
1,500–1,999 miles	4.6	4.6	4.7	4.45		
2,000–and up	4.2	4.2	4.4	4.20		
Terminal Charges	$6.00–$12.00 depending on congestion in city-pair involved	$6.00–$12.00 depending on congestion in city-pair involved	$6.00–$12.00 depending on congestion in city-pair involved	$6.00–$12.00 depending on congestion in city-pair involved	$6.00–$12.00 depending on congestion in city-pair involved Line haul = 6.47¢ Terminal = $20.99	$6.00–$12.00 depending on congestion in city-pair involved
First Class Fares	120% of Coach fare	125% of Coach fare	120% of Coach fare	125% of Coach fare	120% of Coach fare	120% of Coach fare

SOURCE: Derived from U.S. Civil Aeronautics Board, "Report on Meetings Between the Civil Aeronautics Board and the Domestic Trunk Carriers on Domestic Passenger Fares," February 6, 1969; also, air carrier tariff filings.

The Carriers' Strategies in Response to the CAB's Proposals

Each carrier's strategy in approaching the July fare structure meeting can be deduced from Table 3.9. Northwest (a low fare low service[58] carrier) was programmed to become the big winner if any of the six CAB formulas was adopted. The carrier merely had to choose that formula which gave it, relatively, the largest percentage increase. This it did in choosing Formula C.

In contrast to Northwest, TWA saw its competitive position damaged by all of the CAB selections except Formula F. TWA wanted to move the Board away from any notion of holding the line (or actually reducing) long haul fares. The carrier thus filed a proposal which it hoped would placate the Board's desire for more revenue on short haul fares, while still meeting TWA's goal of significant fare improvement in long haul fares.

American's position on the fare formulas is a little more difficult to analyze. This is true because CAB Formulas E and F both gave American a relatively stronger revenue gain position than did its own proposal. What may have occurred is that American was suspicious (as were some of the other carriers) regarding the CAB's sincerity in proposing Formulas E and F. Without the inclusion of these two alternatives, the "best position" of American, TWA and United (three of the Big 4 trunk carriers) would have been significantly reduced as shown in column 8 of Table 3.9. The competitive damage promised by Formulas A to D might have been sufficient to cause these three carriers to challenge the legality of the entire concept of fare construction via formulas from the outset.[59] American may thus have attempted to avoid supporting a formula which it felt was doomed from the beginning, but rather picked its best alternatives from among those remaining.

The positions of Continental and Delta on the fare formulas were relatively clear. They both promised to be big losers if any of the CAB formulas were chosen, so they opted for throwing out the formula approach completely and adopting flat across-the-board increases.

Eastern's strategy in the fare situation was more difficult to understand. It can be rationalized, if not explained, in the following manner. First, if we exclude TWA's proposal,[60] the overall percentage increase in the industry average fare level was by far the highest under Eastern's proposal. Thus, if each carrier were to look not at its *relative* revenue increase (in relation to other carriers) but rather to its *absolute* revenue increase, then nearly every carrier would be better off with the Eastern proposal than with any other. In addition, the Eastern proposal went a long way toward meeting the criticism that fares were going up so high so rapidly in short haul markets (Figure 3.4) that passengers

---

[58] *Business Week,* "Why Northwest Puts on the Ritz," July 5, 1969, pp. 30–32.

[59] This legal question will become more relevant later in the chapter.

[60] Most of the carriers felt that any proposal built on the existing fare structure rather than on a specific "cost-based" formula was doomed. TWA's proposal was thus seen by most carriers as a holding tactic with little chance of success.

would be driven away. Eastern's plan placed the bulk of the increase in medium haul markets (Figure 3.6) where excess service was not now provided, but where the value of service was sufficiently high that passengers would not be lost as a result of fare increases.

On July 21, 1969, the presidents of the airlines met with the CAB in Washington at a closed meeting to discuss the various fare structure proposals. As most

FIGURE 3.6

COMPARISON OF EASTERN'S PROPOSED JET DAY COACH FARE FORMULA
WITH THE INDUSTRY REGRESSION LINE FOR SIMILAR FARES
IN EFFECT AS OF APRIL 1, 1969

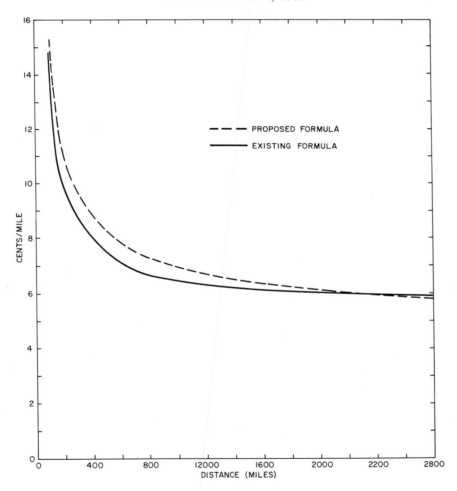

SOURCE: Derived from data in "Eastern Airlines Proposal for a Revised Fare Structure," July 1969, p. 6.11.

carriers' positions had already firmed before the meeting was held, little light was shed at the meeting except to (1) indicate to the carriers that an increase was indeed a strong possibility in the near future[61] and (2) indicate to the Board that few (if any) of the carriers would probably challenge a formula-based fare structure in the courts. At the conclusion of the meeting, the CAB scheduled a second meeting for the carriers on August 14, 1969. It was understood that a number of carriers would formally file tariff proposals prior to that meeting, and that some effort would be made to answer the CAB's concern for the reasonableness of fare increases in the face of declining load factors.

Between July 21, 1969, and the August 14 meeting, six carriers made formal filings for fare increases. The carriers involved were United, Northeast, Western, Continental, and American. Eastern simply filed for the increases that they had proposed informally prior to the July 21 meeting. United made its position clear for the first time by filing a proposal similar to the CAB Formula F. Western followed United's lead with an equivalent proposal soon after. Continental [62] filed a variation of the proposal previously offered by TWA, and American[63] revised its earlier proposal to generate greater taper in the fare curve. Northwest also changed its earlier proposal to reduce the taper in the fare curve—an alteration that would have boosted even higher an already enviable position in the CAB's formulas.

Answering the Load Factor Challenge Posed by the CAB

Prior to the CAB meeting of August 14, 1969, TWA also submitted to the CAB a detailed analysis of the problem of "excess capacity" and declining load factors. The thrust of the report was that declining load factors were in large measure a result of the competitive environment and were, therefore, beyond the control of management.

On August 14, the CAB meeting on fare structure was brief and relatively uneventful. Primarily as a result of pressure from Congressman John E. Moss (D. California) and 19 other Congressmen who were pressing for a general investigation of airline fares, the CAB chose to hold oral public arguments relating to the fare question and scheduled the session for September 4, 1969. Interested persons were invited to express their views "on any aspect of the tariffs that they wish to bring to the Board's attention." [64] Anyone wishing to take a position on the

---

[61] *Aviation Daily*, July 28, 1969; *New York Times*, August 1, 1969, p. 132.

[62] Continental's proposal was first posed rather vaguely in a way that made it look like a straight across-the-board increase. Later, when the proposal was detailed, its revenue implications were substantially different from an across-the-board increase. Continental never released its analysis of the revenue implications for individual carriers, and it appeared that the carrier was trying to cloud the revenue allocation issue.

[63] An industry rumor suggested that American received a phone call from someone at the CAB who requested that American formally submit the proposal which was finally adopted.

[64] Passenger-Fare Revisions Proposed by Domestic Trunklines, Docket #21322, U.S. Civil Aeronautics Board, *Board Order #69-8-108*, August 19, 1969, p. 2.

issue was asked to file a statement of opinion or file a complaint prior to August 28.

On August 20, Representative John E. Moss (backed by the usual 19 other Congressmen) asked the CAB to dismiss all of the general fare increase proposals.

On August 21, Braniff filed a proposal which was equivalent to the previous Eastern filing.

Most of the carriers had already made known their positions prior to the September 4, 1969, meeting, but a few carriers added some additional comments. Delta, obviously feeling outgunned and somewhat helpless, tried to cover all contingencies in a three-tiered plan of retreat:

(1) . . . Delta cannot agree to any of the formulae thus far presented.[65] . . . the needed fare increase should be accomplished by . . . an across-the-board upward adjustment of standard fares. . . .[66]

(2) If existing inequities and inconsistencies in the fare structure are thought to require immediate action, as an interim measure all carriers should be required to bring their standard fares to within plus or minus 4% of the fares which would result from use of the industry computed formula. . . .[67]

(3) If one of the formulas had to be accepted, the Eastern formula would be the soundest in Delta's opinion. . . .[68]

National's position was that "the various fare formulas which have been advanced should not be applied at this time. They are replete with inequities. They have not been thought through." [69] National then requested a flat 5% across-the-board fare increase. Hedging its bets, however, National went on to state that "with the possible exception of United's approach, which has the single redeeming feature of simplicity, the Board should be slow to adopt any formula in the absence of further consideration." [70] Peculiarly enough the United proposal was, on both a relative and absolute basis, the most attractive of all the formulas for National.

Northeast's position was generally in agreement with Eastern's. While the Eastern proposal did not reward Northeast relatively more than the industry average (as did CAB Formula C), in terms of absolute revenue impact it was better for Northeast since the Eastern plan had the highest average rise for the industry. Northeast, a sick carrier (Tables 2.1 and 3.3) thus opted for total revenue increase rather than relative increase.

---

[65] U.S. Civil Aeronautics Board, Docket #21322, Delta Airlines, "Statement of Position and Request to Present Oral Argument," August 28, 1969, p. 7.

[66] *Ibid.*, p. 2.

[67] *Ibid.*, p. 2.

[68] *Ibid.*, p. 7.

[69] U.S. Civil Aeronautics Board, Docket #21322, "Statement of National Airlines, Inc.," August 28, 1969, p. 1.

[70] *Ibid.*, p. 3.

The September 4, 1969, CAB Fare Meetings

The public fare meetings held on September 4, 1969, at the offices of the CAB in Washington produced no surprises. The carriers reiterated the positions that they had taken earlier and, except for a few hassles over the "true" revenue impact of a rival's proposal [71] (and the indignant protests of the most obvious losers), religiously avoided framing their arguments in terms of the one factor about which each carrier was most concerned: its share of the total revenue increase which the CAB planned to allow. The sub rosa issue surfaced at only one or two points in the course of the eight-hour meeting. It was finally broached in a sardonic repartee between the Board's vice chairman and counsel for National Airlines:[72]

MR. MURPHY: (CAB Vice Chairman)	Just so I understand your recommendation clearly, you are saying [that as an interim measure we should] permit carrier management . . . to increase fares . . . by . . . 5%?
MR. MACDONALD: (Counsel for National)	That is correct.
MR. MURPHY:	In the meantime, pursue this course of seeking for the formula, the magic formula, that might do equity and make things a great deal easier and so forth?
MR. MACDONALD:	Yes.
MR. MURPHY:	You are not opposed to that any more than you are opposed to the pursuit of happiness, I take it?
MR. MACDONALD:	No, indeed.
MR. MURPHY:	If we can find the formula, you are not opposed to that. You would participate in this search?
MR. MACDONALD:	Yes, indeed. I would suspect that a formula which would deal perfectly equitably with everybody may never be found.

The vice chairman of the CAB, and later the chairman, then got down to the issue of greatest interest to *them* concerning National's position on rate-making formulas, i.e., whether or not National would challenge the Board's adoption of a formula in a court fight:[73]

MR. MURPHY:	Do you have any view, Mr. MacDonald, as a lawyer, as well as a great student of economics, on the question as to whether or not a formula of this character would conform with or be compatible with the rate-making standards of the statute?
MR. MACDONALD:	I am ashamed to say, Mr. Vice Chairman, but I had not focused on that until I heard you ask that question this morning. [Later.]
CHAIRMAN CROOKER:	Irrespective of the way any particular fares are reached under a formula or otherwise, are you suggesting that there is some legal

---

[71] U.S. Civil Aeronautics Board, Hearing Transcript, Docket #21322, September 4, 1969, pp. 64, 74.

[72] *Ibid.*, pp. 139–140.

[73] *Ibid.*, p. 144.

(of the CAB)	obstacle to the Board approving some tariff *that has now been filed if the Board finds under 1002 [of the Federal Aviation Act of 1958] those amounts are reasonable?* (Emphasis mine.)
MR. MACDONALD:	Mr. Chairman, the only way I could answer that would be I could not answer it without reading the Board's decision and opinion.
CHAIRMAN CROOKER:	(With a smile.) I think that is a sound approach for a lawyer. Thank you.

Toward the close of the fare meeting the CAB chairman read into the record a telegram from Representative John E. Moss (D. California) which was supported by 19 other members of Congress. The essence of the telegram was that since the Board members had already made up their minds (in his view) as to the necessity for a fare increase prior to the September 4 meeting, "the so-called oral arguments become farcical and meaningless." [74] Representative Moss chose, therefore, to present his case elsewhere.[75]

When all of the positions had been aired, the final lineup of carriers at the September Oral Arguments on fares was as follows:

Carrier	First Preference	Second Preference	Third Preference
American	Revised CAB Formula C		
Braniff	Eastern's proposal		
Continental	Flat % increase		
Delta	Flat % increase	±4% increase	Eastern's proposal
Eastern	Eastern's proposal		
National	Flat % increase	United's proposal	
Northeast	Eastern's proposal		
Northwest	Revised CAB Formula C		
TWA	TWA's proposal	Eastern's proposal	
United	United's proposal		
Western	United's proposal	Eastern's proposal	

Clearly, the proposal mentioned most frequently (and the one with some support from both long and short haul carriers) was the Eastern proposal. United's

---

[74] *Ibid.*, p. 206.

[75] The CAB, in May and September of 1969, deferred action on Representative Moss' and other members of Congress' complaints against the two fare increases of 1969. Representative Moss and 31 other members of Congress then filed suit in the U.S. Court of Appeals for the District of Columbia to force an investigation, and to have the fare increases declared illegal. In July 1970, the Court of Appeals found that the October 1969 tariffs approved by the Board were unlawful since the Board had compelled their filing. While the Board held the power to set fares under the rate-making statutes of the Civil Aeronautics Act, this power could only be exercised if certain safeguards assuring "due process" were followed. Since these safeguards were not followed in setting the October 1969 tariffs, the Board had to ask the carriers for a new set of tariff filings which were to be free of any taint of compulsion. Northwest Airlines, the big winner in the October 1969 fare increase (Table 3.9) was the only trunk carrier to refile the same tariffs previously found unlawful by the Court. The Board approved Northwest's filing (which was evidently now purified from the compulsion taint) on September 24, 1970, thereby proving the truth of the adage, "you can't fight City Hall."

proposal and the flat across-the-board percentage increase scheme each merited three mentions.

While Eastern's proposal won the straw carrier vote, the CAB chose the variation of CAB Formula C proposed by American. The "why" of this decision can probably be explained as follows: First, the Board was very interested in (1) getting a basic fare formula approved, and (2) making sure that the formula had sufficient taper to actually reduce many fares in long haul markets. The need to meet these requirements left in the running the CAB staff Formula A to D and the formulas proposed by American, Northwest, and Eastern. Second, as indicated above, the Board members were worried about a legal challenge to a formula approach. They thus wanted to approve *specific tariffs* that were on file from a carrier, and try to avoid the issue of *how* these fares were in fact constructed. This left only the proposals filed by American, Eastern, and Northwest still in the running. CAB concern for the total level of the industry increase (and the Congressional response to that increase) thus led the CAB to select the American formula, the one with the lowest overall percentage increase (Table 3.9).

In the course of winning the fare increases of 1969, the carriers filed, publicly, some 644 pages of fare proposals and defenses with the CAB. Documents filed privately would have undoubtedly expanded the total significantly. The carriers with the greatest need for fare increases carried the bulk of the load [76] in justifying them before the CAB. Indeed, the number of pages submitted by each carrier

TABLE 3.10

PAGES OF DOCUMENTS FILED PUBLICLY WITH THE CAB
IN 1969 IN FAVOR OF FARE INCREASES

	February 20 Increase	±*4% Increase*	*October 1* Increase	*Total*
American	0	10	38	48
Braniff	37	4		41
Continental	23		10	33
Delta			25	25
Eastern	32		85	117
National			9	9
Northeast	41		111	152
Northwest			29	29
Trans World	46	41	51	138
United	14	2	33	49
Western			3	3
Industry Total	193	57	394	644

SOURCE: Derived from data in carrier tariff filing to the CAB.

relating to the increases (Table 3.10) shows an interesting inverse correlation with profitability (Table 3.3).

---

[76] Northeast estimated that the cost of preparing two proposals (95 pages) for the October increase ran to $75,000.

Summary

The economics of competition in the area of setting fares makes the reaching of agreement[77] on fares a near impossibility for the carriers in the absence of "regulatory coercion" from the CAB (Figure 3.3).

While the industry fares have moved steadily toward a cost-related basis (Figure 3.4), the process has been essentially evolutionary. Structural changes have occurred only when the CAB had unusually strong leverage with the industry (i.e., when rate increases were being sought).

While changes in the structure of industry air fares over time show the broad sweep of CAB policy, there is little evidence to support a hypothesis that there exists a well-defined and explicitly timed "grand design" for fare policy at the CAB Board level which has survived the normal turnover of Board personnel.

Over a shorter time span, however, it does appear that a single Board can (and did in 1969) move the carriers to a desired end point position so long as the move is accomplished "incrementally" and its ultimate impact is not immediately apparent to those carriers which would be most damaged.

---

[77] Agreement is again not meant to imply any illegal collusive action on the part of the carriers.

CHAPTER 4

The Fight for Competitive Advantage—Routes

IN THE LICENSING PROCESS[1] there are three basic types of decisions which are of interest to the carriers and the CAB. These decisions relate to (1) the appropriate degree of competition in all markets for the industry in general, (2) the appropriate degree of competition for individual specific city-pair markets, and (3) the designation of the carrier(s) which will be permitted to provide the degree of competition specified by item (2). Each of these decision areas will be investigated separately in this chapter.

CHOOSING AN APPROPRIATE DEGREE OF INDUSTRY COMPETITION

Changes in most industries, particularly large ones, take place within fairly narrow sets of constraints. These constraints are clearly evident in air transportation. For example, questions relating to the "appropriate" degree of competition for the industry are not answered by the CAB in an environmental or historical

---

[1] The process by which the CAB certificates specific carriers to fly in city-pair markets has been the subject of a great deal of scholarly investigation. Two pieces of writing form what might be called the "classics" of the area, and they are drawn upon heavily in this chapter. The two works are (1) W. K. Jones, "Licensing of Domestic Air Transportation," *Journal of Air Law and Commerce,* Part I, Spring 1964, and Part II, Spring 1965, and (2) Samuel B. Richmond, *Regulation and Competition in Air Transportation.* Since this area has been so well researched previously, comparatively less attention has been devoted to it in this work.

vacuum.[2] They are answered, rather, with reference to a specific point in time by either (1) "more," (2) "the same," or (3) "less competition than the industry has today." While Table 2.2 clearly indicates a historic trend toward a greater and greater degree of competition in city-pair markets with the passage of time, this trend has been either accentuated or de-emphasized according to the level and trend of profitability existing in the industry when significant route proceedings were either initiated or decided[3] by the CAB. Indeed, in terms of its ability to *reduce* industry profits, the CAB's regulatory power in the route area represents a very potent tool for controlling industry profitability. To reduce industry profits at a specific point in time the CAB can simply increase the impact of competitive route awards by authorizing a greater number of competitors[4] in a greater number of city-pairs in route cases coming up for a final decision.

When the economic climate for the airlines is favorable, the CAB route policy rationale might appear as follows:

> We need not detail the advantages of competition, nor prove them again in each case. An objective reading of the Civil Aeronautics Act leaves no doubt that the lawmakers considered competition to be [a] desirable objective which should be established whenever it is economically feasible and will contribute to the development of a sound air transportation system.[5]

On the other hand, during periods of industry profit stress, the Board has less flexibility in the route area.[6] About all the Board can do to assist the carriers at

---

[2] For example, measured in the framework of Table 2.2 the "ideal" degree of competition might consist of an industry average fraction of total RPMs flown in COMP80 type markets of 10%.

[3] It is important to distinguish between the scope of a proceeding in the *initiation* and the *decision* stages. This is true because in a typical major route case between two and five years (with perhaps a three-year average) may elapse between the starting date of an investigation into the need for additional service and the actual entry of a new competitor(s) into the market(s) in question. If industry profitability is high when the investigation is first undertaken, its scope may be very broad (i.e., the need for additional competitive service in 18 long haul East-West markets in the southern half of the United States). If industry profitability is greatly reduced by the time the case reaches the point of decision, however, a lesser degree of new competition in a fewer number of city-pairs may be authorized than one would have expected at the outset of the investigation.

[4] Figure 2.1 shows the load factor impact of increased competition, and Table 1.6 (line 1) shows the profit impact of reducing the spread between actual and breakeven load factors.

[5] Southern Service to the West Case, Reopened, 18 CAB, 790, 799–800 (1954) as in Henry J. Friendly. *The Federal Administrative Agencies*, p. 94.

[6] Traditionally, the CAB's prime weapon to *enhance* industry profitability has been its control over price. In 1971, however, the Board broke new ground by approving, for a one-year period, a capacity limitation agreement between American, TWA, and United. This agreement promised to eliminate nearly 30% of the flights linking four transcontinental city-pair markets which accounted for 6.3% of all RPMs generated in domestic service. The objective of the agreement was to raise passenger load factors in the markets from 26–36% to 50–60% and thus produce a cost saving of $60 million for these large but at the time unprofitable carrirers. Board Order #71-8-91.)

these times is (1) to reduce the number of new route investigations actually set for hearing, (2) to slow down the progress of route proceedings already in progress, and/or (3) to reduce the scope and intensity of new competitive authorizations in proceedings which have reached the point of decision. While most of this type of activity is of an informal nature, the Board has occasionally spoken out on the need to reduce its grants of new route authority in times of stress. Under such conditions the CAB shifts gears and argues as follows:

> We would be less than helpful if, at this time, we did not express our considered opinion that further route expansion in our domestic trunk line network would present problems of serious difficulty in view of conditions which presently and during the postwar period have existed in the industry. Certainly the task of providing the public convenience and necessity in satisfying the statutory requirements would place a difficult if not insurmountable, burden upon the air carriers which would undertake to sponsor further route extensions of any substantial character.[7]

While such seemingly erratic behavior on the part of industry regulators can cause legal practitioners great discomfort (as will be discussed in Chapter 6), the economic basis for such behavior is easily understood.

Problems of Profit Regulation via Route Awards

While the obvious and immediate negative profit impact of large-scale route *awards* can easily be derived from an understanding of Figure 2.1, the mere opening of large-scale route *investigations* has a competitive effect which is less apparent but perhaps even more powerful. As one carrier manager has stated:

> It is my belief that there must be a recognition by the CAB that a rash of route cases like that in which we are now involved does much to increase the risk of overcapacity. Obviously, every airline doesn't plan on receiving every route it requests, but at the same time, one does plan on some kind of "batting average" and this does weave its way into the equipment plans of the carriers.[8]

The relevance of this complaint is shown in material presented to the directors of one carrier. The request for authorization to purchase more planes came in the following form:

> There now exist good prospects that we will receive new route authority for nonstop service between (City X and City Y). In addition, other route additions are pending. Three (of the aircraft requested) might be regarded as protection against the probable award to us of these routes.

---

[7] Southern Transcontinental Service Case, 33 CAB, 701, 533–34, as in Henry J. Friendly, *The Federal Administrative Agencies*, p. 94.

[8] J. J. Kerley, "Spotlight: Finance," *Airline Management and Marketing*, January 1968.

CAB members, for their part, disavow any responsibility for the carrier investment behavior induced by its route policies.

It is hard to tell whether all these [aircraft] orders are being placed solely on the basis of sound economic projections, or whether they sometimes may be inflated in anticipation of a large route award. Obviously, if this practice is widespread, somebody ends up with excess airplanes. In this regard there have been situations where carriers have come pretty close to telling us that since they are now so heavily committed for new airplanes, it is somehow up to us to help them out with route improvements.[9]

The carrier managers can and do speak out on the problems engendered by CAB policy at both the initiation and decision stages (as mentioned earlier), but in terms of action alternatives[10] they feel there is little they can do to change either the rules or the outcome of the game by which the degree of competition for the industry is determined.

Choosing Specific Markets for New Service Authorization

While CAB decisions regarding an appropriate intensity of competition for the industry had a substantial impact on overall industry profitability, it was not until CAB choice reached the level of selecting specific city-pairs for new service authorization that questions of competitive advantage between carriers was raised.

The CAB has rarely investigated the need for new service in an area without reaching a positive conclusion that new service was indeed required. The mere fact that the CAB has chosen a city-pair or geographic area for a service investigation thus defines some carriers (the incumbents) as losers in the proceeding.

Relative Profitability of Various Traffic Types

In Chapter 2 (Table 2.5) it was demonstrated that route structure variables were of key significance in determining a carrier's overall relative profitability. In particular, Figure 2.3 suggested that the traffic which fell into the upper right-hand corner of this matrix would be extremely profitable, and that conversely, traffic which fell in the lower left-hand corner might be operated at a substantial

---

[9] John G. Adams, "U.S. Commercial Aviation," speech to the New York Society of Security Analysts, January 12, 1968.

[10] An individual carrier could, of course, choose not to participate in a route investigation by not filing a request for new service authorization (or by withdrawing its request on those cases already under way). Unless every carrier did likewise, however, this alternative would be highly unattractive. In game theory terminology this problem of whether or not to participate in future route hearings when a carrier believes they have become excessive is of the "Prisoner's Dilemma" variety, a category of mathematical games which will be discussed in some detail (but in another context) in Chapter 6.

loss. In point of fact, the variations in the degree of profitability of traffic of various types is extraordinarily wide. The president of Eastern Air Lines stated, for example, that the most profitable one-third of the cities served by the carrier accounted for essentially 100% of its total profit. The remaining two-thirds operated at a declining rate of profit (or increasing rate of loss) so as to reduce the total profit from these cities to zero.[11]

For one of the other carriers, the revenue-profit contribution split was roughly as indicated in Table 4.1.

TABLE 4.1

RELATIVE PROFITABILITY OF TRAFFIC GENERATED
IN DIFFERENT TYPES OF MARKETS

Market Type	Fraction of Total Revenue from These Markets	Cumulative Fraction of Total Revenue from These Markets	Cumulative Fraction of Total Profit from These Markets
Monopoly Medium Haul	6%	6%	25%
Monopoly Long Haul	3	9	35
Competitive Medium Haul	10	19	60
Competitive Long Haul	10	29	85
High Density Markets (Not Included)	19	48	110
All Other Markets	52	100	−10
	100%	100%	100%

SOURCE: Private Carrier Data.

These examples simply demonstrate that at any point in time each carrier has a relatively few generally small and often identifiable[12] markets (accounting for a relatively low fraction of the carrier's total RPMs) which support the operation of a far greater fraction of marginal and/or essentially parasitic markets. The fight for competitive advantage between carriers in the route area thus often centers around either protecting or gaining access to such lucrative markets.

Trigger Points for Selecting Routes Needing Additional Service

The protection of that usually small lucrative fraction of a carrier's total traffic is obviously of great significance to individual carriers. While the CAB has, on

---

[11] *Wall Street Journal*, October 3, 1969.

[12] These are identifiable to competitors and the CAB insofar as it is usually possible to estimate the spread between actual and breakeven load factors in these markets. Except in the case of an unusually short haul market, a 65+% average load factor in a market would be a signal of substantial profitability. As one would suspect, such markets are almost always monopoly or semi-monopoly markets.

occasion, mentioned some specific "trigger points"[13] (i.e. conditions which "might" indicate the need for new service), clearly no market-scanning procedure as precise as the New York Stock Exchange's "stock watch" program is in effect, since any rigid mechanism might encumber the CAB's flexibility in using new service authorizations as a tool to reduce industry profitability by increasing the intensity of city-pair competition.[14] Mechanical rules would also endanger the ability of the CAB to regulate the relative profitability of specific carriers by "premature" or "tardy" investigation of the carrier's most lucrative routes. As Richmond has observed,

> The Civil Aeronautics Board must, as it has already recognized (e.g., The Denver-Kansas City Route in the Denver Service Case, where Continental's monopoly was maintained), view the problem of the optimum amount of competition on a route as a function of the importance of that route's excess profitability to the overall profitability of the existing carrier on that route.[15]

While the profitability of traffic in various city-pairs on a carrier's routes varies extremely widely, the CAB, in its Hearings and Board Orders has traditionally insulated itself from criticism arising from the elimination of a substantial fraction of a carrier's profit (via new service authorizations to competitors) by entertaining arguments relating only to the *revenue* diversion rather than the *profit* diversion impact of added service upon the incumbent. For example, in July 1969, the Board increased from three to seven the number of carriers serving mainland-Hawaii markets. In the following year, Pan American suffered a revenue reduction of $73 million and a decrease in operating profit equal to $25 million on these routes as a result of the added competition. In the decision which led directly to this profit debacle, the Board had dismissed Pan American's prediction of "unprecedented" damage to its financial health by stating that Pan American's estimated revenue loss on its mainland-Hawaii traffic, when measured in relation to the carrier's total revenues of over $1 billion, could be made up in only $4\frac{1}{2}$ months of normal system revenue growth.[16]

---

[13] For instance, some traffic density "triggers" indicated in the Gulf States-Midwest Points Service Investigation included (1) first *competitive* nonstop service in markets generating at least 100 passengers/day, and (2) first *nonstop* service in those markets which generated in excess of 50 passengers/day (Board Order #E24202). These levels were so low that the industry protested the figures vigorously. A load factor trigger was mentioned in the Southern Transcontinental Service Case, "at the point where load factors on a given segment reach an average level of 75%, a space available problem is created. Moreover, the Board has recognized that high average load factors are an important criterion in assessing the shortcomings of existing operations and the need for additional competitive service" (33 CAB 701, 837).

[14] By explicitly defining various trigger points, the CAB might also run the risk of encouraging incumbent carriers to keep traffic artificially below these "triggers" to delay the certification of added competition.

[15] Samuel B. Richmond, *Regulation and Competition in Air Transportation*, p. 253.

[16] Transpacific Route Investigation (Domestic Phase—On Reconsideration) Board Order #69-7-105, July 21, 1969, p. 16.

The notion that a dollar of revenue might carry with it different levels of cost and therefore different levels of profit contribution (depending on the condition of the market in which it is earned) was completely absent from the line of logic disclosed.

The Carriers' Role in Initiating Route Investigations

Over the years the carriers have tried a number of strategies in trying to influence the CAB's selection of markets for route investigations. In the 1940s and 1950s, the Board was somewhat responsive to carrier initiated requests for investigations in particular market areas.

> The selection of applications for processing involves important policy determinations. In theory at least the Board used to process applications in the order in which they were filed, although reserving power to make exceptions and expedite later-filed cases where special reasons require their early disposition. But the small number of route cases currently heard in relation to the Board's large backlog of pending applications had tended to make the exceptions more important than the general rule. . . . The net result is that. . . . It is the Board and not the applicant which, in a realistic sense, controls the initiation of licensing proceedings.[17]

In more recent years, the Board has assumed even greater responsibility[18] in the initiation area, and the carriers see quite limited competitive benefit[19] in making costly but highly speculative initiations for route investigations.

Strategies for Delaying the Inevitable

Once a route investigation is undertaken by the CAB, the losers in the proceeding are (as mentioned earlier) already defined. The timing and extent of their loss is still subject to some management control, however. As the period between the initiation of a route investigation and the initiation of added service is almost always measured in years, even small percentage delays caused by incumbent carriers can mean many dollars of additional profit. The Transpacific case, for exam-

---

[17] W. K. Jones, "Licensing of Domestic Air Transportation," *Journal of Air Law and Commerce*, Spring 1964, p. 134.

[18] In September 1969, the Board directed the carriers to supply it monthly with magnetic tape passenger and capacity data for each flight stage by flight number. Relative to the data previously supplied by the carriers (aggregate system data only for load factors) this change represented a "quantum leap" for the CAB. It gave the Board a computer-based overall route scanning capability that was more comprehensive than that enjoyed by any single carrier management. It also allowed the CAB to uncover with *far* greater ease than was previously possible each carrier's high profitability market segments. Armed with such data, the CAB can presumably operate more aggressively in the initiation of service investigations, thus giving it an even greater degree of control over the relative profitability of individual carriers.

[19] There are some "Ashbacker" benefits involved in having applications in for areas in or near a carrier's most lucrative routes, and these will be discussed later in the chapter.

ple, took almost 10 years to complete. This inordinately long time span, while certainly resulting from many factors in addition to carrier delay, may have given Pan American the opportunity to earn tens (if not a hundred) or more millions of dollars of profit than the carrier might otherwise have achieved during this period. This delay was clearly of enormous historic importance to Pan American.

One final way in which the carriers can influence to some degree the choice of markets at issue in an investigation is through an "Ashbacker" [20] pleading that additional markets must be consolidated in the case at issue in order to guarantee the fairness of the proceeding.

(1) Parties seemingly excluded from the proceeding fight vigorously to have their applications included in order (1) to obtain an early decision on their applications, and (2) to prevent their own applications from being prejudiced by grants of applications in the pending proceeding.
(2) Parties clearly included in the proceeding fight just as hard to exclude additional applications so as not to encumber the proceeding.[21]

The barrier which has to be breeched in the consolidation issue is similar in many ways to the problem of nuclear nonproliferation described by numerous writers.[22] The option to try and expand the proceeding endlessly via Ashbacker is clearly one important part of an incumbent carrier's arsenal of delay tactics, and it leads, ultimately, to a pattern of regulatory behavior (i.e., an increasing requirement for tight regulatory control over proceedings) which the carriers individ-

---

[20] The Ashbacker case involved an application to the FCC for authority to construct a new radio station to operate on 1230Kc filed by Fetzer Broadcasting Co. Subsequently Ashbacker Radio Corp. filed its application to change the frequency of its existing station to 1230Kc. Before Ashbacker filed, the Commission had taken no action on the Fetzer application. In an ex parte proceeding Fetzer's application was unconditionally granted by the FCC. Such grant, the Commission noted, did not preclude it from taking subsequent action on Ashbacker's application. The Supreme Court held that the Ashbacker application was effectively denied by the granting of Fetzer's application. Congress had expressly guaranteed the right to a hearing before an application is denied. The applications were mutually exclusive, and the Court held that the Commission exceeded its authority by granting the Fetzer application without hearing Ashbacker's. The Court reasoned that a subsequent hearing, as the FCC suggested was possible, would amount to a hearing on the revocation or modification of an outstanding license. Because of the difficulty in displacing an established licensee, granting the Fetzer petition imposed a greater burden on Ashbacker. Under the circumstances this increased burden was unwarranted—Ashbacker should have been allowed a hearing for an available frequency. Source: Joseph H. Lazara, "Administrative Law-Ashbacker Doctrine-CAB Discretion," *Journal of Air Law and Commerce,* 1969, p. 269.

[21] William K. Jones, "Licensing of Domestic Air Transportation," *Journal of Air Law and Commerce,* Spring 1964, p. 139.

[22] Political scientists have noted a dramatic shift in the interest shown by nations in the problems of nuclear nonproliferation immediately *after* they have joined the "nuclear club." See, for example, National Planning Association, "The 'Nth Country' Problem and Arms Control," 1959, or Arthur L. Burns, "Power Politics and the Growing Nuclear Club," Princeton University, 1959.

ually abhor, but collectively encourage. A similar basic force was found to exist in the fare area (Figure 3.3).

CARRIER SELECTION IN NEW ROUTE AUTHORIZATIONS

Once the CAB has reached a final decision regarding the scope of an investigation, the parties to be included, and the markets requiring new carrier authorization, the problem has reached, competitively speaking, its most important stage, i.e., that of selecting the carrier(s) to actually provide the new service. In one paragraph the CAB has caught the flavor of this problem.

> With respect to [carrier selection] the record is beset with a multiplicity of preoccupations: some wise, some petty, most of them self-serving, and almost all of them in hopeless conflict. The preoccupations range, in the case of the air carrier parties, from insistence on the part of certain of the large applicants that they alone have the equipment and resources and the connecting service patterns which can assure satisfactory service in the major markets for both passengers and cargo, to desperate pleas by each of the smaller carriers for more mileage, more markets, and more traffic to assure survival. . . .[23]

While the carrier selection process has its own distinctive flavor in each individual route case, there is certainly some broad pattern of consistency in decisions which seems to sweep over the record. As shown in Figure 4.1 the CAB decision process in most route cases apparently incorporates a scanning and sifting process in which first markets, then broad classes of carriers, and finally specific carriers are passed through a successively finer and finer series of test grids until the carrier(s) to provide new service in a specific market is the sole survivor of the various tests.

Narrowing the List of Carrier Participants in Specific Investigations

In the previous section of this chapter it was mentioned that the selection of markets for new service defined, in some manner, the universe of carrier participants in the proceeding. At the broadest level, the class(es) of carriers participating in a route proceeding may be narrowed by considering the nonstop hop length over the route in question and/or the density of traffic on a route. Local service carriers, for instance, would probably not participate in an investigation of the need for added nonstop service between New York and Los Angeles.

Considerations relating to "historic interest" in an area tend also to exclude from a proceeding any carrier without at least one existing station in the market area under investigation. Thus, Northeast Airlines would probably not be a party to a route investigation in the Pacific Northwest. While historic interest in an

---

[23] Southern Transcontinental Service Case, 33 CAB, 701, 899.

area would tend to be reflected in profitability considerations in any proceeding, and thus be tested later in the grid (Figure 4.1), the profit implications of gaining entry into markets totally nonintegrated into a carrier's system are obviously so high as to preclude the need for any further consideration.

FIGURE 4.1

BROAD FACTORS CONSIDERED BY THE CAB IN THE LICENSING PROCESS
FOR NEW DOMESTIC ROUTE AUTHORITY

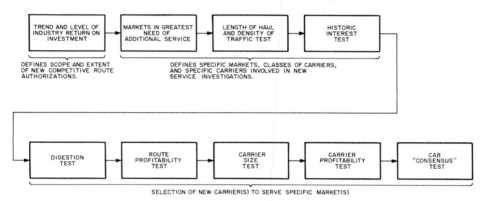

Once the carriers with a legitimate interest in a proceeding have been defined, specific carrier choice tends to revolve around five factors: Problems of Digestion, Route Profitability, Carrier Size, Carrier Profitability, and CAB "Consensus" (Figure 4.1).

Importance of the Digestion Factor in Carrier Choice

The "digestion" factor has both a resource and political dimension. Along the resource dimension, a carrier must

(1) Have available (or be able to acquire within a reasonable period of time) the equipment necessary to operate the routes.
(2) Be strong enough to finance any "market entry" [24] cost involved in getting a position in the market.
(3) Have available the management resources necessary to undertake an active role in developing the route.

The Route Profitability in Carrier Choice

In most cases it is not very meaningful to discuss the expected profitability of certain markets independent of the carriers proposing to service those markets.

---

[24] This might be gauged, for instance, in terms of the size of the route involved in relation to the newly authorized carrier's overall industry market share.

This is true since different carriers would estimate, and indeed realize, widely different returns from operating the same markets. These variations arise primarily from

(1) Differing carrier estimates regarding the degree of traffic stimulation which will be realized by the new service proposed.[25]

(2) Differing carrier estimates regarding the amounts of available connecting traffic from their existing service in the area.[26]

(3) Differing carrier estimates of the level of incremental *costs* involved in serving the market (due, for instance, to the fact that one or more of the carrier candidates may already operate flights out of both stations involved in the market).

Carrier Size and Overall Profitability

As route hearings are essentially economic proceedings, the CAB pays a great deal of attention to the economic impact of the available decision alternatives. The nature of the decision grid at this point in the analysis is, however, by no means obvious, so it is described in greater detail in Figure 4.2. Carrier size and overall profitability is inextricably wound up with route profitability in the carrier selection process. As a general rule, the CAB will award routes to (1) local service carriers over domestic trunk carriers if a reduction in government subsidy is involved (i.e., the route could be profitable to a local service carrier); (2) Little 7 carriers over Big 4 carriers if the route would be profitable to either, but is not an obvious integral part of the larger carrier's system (a fact which might be reflected in far greater potential profitability for the larger carrier).

The Importance of Consensus in Carrier Choice

The decision problem in most route cases is rarely clear cut. One industry lawyer with considerable experience in route investigations observed, "After all the evidence is in on a route case, it's pure luck if you can guess who will get access to which markets." Indeed, the "Consensus" variable is probably the most important in many route proceedings (Figure 4.2); it consists solely of getting three out of five members of the Board to agree to a final decision of any sort.

If a route case can be resolved by any number of solutions, and if Board members reach determinations on highly individualized grounds, the Board's efforts in a

---

[25] In recent years American has been the most aggressive of the Big 4 carriers in estimating traffic growth in markets where it is competing for new route authority. This aggressiveness tends to place American in the position of initially proposing to offer more new flights than its fellow applicants. In periods of high industry profit, this tactic may have given American an occasional edge over its less aggressive Big 4 rivals since the CAB may have been occasionally swayed in American's direction by the potential improvement in quality of service suggested by a greater number of flights.

[26] Both (1) and (2) lead to pronounced differences in the estimated incremental revenue each carrier might hope to receive if it won authority to serve the markets at issue.

FIGURE 4.2

SOME AREAS OF RELATIVELY CLEAR DECISION CHOICE IN THE CAB
LICENSING PROCESS FOR NEW DOMESTIC ROUTE AUTHORITY

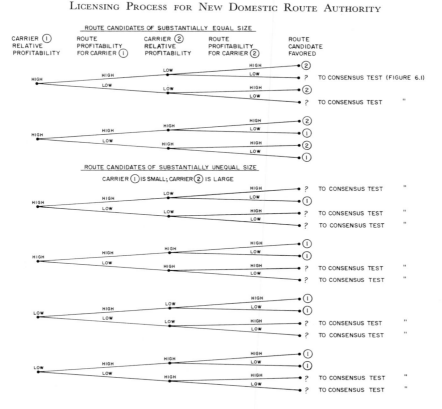

particular case are likely to involve, first, a struggle to reach a composite result—points to be served, carrier(s) to be chosen, restrictions to be imposed—to which a majority will adhere; and, second, an effort to state a theory upon which the result may be justified. The first step is probably the one which absorbs most of the collective energies of the Board. The latter task, the statement of a rationale, is not only of secondary importance but is often highly generalized and inconclusive because the grounds of individual members in the majority are not the same and the result may reflect no consistent policy approach, but rather a compromise of conflicting individual solutions incapable of mustering a majority.[27]

Carrier Response to the Pattern of CAB Decision Making

Probably because of the enormous range of uncertainty in route proceedings, carrier managers seem to concentrate their effort on those variables which would

[27] William K. Jones, "Licensing of Domestic Air Transportation," *Journal of Air Law and Commerce*, Spring 1965, p. 92.

tend to make the choice problem quite clear cut (Figure 4.2) and thus allow the
case to be decided before reaching the "Consensus" stage. Thus, large carriers tend
to stress the need for a strong source of connecting traffic to make a route
profitable (since this is an area where larger carriers generally have a substantial
edge), and the small carriers tend to exaggerate the potential market stimulation
which results from added service in order to make the route look profitable without any connecting traffic. From this melange, the CAB must then make its final
determination.

SUMMARY

In the three areas of greatest concern to the carriers in the licensing process, it
is clear that the CAB has almost complete decisional control. In addition, it
appears that the trend of events portends an ever-greater control in these areas
in the future (footnote 18). The one area in which an incumbent carrier on a
route still has some room to maneuver lies in the length of time needed to bring a
new service investigation to a conclusion. While there is a broad, purposive and
well-defined pattern to the CAB's granting of route authority, most carrier managers involved in this aspect of the business seem to feel that there is little they can
do to influence CAB decision making. Indeed, many of these men feel no more able
to predict the outcome of a service investigation from the complete record than
they could guess the outcome of a single roll of dice. One knows that in a long
series of fair rolls of dice, the outcomes will show a clear and distinct pattern. The
outcome of any single roll, however, is strictly a matter of chance. The granting of
route authority shows a similar pattern of behavior (with the smaller carriers
winning on the vast majority of rolls for reasons which will be outlined in Chapter 6).

Other important factors which come out of the chapter relate to the CAB's use
of route authorizations to regulate first *industry* and then *individual carrier* profitability. The use of route authority to regulate industry profitability has extremely
undesirable side effects, as at the industry level it generates a substantial impetus
for the purchase of an excessive amount of new capacity. This problem will receive greater attention in Chapter 5.

At the individual carrier level the discretionary profit allocation impact of route
awards raises some serious policy questions which the CAB has consistently refused
to face.

> It has never cast a dispassionate, retrospective eye over the consequences of
> using route awards to change the size and profitability distribution of firms in the air
> industry.[28]

The CAB has shown a somewhat schizophrenic behavior pattern on this topic. In
the Transpacific Case the Board awarded new authority to Braniff, and in justify-

---

[28] Richard E. Caves, *Air Transport and Its Regulators*, p. 230.

ing this pointed to relative indicia of route strength for the carriers which were quite similar to those used for the relative profitability study in Chapter 2.

> Thus, Eastern in 1967 originated an average of 498 daily passengers in domestic scheduled service for each point it served as against 451 for Delta and only 369 for Braniff. (Braniff showed the least improvement in this index between 1960 and 1967 of any trunkline applicant.)[29]

In the same opinion, the Board emphasized the importance of such indices to a carrier's relative profitability.

> Braniff's system also suffers from a predominance of short-haul, short-hop operations which (other things being equal) tend to be less profitable than long-haul, long-hop markets.[30]

When challenged to "own up" later on to the link between route strength indices (which the CAB admittedly used in its decision making) and profit distribution within the industry, however, the CAB "begged off" with the following:

> Contrary to Delta's suggestion, the Board has never assumed that route strength is the sole determinant of carrier profitability. . . . This is why citations to past carrier profits have been avoided as an indicium of route strength. . . .[31]

The problem raised by the CAB's implicit profit allocation activity is a serious one, and a proposal aimed at reducing the dimensions of the difficulty will be defined in Chapter 6.

---

[29] Transpacific Route Investigation (Domestic Phase) Board Order #69-1-11, January 4, 1969, p. 48.

[30] *Ibid.*, p. 48.

[31] Transpacific Route Investigation (Domestic Phase—On Reconsideration) Board Order #69-7-105, July 1969, p. 50.

CHAPTER 5

The Fight for Competitive Advantage—Capacity and Equipment Purchases

CHAPTER 2 OF THIS BOOK indicated that the relative profitability of individual carriers was heavily influenced by their route structure. Small carriers which enjoyed a substantial fraction of monopoly and/or long haul routes, e.g., Delta Airlines[1] (Tables 2.2 and 2.3) realized higher passenger load factors and higher spreads between yields and costs and achieved higher relative profitability than large carriers which flew on more highly competitive and/or shorter routes, e.g., Eastern Airlines. While carrier managers tried to improve their route structure through CAB petitions for new route authority, most felt that they could exercise only limited control over this important aspect of the competitive environment.

Given the routes determined by the CAB, airlines individually and collectively had some effect on the total demand for air transport because of their influence on the departure frequency, speed, and comfort of air travel vis-à-vis the alternative modes of transportation and the alternative of not traveling at all. However, the CAB retained a major element of control over total demand on any route or routes, since it regulated rates.

At times, airline managers had to decide between equipment differing signifi-

---

[1] "So Rich It Hurts," *Forbes* magazine, January 15, 1969, p. 20.

cantly in features that might influence consumer demand and costs. These decisions often involved major gambles on (1) the general pace of aircraft technology, (2) the design and production skills of a particular airframe or engine manufacturer, and/or (3) the financial strength of a particular airframe or engine manufacturer. As an example of the first problem area, in the early 1950s many airlines invested in the turbine-propelled Lockheed Electra despite the chance, which materialized, of rapid obsolescence due to the appearance of the pure-jet Boeing 707s. An example of the second gamble was that faced by each carrier in deciding in the early 1960s between the Boeing and Douglas jets and the Convair 880 and 990 jets, which failed to measure up to their buyer's expectations. An example of the third problem area came when major decisions had to be made by individual carriers on the Boeing 747s and the competing airbuses of McDonnell Douglas and Lockheed. For buyers of the Lockheed 1011, this decision turned out to be a gamble on the financial strength of both Rolls Royce and Lockheed. For Eastern Airlines and TWA, with $72.8 million and $101.3 million, respectively, at risk in the form of unsecured advance payments on their Lockheed 1011 orders, the gamble was truly of the "you bet your company" variety.[2]

Even in situations where new flight equipment ordered by a carrier was produced successfully and turned out to be competitive, an important element in the equipment *type* decision was the fact that an airline ordering early in the design and prototype stages of an aircraft was given early delivery positions. If, during the late design or early production stages, it became clear that the new aircraft was superior in consumer acceptance or costs to other equipment, competing airlines could place orders for the new type of aircraft. But the airline ordering early might well have had enough early delivery positions locked up to give it a significant equipment advantage for a year or more after delivery began. This was important because, as discussed in Chapter 2, the relative "quality" of a carrier's fleet was an important determinant of airline profitability.

Although airline managers had only limited influence on route structure, total demand for air transportation, and rates, there were no regulatory restraints on the amount of equipment an airline could fly on the routes it served. Industry experts believed that, given no great differentials in type of equipment, the single most important determinant of a carrier's market share was that carrier's share of the seat capacity offered on that route. Although marketing and promotion did influence market share, they were believed to play a secondary role. Thus, by varying the number of flights allocated to a particular route, the airline managers felt that they could exercise some control over their market share on that route.

Equipment policy decision making represented about the only area of undisputed management prerogative where explicit choice offered the hope of giving a

---

[2] By way of comparison with the size of their advance payments, Eastern and TWA had total net worths of $227 million and $262 million respectively as of March 31, 1971. Should their advance payments have been lost as a result of a Lockheed bankruptcy (an outcome that looked highly plausible in mid-1971), either or both of these carriers might easily have followed Lockheed into reorganization.

carrier some measure of control over its own destiny. Since competitive opportunity rests in this area, much management attention is focused on the strategic importance of equipment planning. This chapter carefully examines the capital budgeting dimension of equipment planning, and points up the relevance of a "game theory" approach to decision making in the oligopoly environment facing the airlines.[3] The research question addressed by this chapter is thus

How do firms do their capital budgeting when the competitive environment explicitly makes a "game theory" approach to the problem relevant, and to what extent do the decisions of one firm influence those of competitors within the same industry?

Pressures for Excess Capacity Purchases

The *air transportation* industry provides what is perhaps currently the most interesting example of "game theory" in capital budgeting. This is true because in the aggregate, market share in air transportation seems to follow capacity share much more closely than it does in most other industries. "Fly the seats and you get the passengers" is an appropriate description of the competitive situation. To gain market share, then, an air carrier's strategy might simply be to increase his share of industry capacity through massive purchases of air equipment. One might expect air carriers to compete strongly along the capacity dimension simply as a result of this basic phenomenon. In point of fact, the economics of capacity competition are even more unstable than indicated above. It is a characteristic of the airline industry that on a competitive route served by two carriers, an air carrier in a minority position (e.g., that of providing 30% of the available seats flown on

---

[3] There is certainly no shortage of industries in which the fixed plant decisions of participating firms provide an equally interesting scenario for investigation. The fertilizer and fiber industries might all serve as rich examples for a game theory approach to capital budgeting.

Fertilizer would present an interesting situation since the industry exploded so rapidly that many of the recent entrants seemed not to realize (or take into account) the capacity plans of competitors. (Thomas O'Hanlon, *Fortune*, June 1, 1968, pp. 92–94.) The capital budgeting for each firm planning to participate in the industry was evidently performed in a competitive vacuum.

The *polyester fiber* industry presents a similar fruitful area for investigation. Here during a surge in market growth the principal participant (Du Pont) made all the appropriate public announcements staking out its permanent claim on a very large market share. Enormous plant expansions, large price cuts and threats of future cuts, etc., were undertaken in order to discourage entry [William E. Fruhan, "Midland Ross Corporation (B)," EA-F 329, Harvard Business School, 1968]. Yet in the face of this evidence (to their present dismay), a number of firms entered the competitive arena with plants small enough to be uneconomic but large enough to represent a substantial commitment for the new entrant. Unlike the fertilizer situation, in the polyester industry at least one powerful participant understood (and indeed set the terms of) the "game" and endeavored to warn potential participants to keep out. Many did, but those who failed to understand the economics of the competitive environment suffered consequences.

the route) will very often get a substantially smaller share of the total passengers flown on the route (e.g., a little more than 20%). The carrier providing 70% of the total available seats flown will then get a disproportionately larger share (about 80%) of the total passengers flown. Figure 5.1 shows how a carrier's *market*

FIGURE 5.1

MARKET SHARE VERSUS CAPACITY SHARE ON A TWO-CARRIER ROUTE

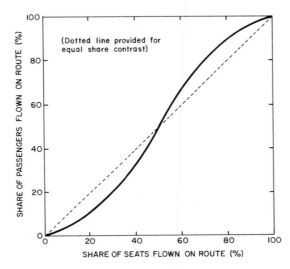

share varies in relation to the share of *seat capacity* which the carrier provides on the route.[4]

This imbalance in passenger patronage is probably a result of the fact that a traveler telephones the dominant carrier first in search of a reservation, expecting to find departure and return times there which are closest to the ones desired.

Since a passenger load factor of about 50% is required for breakeven operation, it is clear that a carrier in a 30% minority share position will usually be losing money unless revenue yields or passenger load factors are unusually high on the route. Indeed, the passenger load factor on the overall route would have to be above 75% in order for the minority carrier mentioned above to fly with a 50% passenger load factor, and this is a highly unlikely situation.

---

[4] This market share-capacity share relationship is actually just a market share-flight frequency share relationship in which carriers on the same route fly equipment of roughly equal size.

A number of airline analysts have found this S-curve relationship between market share and flight frequency share in statistical studies. Among these are: N. K. Taneja, "Airline Competition Analysis," Massachusetts Institute of Technology Flight Transportation Laboratory, FTL Report R-68-2, September 1968; D. B. Bibeault, "Market Share Dependency Study," unpublished manuscript, March 31, 1969; S. Barcun, et al., "Airline Seat Share: An Optimizing Model," unpublished manuscript, 1970.

Competitive Responses and Market Share Changes

Let us assume initially that on a hypothetical route served by two carriers the overall passenger load factor is 55%. Assume further that the carriers together fly 100,000 seats per year on this route. The carriers' competitive positions are then as indicated in Table 5.1.

TABLE 5.1

INITIAL COMPETITIVE POSITIONS

Carrier	Seats per Year	Share of Seats	Share of Market	Passengers Flown	Passenger Load Factor	Overall Passenger Load Factor
Minority	30,000	30%	20.5%	11,300	37.6% ⎫	
Dominant	70,000	70%	79.5%	43,700	62.4% ⎬	55%
	100,000			55,000		

The load factors show that the minority carrier is operating at well below breakeven on the route (which we assume to be 50%), but that the dominant carrier is operating at a substantial profit. Assume now that (1) the minority carrier increases his seat capacity by 50%, (2) passenger traffic grows by 15%, and (3) the dominant carrier makes no competitive response in terms of equipment additions. According to Table 5.1, the competitive situation would then shift to the one shown in Table 5.2, in which the incremental 15,000 seats added by the minority

TABLE 5.2

LATER COMPETITIVE POSITIONS

Carrier	Seats per Year	Share of Seats	Share of Market	Passengers Flown	Passenger Load Factor	Overall Passenger Load Factor
Minority	45,000	39.1%	32.8%	20,800	46.1% ⎫	
Dominant	70,000	60.9%	67.2%	42,500	60.7% ⎬	55%
	115,000			63,300		

Incremental passengers flown by minority carrier	9,500
,, ,, ,, ,, ,, ,, due to traffic growth	1,695
,, ,, ,, ,, ,, ,, due to capacity addition	7,805
Passenger load factor on incremental seat additions	52%

carrier are operating above breakeven in spite of the fact that in overall terms the minority carrier is still operating below breakeven and losing money.

This kind of exercise can be carried out to include additional competitive developments, but the net result would indicate that in the long run, the carrier with the financial resources to purchase the planes required to achieve a dominant capacity share might well come out ahead by using its financial power to purchase the equipment necessary initially to achieve or continue to maintain this objective. Indeed, Tables 5.3 and 5.4 carry the hypothetical example further by tracing over a period of years the profit implications and the financial resources required by competitors under varying assumptions concerning their market share strategies on individual routes.

Strategy 1: Maintaining a Route's Overall Passenger Load Factor

Table 5.3 assumes that the minority carrier (Carrier 1) makes annual capacity additions which are sufficient in size (assuming no competitive response) to keep the route's overall passenger load factor at 55% as passenger traffic grows 15% annually. The initially dominant carrier (Carrier 2) does not react competitively to the minority carrier's encroachment upon his market share, since to do so would "spoil" the market by driving the route's overall passenger load factor downward.

The trends of lines 14 and 16 of Table 5.3 clearly demonstrate that a carrier who "stands pat" in the face of competitive capacity additions does not merely fail to expand his profit base as might be the case in many industries. In spite of the fact that the *overall* passenger load factor on this robustly growing route remains unchanged (line 4 of Table 5.3), a carrier adopting such a strategy will rapidly find himself losing both profit and passengers on an absolute basis.

Strategy 2: Maintaining Market Share at Any Cost

Table 5.4 starts with the carriers in the same initial positions which they occupied in Table 5.3. Carrier 2 has changed its competitive strategy, however, and now has determined to maintain its market share (line 8) regardless of the size of the capacity additions necessary to match the competitive thrusts of Carrier 1. In this example (Table 5.4), both carriers find their losses (lines 12 and 14) mounting rapidly as the route's overall passenger load factor declines (line 4). If Carrier 2 were the financially weaker carrier, however, it is not difficult to see where the competitive game would end.[5] The scheduling practices of the larger carriers have,

---

[5] This situation is explored in some detail in Chapter 6. Barcun's model (footnote 4) shows the carriers in a similar situation reaching an equilibrium in which each carrier continues to incur losses from operations on the route which are slightly in excess of 20% of its revenue generation on the route.

The S-shaped curve relating market share to capacity share in air transportation seems to have a corollary in several other industries where profitability exhibits an S-shaped relationship to market share. This pattern can result in unusually high returns on investment for the dominant firm in a business showing a high degree of market concentration. Documented

TABLE 5.3

ROUTE COMPETITION BETWEEN TWO CARRIERS—STRATEGY 1 (RETREAT)
(All Figures in Thousands Except for Decimals)

		1	2	3	4	5	6	7
1	Year	1	2	3	4	5	6	7
2	Total passengers flown on route	55	63	73	84	96	111	127
3	Available seats flown on route	100	115	132	152	174	198	225
4	Route's overall passenger load factor	.55	.55	.55	.55	.55	.55	.55
5	Carrier 1 Share of seat capacity	.30	.39	.47	.54	.60	.65	.69
6	Carrier 2 Share of seat capacity	.70	.61	.53	.46	.40	.35	.31
7	Carrier 1 Share of passengers flying route	.20	.33	.45	.56	.66	.73	.78
8	Carrier 2 Share of passengers flying route	.80	.67	.55	.44	.34	.27	.22
9	Carrier 1 Passenger load factor on route	.37	.46	.53	.58	.60	.63	.64
10	Carrier 2 Passenger load factor on route	.62	.61	.57	.52	.47	.43	.40
11	Carrier 1 Cost of equipment committed to route (dollars)	915	1,373	1,891	2,502	3,188	3,905	4,725
12	Carrier 1 Book pretax profit on route (dollars)	−204	−170	−86	22	137	270	405
13	Carrier 2 Cost of equipment committed on route (dollars)	2,135	2,135	2,135	2,135	2,135	2,135	2,135
14	Carrier 2 Book pretax profit on route (dollars)	141	97	7	−116	−239	−334	−423
15	Carrier 1 Passengers flying route	11	21	33	47	63	81	99
16	Carrier 2 Passengers flying route	44	42	40	37	33	30	28
17	Carrier 1 Available seats flown on route	30	45	62	82	104	129	155
18	Carrier 2 Available seats flown on route	70	70	70	70	70	70	70

Strategy of Carrier 1: Add sufficient capacity on the route each year to provide seats (at a 55% load factor) for *all* of the annual growth in passenger traffic.

Strategy of Carrier 2: Add capacity whenever Carrier 1 allows the route's overall passenger load factor to rise above 55%.

Where this strategy is coupled with the strategy of Carrier 1, no new capacity will be added by Carrier 2 on this route.

SOURCE: Hypothetical example based on relationships shown in Figure 5.1 and operating economics of the New York to Chicago route with 1968 fares.

for example, occasionally caused considerable furor in the industry. Northeast once filed a complaint with the CAB alleging that Eastern (on its Florida routes) planned to schedule 30% more seats in the winter of 1962 than in the prior season, in spite of Eastern's own projection of only a 1.4% growth in traffic. "Eastern has deliberately overscheduled with the result of producing lower load factors for

examples of businesses showing this characteristic include food manufacturing and food retailing.

It can probably be argued that the main frame computer manufacturing industry shows similar characteristics, and that the General Electric Company probably left the computer industry in 1970 because GE's management felt that the prospect of achieving a Table 5.3 type outcome (in which GE's computer market share could be substantially increased in a content with IBM) was extremely remote. (William E. Fruhan, "General Electric 1970," EA-F 383, Harvard Business School, 1971.)

TABLE 5.4

ROUTE COMPETITION BETWEEN TWO CARRIERS—STRATEGY 2 (MATCHING)
(All Figures in Thousands Except for Decimals)

			1	2	3	4
1	Year		1	2	3	4
2	Total passengers flown on route		55	63	73	84
3	Available seats flown on route		100	150	207	273
4	Route's overall passenger load factor		.55	.42	.35	.31
5	Carrier 1	Share of seat capacity	.30	.30	.30	.30
6	Carrier 2	Share of seat capacity	.70	.70	.70	.70
7	Carrier 1	Share of passengers flying route	.20	.20	.20	.20
8	Carrier 2	Share of passengers flying route	.80	.80	.80	.80
9	Carrier 1	Passenger load factor on route	.37	.29	.24	.21
10	Carrier 2	Passenger load factor on route	.62	.48	.40	.35
11	Carrier 1	Cost of equipment committed to route (dollars)	915	1,372	1,891	2,502
12	Carrier 1	Book pretax profit on route (dollars)	−204	−446	−719	−1,042
13	Carrier 2	Cost of equipment committed to route (dollars)	2,135	3,203	4,413	5,838
14	Carrier 2	Book pretax profit on route (dollars)	141	−330	−861	−1,493
15	Carrier 1	Passengers flying route	11	13	15	17
16	Carrier 2	Passengers flying route	44	50	58	67
17	Carrier 1	Available seats flown on route	30	45	62	82
18	Carrier 2	Available seats flown on route	70	105	145	191

Strategy of Carrier 1: Add sufficient capacity on the route each year to provide seats (at a 55% load factor) for *all* of the annual growth in passenger traffic.

Strategy of Carrier 2: Add sufficient capacity each year to maintain a 70% share of the total seats flown on the route.

SOURCE: Hypothetical example based on relationships shown in Figure 5.1 and operating exonomics of the New York to Chicago route with 1968 fares.

both Eastern and its competitors as well as reduced earnings or substantial losses which Eastern was prepared to endure until it drove Northeast out of business." [6] In a later fracas on the Denver-St. Louis route, Frontier Airlines accused TWA of excessive scheduling. Reports in the trade press were as follows:

> In response to (Frontier's) complaints about Trans World's "unreasonable" competition . . . one Trans World official scoffed, "He (Frontier) has just wandered in over his head, and he's running scared. TWA is doing nothing that it would not against any competitor."

> Another trunkline official commented, "If they (the local service carriers such as Frontier) want to become trunks (like TWA), they will have to compete with us on our own terms."

[6] Complaint of Northeast Airlines, Inc., against Eastern Airlines, Inc., Board Order #E20421, January 31, 1964, p. 6.

Still another trunk official cautioned: "The locals must be careful in choosing their spots. They just are not qualified to compete on a wholesale basis with the trunks." [7]

In a second example involving Frontier, in 1967 the carrier . . .

won a route from Denver to Kansas City in direct competition with Continental. Mr. Six [Continental's president] immediately placed a call to congratulate Lewis Dymond, Frontier's president, then hung up and ordered a massive marketing effort to squash Frontier. "We never let them get off their knees," chortled Mr. Six.[8]

Competition at the Industry Versus the Route Level

For a carrier to increase (or maintain) its market share on the particular route it flies, according to Figure 5.1 the carrier must expand its seat capacity faster than (or at least as fast as) its competitors. As a practical matter "competitive" capacity additions, particularly those of medium-range jet aircraft, are hard to identify in advance. For example, when Boeing announces that American Airlines has ordered three new 727 jets, United Airlines cannot be sure whether these planes will be placed on the New York-Chicago route on which United competes with American, or on the Chicago-Dallas route on which American and United do not compete. To be operationally effective, then, for the large carriers the objective of increasing capacity share on the individual *route* level must be translated into increasing capacity share on the *industry* level. Thus we find that the directors of one major air carrier were asked to approve the purchase of additional aircraft not because of revisions in traffic growth expectations on its routes, or because particular aircraft orders of other carriers "gamed out" [9] to be competitive, but rather because:

Other carriers have committed for larger fleets than we expected when the five-year plan was developed. This added competitive capacity, and resulting ability to compete more effectively against us can only erode our competitive position. Additional aircraft are required to offset the intensified competitive threat.

By adding the equipment requested, the carrier in question planned to *match* the competitive threat and simultaneously increase its industry share of capacity by almost two percentage points, thus escalating the capacity battle.

The relationship between market share and capacity share, shown in Figure

---

[7] H. D. Watkins, "New Routes, Costs Test Local Airlines," *Aviation Week and Space Technology*, March 18, 1968.

[8] W. S. Pinkerton, Jr., "Last of a Breed," *Wall Street Journal*, June 30, 1970.

[9] When an air carrier and/or an airframe manufacturer announces an order for equipment, the planning departments of competitive carriers try to determine ("game out") the routes on which the new planes will probably be used.

5.1, leads one to predict a strong tendency toward capacity competition among the air carriers. Indeed, the economic presumption that capacity share will be translated into market share which will in turn be translated into profit share might present an attractive prescription for capacity expansion to any carrier. Before embarking on an aggressive capacity strategy, however, an air carrier manager might need some assurance about the last link in this line of reasoning. A carrier manager might assume *first* that at some time in the future profits will be maintained at a satisfactory level for the industry at large; *second,* that the capacity "game" will end sometime in the future because participants agree that it is simply no longer economic to play; and *third,* that a current effort to increase market share via capacity additions is sufficiently attractive to warrant the expenditure necessary to achieve it. The rationality of these necessary assumptions is greatly enhanced by (1) a projected rapid growth in air transportation, (2) an expected reduction in the rate of growth 10 to 15 years in the future, and (3) the general availability of high debt leverage to the air carriers.

Numerically, it is possible to evaluate only the third assumption relating to the value of an immediate increase in market share. From this evaluation it is possible, however, to conclude that at some future date (due to a slowdown in traffic growth) market share assaults will become economically less attractive—thus making our second assumption (that market share duels will subside) intuitively more attractive.

The Value of a One Point Increase in Market Shares

In Table 5.5 it is assumed that air traffic (RPMs) will grow at the rate of (1) 15% annually between 1968 and 1972, (2) 10% annually between 1973 and 1977, and (3) 5% in 1978. It is further assumed that the industry's total investment (defined as equity plus long-term debt and lease equivalents) will grow at comparable rates from a base of $6.8 billion in 1967. Finally, it is assumed that the industry will be able to earn 10% after taxes on its investment base.[10]

Given these assumptions, line 4 of Table 5.5 shows the profit in excess of capital costs which a carrier would earn each year if (1) it were able to "buy" an extra point in market share at the end of 1967 and (2) it had a "cost of capital" one full percentage point below its investment rate. The net present value in 1967 of the stream of additional profits shown in line 4 could be determined by discounting the stream at the carrier's "cost of capital." Since we have assumed a 10% return on investment, and a one percentage point spread between the investment rate and the "cost of capital," this stream should be discounted at our assumed 9% cost of capital.

While in theory the inflows of line 4 should be continued indefinitely, for the

---

[10] In the 1970 Domestic Passenger Fare Investigation, the Board concluded that the carriers should be permitted to earn 12% on invested capital. The 10% rate assumed here is thus fairly conservative. (U.S. Civil Aeronautics Board, Board Order #71-4-58, April 12, 1971.)

TABLE 5.5

NET PRESENT VALUE OF A 1 PERCENTAGE POINT INCREASE IN A DOMESTIC TRUNK CARRIER'S INDUSTRY MARKET SHARE

Pro-Forma	1967 Actual	1968	1969	1970	1971	1972	1973 Pro-Forma	1974	1975	1976	1977	1978	...	2008
1 Projected Growth in Industry RPMs	—	15%	15%	15%	15%	15%	10%	10%	10%	10%	10%	5%	...	0%
2 Asset Base Required (Millions of Dollars)	$6,885	$7,920	$9,100	$10,470	$12,050	$13,880	$15,250	$16,780	$18,460	$20,300	$22,330	$23,450	...	$23,450
3 Asset Base Required Per 1 Percentage Point Increase in Industry Market Share (Millions of Dollars)	$ 68.8	$ 79.2	$ 91.0	$ 104.7	$ 120.5	$ 138.8	$ 152.5	$ 167.8	$ 184.6	$ 203.0	$ 223.3	$ 234.5	...	$ 234.5
4 Profits Earned in Excess of Capital Costs Per 1 Percentage Point Increase in Market Share—Assuming Investment Returns are 1 Percentage Point Higher Than Capital Costs (Millions of Dollars)		$ .792	$ .910	$ 1.047	$ 1.205	$ 1.388	$ 1.525	$ 1.678	$ 1.846	$ 2.030	$ 2.223	$ 2.345	...	$ 2.345
5 Net Present Value of Flows in Line 4 (Continued Through Year 2008 at the 1978 Level) Discounted at 9% = **$19.3 million.**														

Cost of Capital Assumptions Used in Discounting the Cash Flows in Line 4

6 Equity	$ 40 @ 17.2%	= $6.90
7 Debt and Leases	$ 60 @ 3.5%	= $2.10
8 Total Capital	$100 @ 9.0%	= $9.00

calculation in line 5 the 1978 return was repeated for a total of 46 years, at which point the stream had a net present value of $19.3 million. This calculation implies that the "right to invest" up to $235 million (at a return one percentage point greater than "cost") should be worth $19.3 million to a carrier in 1967. The carrier could thus afford to "throw away" that amount of money in terms of profit reduction in 1968 in order to achieve an extra point in its industry market share. Of course, this assumes a "cost of capital" equal to a full percentage point below the investment rate, but this does not seem unreasonable since with a 1.5 to 1 debt/equity ratio a 9% charge for total capital (assuming a 3.5% after-tax debt cost) leaves the equity with a return of more than 17% (line 6 of Table 5.5).

Market Share Now Versus Later—a Comparison

Since a carrier always faces the question "market share now versus market share later?" a few words on the subject might be useful. It is fairly clear that if a carrier waited until market growth slowed in 1978 to try to gain a 1 percentage point increase in market share, the "cost" of achieving this goal would probably be far higher than it would have been in 1968. This would be true for two reasons. First, by 1978 the amount of revenue represented by a 1% share of the market would be three times higher than it was in 1968. The cost of attracting the revenues contained in this 1% market share would thus be much higher in 1978. Second, in 1968 market share growth for an aggressive carrier could be achieved by preempting some portion of a less aggressive carrier's normal anticipated growth. At the later date, however, such growth would require the less aggressive competitor to suffer an absolute revenue shrinkage, an outcome which most firms, even nonaggressive ones, would vigorously contest. These two qualitative arguments suggest that market share duels ought to occur during the robust stages of market growth in an industry. So do the quantitative arguments. The present value (in 1968) of 50 annual payments starting in 1979 at the 1979 rate (line 4 of Table 5.5) is not much greater than the present value (in 1968) of an outlay of $19.3 million in 1978. Thus, it would be relatively cheaper to "buy" market share in 1968 than it would be 10 years later.[11]

Another factor which came out of this analysis is the importance of expected rates of growth to the value of market share increases. A 50% reduction in anticipated traffic growth would cut the value of line 5 in Table 5.5 down to $12.0 million. We might expect the air carriers to compete less vigorously when the re-

---

[11] The notion that it is cheaper to acquire market share early in the life cycle of a growing business has substantial empirical support. Citing the computer business again as an example, at several points in time between 1956 and 1970, the General Electric Company could have made a major push to increase its relatively small (less than 5%) market share in computers. In relation to GE's asset base, however, the phenomenal growth in computers between 1956 and 1970 tied a financial burden to the option of expanding market share in computers in 1970 that GE was probably unable to bear. GE thus chose to leave the business rather than fight what the company may have perceived as a losing battle with the dominant firm, IBM.

wards anticipated from success decline. As the industry matures and growth slows, we might thus expect the intensity of market share battles to subside.

Capacity Stimulating Impact of High Profitability

While the objective of achieving long-run growth in market share is probably the most powerful economic force driving the air carriers toward overcapacity in their equipment planning, a second force also compels them to move in a similar direction during periods of high profit. Averch and Johnson have shown that economic forces can tend to encourage regulated firms to adopt a posture of overinvestment in fixed assets.

> . . . if the rate of return allowed by the regulatory agency is greater than the cost of capital but is less than the rate of return that would be enjoyed by the firm were it free to maximize profit without regulatory constraint . . . [then] . . . the firm has an incentive to expand into other regulated markets, even if it operated at a (long run) loss in these markets.[12]

The following example is offered to demonstrate this effect. Assume that in 1967 a regulated firm had an investment base of $200 and a profit (as defined by the regulator) of $20. Assume further that the regulator allowed a 10% return and that the firm's cost of capital was 8%. Now assume that profits start to move above the allowed return, and that the firm foresees that if it could avoid a rate reduction its position for 1968 would be as follows:

	Actual 1967	Pro-forma 1968
Investment Base	$200	$200
Profit	$ 20	$ 22
Actual Rate of Return	10%	11%
Allowed Rate of Return	10%	10%
Cost of Capital	8%	8%

Since the regulator would not permit the firm's return to exceed 10%,[13] the firm could either (1) look forward to a rate decrease, or (2) build its asset base by expanding into less profitable (or even *unprofitable*) areas.

Assume that the only expansion available to the firm in the regulated business consists of an investment of $20 which will yield a net loss for each year of its projected life equal to $.2. The question facing the firm is, "Should it invest?" The example below shows the answer.

---

[12] Harvey Averch, and Leland L. Johnson, "Behavior of the Firm Under Regulatory Constraint," *American Economic Review*, December 1962, 52, 1052–69.

[13] In practice, "regulatory lag" and arguments relating to averaging returns over a period longer than one year might ordinarily delay a price response, but as indicated in Chapter 4, the CAB can use route proceedings to accomplish a similar end with a very little time lag.

	Without "loss" investment		With "loss" investment
	(Before Regulatory Response)	*(After Regulatory Response)*	
Investment Base	$200	$200	$220
Profit	$ 22	$ 20	$ 21.8
Actual Rate of Return	11%	10%	9.9%
Rate of Return on "Loss Investment"	—	—	9%

While the investment results in an overall economic loss of $.2, the existence of the regulatory ceiling on returns places the project in the acceptable category for the firm since, on a comparative basis, the return is $1.8/$20 = 9%, an amount higher than the firm's cost of capital.

From the standpoint of an air carrier, this phenomenon has relevance, since it encourages the carriers to bury profits, at least in the short run, by market share assaults (implemented via excess equipment purchases), when profits are relatively high. The phenomenon of "buried profits" for the industry as a whole occurs only in periods of high aggregate profit such as in 1965. For a few of the well-situated individual carriers, however, the problem has longer range significance. The trunk airlines as an industry have rarely approached the 10.5% permitted rate of return, but some individual carriers have faced an embarrassment of riches over a substantial period of time. In spite of the fact that the CAB's return guidelines relate to the industry as a whole (and not individual carriers), extremely high profits carry a risk of encouraging the CAB to bolster weaker carriers by making route awards in the high profit carriers' most lucrative markets.

The choice facing the high return carriers is thus to risk competition on lucrative routes earlier than it might otherwise occur (if profits were lower), or to bury profits by excess equipment purchases and increased market penetration in competitive markets. While high return carriers can and have buried profits by adopting extremely conservative acounting practices (Table 2.7), excess equipment purchases offer a less transparent means to a similar end.

Level of Analysis Conflicts and the Overcapacity Spiral

Table 5.3 showed the penalty which one carrier would sustain by refusing to engage in a capacity duel with a route competitor. If a carrier has no desire or expertise enabling it to move investment capital into other business areas, but rather wishes to stay in the air transportation business, according to this exhibit the carrier cannot afford to let an aggressive competitor make serious inroads upon his capacity share. A carrier's corporate strategy would almost have to include a strong competitive response whenever his capacity share was threatened.

While equipment purchases made to increase or maintain a carrier's share of capacity may appear to have a very long-run strategic justification at the corporate level (as suggested in Table 5.5), at both the route level and the industry level such purchases can appear to be self-defeating. Focusing at the individual route level for a moment, when lines 14 of Tables 5.3 and 5.4 are compared with lines 13 of these same tables, as is done in Table 5.6, one fact is clear. If Carrier 2 based its

TABLE 5.6

Carrier 2 Pretax Profit and Investment Commitments Associated with Different Responses to Competitive Capacity Additions
(*Thousands of Dollars*)

	Year	1	2	3	4
1		1	2	3	4
2	Pretax Profit—Matching Strategy (Table 5.4, line 14)	141	−330	−861	−1,493
3	Pretax Profit—Retreat Strategy (Table 5.3, line 14)	141	97	7	−116
4	Losses Avoided if Retreat	0	427	868	1,377
5	Equipment Investment—Matching Strategy (Table 5.4, line 13)	2,135	3,203	4,413	5,838
6	Equipment Investment—Retreat Strategy (Table 5.3, line 13)	2,135	2,135	2,135	2,135
7	Investment Outlay Avoided if Retreat	0	1,068	2,278	3,703

Source: Tables 5.3 and 5.4.

capacity decision for the route on a discounted cash flow analysis (lines 4 and 7 of Table 5.6), the carrier would never commit any new equipment to the route since it would operate at an enormous loss. Indeed, a series of independent equipment purchase decisions based on return on investment (ROI) calculations at the individual route level might well lead a carrier not to purchase any new planes for any of its routes. A series of independent route equipment decisions might very well take the carrier out of the air transportation business altogether.

At the industry level, Table 1.10 demonstrates the profit penalties caused by purchases of equipment which are in excess of that required by traffic growth. In any year when the value in column 4 (which represents capacity growth) is larger than the value in column 5 (which represents traffic growth), actual passenger load factors (column 6) decline. The resulting reduction in spread above breakeven narrows overall industry profits (column 9). Clearly, if everyone plays the "market share via extra capacity" game nobody gains any advantage and the industry participants suffer together.

If this analysis of the airline industry is correct, and the nature of this environment is well understood by the industry participants, we might expect to find a history of unrestrained capacity competition reflected in low ROIs among the air carriers. If we look at the record (column 10 of Table 1.10) this hypothesis is not entirely rejected, but it clearly needs modification. The high returns of the early to mid-1950s and the period between 1964 and 1966 clearly need to be explained. Perhaps some usually dominated force external to the industry came into play during these periods and restrained equipment competition. Information on this possibility might be forthcoming if we zeroed in on an industry participant to see how the capital budgeting process is actually carried out within the firm.

Capital Budgeting at XYZ Airlines

Forecasting Equipment Needs—The Bottom Up Approach

In forward equipment planning at XYZ, the carrier's periodic seat-mile capacity additions were determined from an analysis of total equipment needs derived from two independent approaches which are presented pictorially in Figure 5.2. The first approach, labeled the "bottom up" analysis is represented by the Marketing, Equipment Planning and Research, and Financial triangle in the figure. In this analysis, the traffic growth potential on each of 150 to 200 routes flown by XYZ was estimated by the corporate marketing staff. These growth estimates varied quite widely on routes between differing city-pairs. For instance, the annual traffic growth expectation for the New York-Chicago route might be only 10%, while the expected traffic growth on a route linking Boston to Atlanta might range as high as 25%.

Once growth estimates at the individual route level were determined by XYZ's marketing staff, the carrier's top marketing management set market share targets for each individual route. The marketing staff personnel would then estimate the load factor which XYZ could expect to achieve on each route in meeting its market share goal. This estimate would take into account the carrier's historic market share, its image on the route, and anticipated capacity additions of competitors. After establishing projections for (1) total traffic growth on the route, (2) an XYZ target market share on the route and (3) a passenger load factor associated with the target market share, XYZ's marketing staff could then calculate the additional ASMs of capacity needed on each of the carrier's routes, and forecast the incremental revenues which would be generated by the new aircraft purchases. This forecast would include incremental revenues on the route in question as well as any revenue which might be added and identified elsewhere in the system as a result of the equipment addition. XYZ's equipment planning and research group could then translate the capacity requirement into a specific level and type of equipment purchases.

The incremental revenue projections (supplied by the marketing department) and the operating cost and equipment purchase price data (supplied by the equipment planning and research department) were then forwarded to the financial staff for a "price out." At this point in the information flow, the discounted cash flow rate of return on investment for equipment dedicated to specific routes was calculated. XYZ's top financial officer was then presented with (1) the total amount of capital required to purchase the equipment specified in the analysis and (2) the DCF-ROI calculations for the equipment to be dedicated to each of

FIGURE 5.2

XYZ Airlines—The Equipment Acquisition Decision

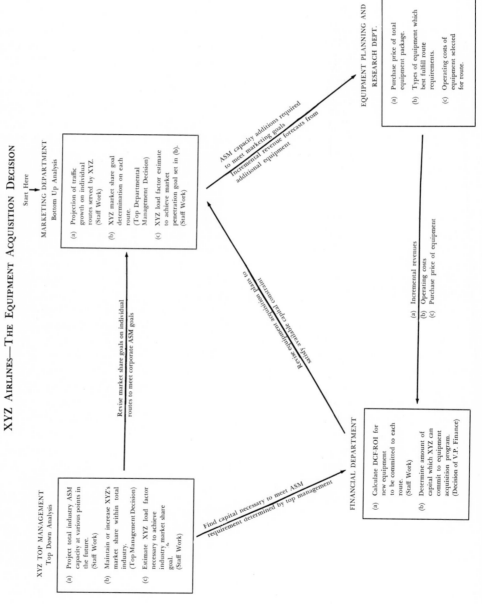

TABLE 5.7

XYZ AIRLINES

PROJECTED INVESTMENT AND ADDITIONS TO EARNINGS (AS REPORTED TO SHAREHOLDERS) DUE TO 40 AIRCRAFT ACQUISITION PROGRAM, 1968–1971

	1967	1968	1969	1970	1971	Five-year Summary
		(*Millions of Dollars*)				
Cash Outflows for Capital Equipment	14.5	63.7	197.6	55.7	134.7	466.2
Contribution to Overhead and Profit	—	(.3)	10.8	32.5	43.2	86.2
Allocated Corporate Overhead	—	.8	9.8	16.2	24.5	51.3
Profit Before Taxes	—	(1.1)	1.0	16.3	18.7	34.9

SOURCE: Private Carrier Data.

XYZ's routes, and (3) the projected impact of the equipment purchases on XYZ's operating earnings (see examples in Tables 5.7 and 5.8).

The point where limitations were first imposed on the planned volume of equipment purchases was at the level of XYZ's financial vice president. Each time the equipment purchase decisions came up for review, a complete "bottom up" analysis

TABLE 5.8

XYZ AIRLINES

DISCOUNTED CASH FLOW RATE OF RETURN
ANALYSIS FOR XYZ'S 40 AIRCRAFT ACQUISITION PROGRAM

Quantity of Aircraft Purchased	Model of Aircraft Purchased	Cost of Aircraft (*Millions of Dollars*)	DCF-ROI without Overhead Allocation	DCF-ROI with Overhead Allocation	DCF-ROI with Overhead Allocation and Removal of ITC**
10	747	251.6	14.6%	8.7%	7.7%
1	707-331B	8.3	8.9	*	*
2	707-331B	*	27.6	20.6	*
7	707-331B	*	*	*	*
2	707-331C	*	*	*	*
3	707-120	*	*	*	*
2	707-131B	*	19.6	14.1	13.1
1	727-31	5.4	9.7	*	*
3	727-31	17.0	12.7	*	*
3	727-231	*	*	*	*
2	727-231	*	32.2	26.7	*
4	727-231	*	*	*	*
40		466.2	17.5%	*	*

* Return calculated but not available.
** ITC refers to the 7% investment tax credit.

SOURCE: Private Carrier Data.

was run under a variety of assumptions relating to the availability of funds. The first run always assumed that the firm had unlimited capital resources. Given such free reign, the marketing staff usually submitted requests for equipment the cost of which far exceeded the firm's resources. A second run would then be made using the assumption that a fixed dollar amount of capital would be available to the firm for equipment purchases. This dollar limit was determined by XYZ's financial vice president, and it generally equaled the amount of cash that he felt the corporation could generate internally plus the debt and lease additions which he felt the corporation would be able to raise externally. The results of this second run, in a form such as that presented in Tables 5.7 and 5.8, were then presented to XYZ's top management for review.

Forecasting Equipment Needs—The Top Down Approach

At this point in the decision process, XYZ's top management compared the level of equipment purchases indicated by the "bottom up" analysis to a second total purchase figure established by a "top down" analysis. In the "top down" analysis (represented in the top left corner of Figure 5.2), XYZ's planning staff examined the announced and projected equipment orders of all the domestic trunk carriers and Pan American. From a study of these orders, their related delivery dates, and equipment retirement estimates, the planning staff projected forward the industry's total seating capacity, and each carrier's share of that capacity at various future dates. These projections could be made with considerable accuracy over the near term (six months in the future), and with reduced accuracy as far as four or five years into the future. Using these projections, XYZ's top management could revise the firm's equipment purchase plans in order to meet corporate goals with regard to XYZ's share of the industry's total available seat-mile capacity.

Corporate ASM Goals—The Strategic Capacity Decision

In forecasting capacity purchase goals, XYZ's top management tried first to preserve the carrier's capacity share within the industry (Figure 5.3). This would usually be attempted even if the necessary capital could not be met without resorting to some type of equity financing. Once this minimum constraint had been satisfied, however, the decision to purchase additional equipment was seasoned by a number of other factors, such as XYZ's "then current" profit/investment ratio. If this figure were relatively high (say 9%) the carrier would usually "invest" in market share expansion via extra equipment additions. If the figure were low, however (say 5%), the carrier would adopt a more conservative posture in adding extra equipment.

XYZ's top management also had to keep an eye on the firm's profit/investment ratio in relation to the industry average in order to make sure that the carrier did not get too far out of line with the industry as a result of rapid equipment additions. In order to keep the visibility of a market share assault low (and thus reduce

FIGURE 5.3

XYZ AIRLINES
Decision Constraints for Equipment Capacity Purchases*

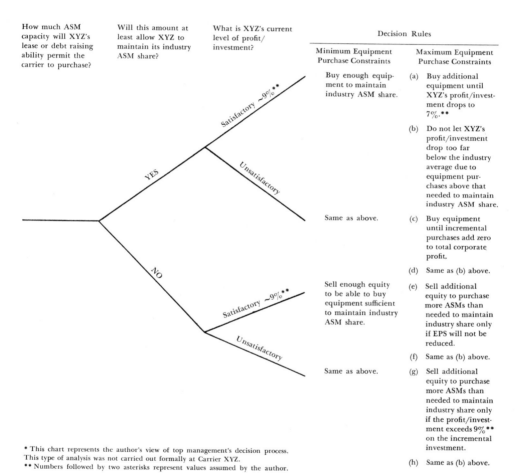

How much ASM capacity will XYZ's lease or debt raising ability permit the carrier to purchase?

Will this amount at least allow XYZ to maintain its industry ASM share?

What is XYZ's current level of profit/investment?

Decision Rules

Minimum Equipment Purchase Constraints	Maximum Equipment Purchase Constraints
Buy enough equipment to maintain industry ASM share.	(a) Buy additional equipment until XYZ's profit/investment drops to 7%.**
	(b) Do not let XYZ's profit/investment drop too far below the industry average due to equipment purchases above that needed to maintain industry ASM share.
Same as above.	(c) Buy equipment until incremental purchases add zero to total corporate profit.
	(d) Same as (b) above.
Sell enough equity to be able to buy equipment sufficient to maintain industry ASM share.	(e) Sell additional equity to purchase more ASMs than needed to maintain industry share only if EPS will not be reduced.
	(f) Same as (b) above.
Same as above.	(g) Sell additional equity to purchase more ASMs than needed to maintain industry share only if the profit/investment exceeds 9%** on the incremental investment.
	(h) Same as (b) above.

Satisfactory ~9%**

Unsatisfactory

YES

NO

Satisfactory ~9%**

Unsatisfactory

* This chart represents the author's view of top management's decision process. This type of analysis was not carried out formally at Carrier XYZ.
** Numbers followed by two asterisks represent values assumed by the author.

the competitive response), the carrier also attempted to limit its capacity share growth in any year. This tactic was generally followed unless an immediate competitive response was impossible due to the unavailability of equipment deliveries.[14]

Reconciling the "Top Down" and "Bottom Up" Equipment Analyses

Whenever the cost of equipment purchases needed to fulfill top management's capacity share goals differed from the total cost of the equipment purchase plan produced in the "bottom up" analysis, a recalculation was required. Assume, for example, that the "bottom up" analysis produced aircraft purchase proposals costing $400 million (the maximum that the financial vice president felt could be raised between 1968 and 1971 without resorting to outside equity financing). If the "top down" analysis indicated a need for $450 million in expenditures to meet strategic ASM capacity goals set at the corporate level, then the market penetration target established by XYZ's marketing management on particular routes would be raised and the "bottom up" analysis recalculated. This procedure would be repeated until the capacity requirements indicated by the two types of analysis were equal. The financial vice president would then face the problem of finding the capital necessary to pay for the volume of equipment purchases finally agreed upon.

The Use of DCF-ROI in Equipment Planning

XYZ used the technique of discounting cash flows to arrive at an overall return on investment in the formal economic analysis used to justify new equipment purchases. Aircraft orders were usually earmarked for use on specific routes. The discounted cash flow return on investment (DCF-ROI) associated with the purchase of each aircraft was thus geared primarily to specific route economics.[15] Since aircraft were often shifted around, however, XYZ tried to predict an aircraft's revenue and expense streams for only the first three years of its life. For the remainder of the aircraft's expected life, the revenue and expense streams were simply assumed to be equal to the third year expected performance.

The Relative Importance of Market Share and DCF-ROI Considerations in Equipment Planning

One of XYZ's financial planners made a number of observations with regard to the company's equipment plans.

---

[14] For example, Pan American planned to expand capacity greatly as evidenced by its B-747 order, but an immediate capacity response by competitors was impossible since the early delivery positions for the plane were taken by Pan American.

[15] Whenever it could be demonstrated that adding equipment to one route would result in traffic increases elsewhere, the incremental revenue would be credited to the new aircraft. Such "bonus" traffic was hard to identify, however, so it was included only in unusually clear situations.

Because of competitor's equipment programs the equipment purchase decision at XYZ is probably tied more closely to our defensive and/or offensive posture vis-à-vis market share than it is to a DCF-ROI calculation. In all of our equipment planning, top management has made two specific assumptions; *first,* that growth of the air transportation industry will stabilize sometime in the future (and the time horizon here may be 5, 10 or even 15 years) and *second,* that if we ignore the effects of dissimilar route structures the total profits earned by each carrier at that time will be geared closely to that carrier's overall industry market share. Given these basic assumptions, the equipment purchase decision becomes much less complex. The first question that you have to answer is, "Are we buying enough capacity to maintain our industry share?" Having answered this question we can then move on and ask the question, "Can our income statement and balance sheet stand the strain caused by an effort to improve our market share?" In essence, what I'm saying in this discussion of equipment strategy is that you may have to accept some short-term deviations from profit objectives when a carrier, due to competitive pressure and long-term economics, makes capacity decisions in this manner, but the penalties associated with the long-term loss of market share in this business look even worse. It doesn't make too much sense from the standpoint of your overall equipment planning effort to look at the DCF-ROI calculation for a single aircraft tied to a specific route. It's just too difficult to factor into such a calculation the revenue benefits which might occur elsewhere in the system immediately or at some later date. You have to broaden the perspective and look at the aggregate return which you expect to earn on a large package of equipment purchases. Given this planning viewpoint you do wind up purchasing some aircraft which appear to have lower than objective DCF-ROIs, but competitive requirements and public convenience[16] compel you to do so.

Where your competition is expanding as rapidly as it is in air transportation, the stakes are too high to let market share slip away from you due to the fact that a DCF-ROI calculation looks too low. Of course this approach to equipment planning can and does give you a certain amount of profit pressure. But in the future the air transportation industry will mature, growth will slow down, and market shares will stabilize. At that time the carriers will be able to earn a better return on their investment. When this occurs, we want to be sure that XYZ is a major factor in the air transportation industry.

AIRLINE PROFITABILITY CYCLES

In the first half of this chapter it was hypothesized and argued that very basic economic factors tend to force United States air carriers into excess equipment purchases, and Tables 5.3, 5.4 and 5.5 demonstrated how a game theory type analysis could be applied to air carrier equipment competition. On the basis of this hypothesis, it was tentatively concluded that given the unstable economic climate, one might reasonably expect to find among the carriers a history of chronic equip-

---

[16] Under the CAB doctrine of "public convenience and necessity," carriers were required to provide some service on specific routes even if the amount of traffic carried was insufficient to support profitable operation on the route.

ment competition, failures among the financially weaker industry participants, and consistent unsatisfactory levels of return on investment. Column 10 of Table 1.10 appeared to rule out this rather simplistic hypothesis, so additional analysis was undertaken in the second half of the chapter which aimed at discovering moderating influences to capacity competition.

The second part of the chapter thus began by focusing on one industry participant's equipment purchase procedure, and discovered a strong similarity in this process to a simple linear programming model (Figure 5.3). By examining the constraints on the purchase decision in this model, it would be possible to isolate the external forces moderating equipment competition and then incorporate these findings explicitly into a new hypothesis describing industry behavior.

In particular, two important factors come out of the Figure 5.3 decision grid. *First,* the availability of debt capital plays a crucial role in a carrier's expansionist tendencies. The carriers seem to be willing to spend for new equipment until the creditors force them to stop. *Second,* in any period a carrier's expansionist tendencies seem to be rather directly related to its then current profit/investment ratio.

The incorporation of these two constraints in our hypothesis carries us a long way toward explaining the pattern of industry returns shown in column 10 of Table 1.10. The period of air carrier prosperity in the early to mid-1950s might then be explained by the fact that traffic growth was so rapid (column 5, Table 1.10) and debt availability so low (column 13, Table 1.10) that the carriers could not raise the capital necessary to expand capacity fast enough to maintain passenger load factors let alone engage in capacity duels.

It was only when creditors began to accept the air transportation industry as a secure credit risk, and permitted debt/equity ratios to expand rapidly, that the industry had the wherewithal to get into difficulty. Between 1955 and 1962, debt/equity ratios expanded fourfold, and sufficient capacity was purchased to drop passenger load factors nearly 11 percentage points. By 1962, industry creditors had called a halt to credit expansion, traffic growth had slowed to a point where market share gains did not hold the promise of great future reward, and returns had gotten so low that the carriers themselves might have called a halt to the game even if creditors had not. The carriers then enjoyed the fruits of their involuntary restraint until 1966 (some industry analysts claim that traffic simply grew faster than anyone anticipated, leaving the carriers unable to "overbuy" equipment due to miscalculation and long order lead times). By 1966, however, profits had risen to the point where the carriers once again collectively assumed more aggressive equipment postures. In response to this aggressiveness the overcapacity forces were once again brought into play reducing industry ROI to the lowest point in history by late 1970 and early 1971 (column 10 of Table 1.10, and Table 3.3).

The Revised Hypothesis

As a result of the findings in the second half of this chapter, the new hypothesis used to describe air carrier equipment competition becomes that:

Basic economic factors tend to force each of the U.S. air carriers into a posture of making excessive equipment purchases in an effort to build market share. This dynamic force is accentuated by periods of rapid traffic growth since at such times carrier managers' anticipations of future growth are revised upward and the expected value of a one percentage point increase in market share (Table 5.5) increases. In addition, during periods of high traffic growth the carriers' rates of return tend to approach the level allowed by the CAB, and this further encourages overbuying as a means of burying profits as mentioned on page 137.

The normal tendency of air carriers to expand capacity at a pace more rapid than traffic growth is muted by (1) the tightening of industry credit when profits turn down sharply, (2) carrier managers' miscalculations (underestimations) of industry growth, and (3) supplier inability to immediately respond to capacity demands.

Using the above hypothesis, one can "explain" several distinct cycles of airline profitability:

I—The relative profitability of the air carriers and the absence of capacity competition during the period 1950–1956 might be explained by the following:
  (a) Repeated underestimation of traffic growth during this period masked what otherwise would have been strong competition (and low industry profits) if the traffic growth anticipated by the carriers had in fact materialized.
  (b) Lenders were unwilling to advance the debt capital which the air carriers would have required to engage in equipment capacity (i.e., asset) competition.
  (c) Traffic growth and aircraft delivery demands were so great that airframe manufacturers were unable (or unwilling) to expand their production facilities rapidly enough to meet the total demands of the carriers which were in fact higher than deliveries indicate. (The Korean War may have contributed to an equipment shortage.)
II—The relative profitability of the air carriers and the absence of severe capacity competition during the period 1964–1966 might be explained by the following:
  (a) After the nerve-shattering unprofitability of 1961, creditors shut off the source of additional debt capital (freezing the industry's total debt at $1.4 billion for 4 years as shown in Table 1.12) "forcing" the carriers to return to profitability since they could no longer command the capital resources necessary to engage in equipment capacity competition.
  (b) The distant future traffic growth projections of carrier managers were so relatively pessimistic in the early 1960s that market share gains appeared to be less attractive (as demonstrated on page 135) and the carriers voluntarily desisted from equipment capacity competition in determining their fleet sizes, since the rewards for successfully capturing a larger market share did not appear to be particularly great.
  (c) Same as I (a)
  (d) Same as I (c)

Data are not available to prove the significance of all the factors contributing to the airline equipment and profitability cycle during each of the periods mentioned. Data are available, however, to demonstrate the significance of these factors at one point or another during the 1963–1970 period.

Misestimates of Traffic Growth

There is clear evidence, for instance, that at least one[17] of the larger carriers was overly pessimistic in its traffic projections for the mid-1960s (Table 5.9), probably

TABLE 5.9

CARRIER XYZ DOMESTIC TRUNK FORECAST
Revenue Passenger Miles (Billions)

Year Forecast Was Made		1964	1965	1966	1967	1968	1969
1963	Forecast	36.4	37.2	—	—	—	—
	Actual	41.7	49.0	—	—	—	—
1964	Forecast	—	41.9	44.4	—	—	—
	Actual	—	49.0	56.8	—	—	—
1965	Forecast	—	—	48.0	51.6	—	—
	Actual	—	—	56.8	71.0	—	—
1966	Forecast	—	—	—	69.0	75.7	—
	Actual	—	—	—	71.0	81.6	—
1967	Forecast	—	—	—	—	80.1	90.2
	Actual	—	—	—	—	81.6	89.4
1968	Forecast	—	—	—	—	—	91.5
	Actual	—	—	—	—	—	89.4

SOURCE: Private Carrier Data.

as a result of the low RPM growth experienced from 1959 to 1962. This table also makes clear the same carrier's shift to progressively more and more optimistic traffic growth forecasts for the later 1960s as RPM growth and the profit situation improved in the mid-1960s. The carrier's two-year projections of industry RPMs moved from 24% below actual for the 1963 forecast to slightly above actual for the 1967 forecast as annual RPM increases grew in the early to mid-1960s. This demonstrates the significance of points I (a) and II (b) mentioned earlier.

Aircraft Availability

Aircraft availability (or more appropriately aircraft scarcity) has a significant impact on airline profitability. During the 1965–1967 period, airframe manufacturers' backlogs of orders were so high that additional aircraft could not be

---

[17] The traffic projections which the Big 4 carriers submitted to the ATA for use in "Major U.S. Airlines, Economic Review and Financial Outlook 1969–1973," were all very tightly bunched together, leading one to believe that all of the carriers probably made their estimates in the same basic way.

squeezed out of production lines. Indeed, the Douglas Aircraft Company nearly faced bankruptcy at one point because "the company had accepted more orders than its financial resources, work force, and suppliers could handle." [18] Boeing got into trouble later due to the inability of suppliers to meet jet engine delivery deadlines. Airframe manufacturers were strained to the breaking point in the mid-1960s. Had they been available, the carriers would have taken many more aircraft than were actually delivered during this period.[19]

Indicative of the importance of (1) airframe manufacturers' production schedules and (2) the carriers' desires to maintain their industry capacity shares individually was an analysis made by one carrier in 1966 which showed that the carrier's capacity position for the next two years was relatively secure since its orders had been pegged to a percentage of total airframe manufacturer capacity! The competition for aircraft in the mid-1960s was so great that it was necessary to step the equipment planning analysis back even further than simply reviewing the order positions of one's competitors. If a carrier waited too long to order its full complement of aircraft, planes would simply not be available at all. The constraint here was not credit availability, it was the manufacturers' productive capacity. This demonstrates the importance of points I (c) and II (d) mentioned earlier.

The factors noted in the previous pages help to explain occasional peaks of adequate profitability in the airline industry profit cycle, but the factors which help to limit the depth of the valleys in the cycle of airline industry profits have not yet been explored in detail. The 1970 collapse in airline profits presents a particularly appropriate example for study in this regard.

Debt Availability

Debt availability has already been mentioned as a major constraint to capacity wars and the loss in airline profitability arising therefrom. On the question of debt capital availability, in August of 1969 Western Airlines canceled orders for $150 million worth of Boeing aircraft due to the carrier's inability to arrange financing. Five of the twelve planes covered in the transaction had delivery dates of only two to five months from the date of the cancellation.[20] Flight equipment order cancellations were rare for the trunk carriers. The impact of credit restraint was usually felt before, not after, equipment orders were placed. Indeed, most of the larger carriers usually had their financing sources lined up at least tentatively for deliveries well into the future. Once an equipment order was actually placed, credit questions were generally of a price rather than of a quantity variety.

While the Western example shows the impact of credit discipline in its severest form, New York State Insurance Law poses a subtler but perhaps more far-reaching credit constraint. Insurance companies have traditionally been the greatest source of industry credit (Table 1.14) and all of these companies were subject in

---

[18] *Business Week,* January 11, 1969, p. 100.

[19] *Aviation Daily,* December 4, 1967, p. 178.

[20] *New York Times,* August 16, 1969, p. 35.

one way or another to New York's regulations regarding the legality of various investments. Subsection 2 "corporate obligations" of #81 of the New York Insurance Law states that obligations secured by adequate collateral security are a proper investment if the net earnings of the guaranteeing corporation in each of any three of the preceding five years, including either of the last two years have been not less than 1¼ times the total of its fixed charges. Because of this limitation, the debt securities of Northeast, Eastern, Western and TWA[21] did not qualify during 1970 as legal new investment securities for insurance companies.[22] Undoubtedly, this fact, if not the general decline in industry profitability, induced capacity restraint from these carriers. If other carriers tied their equipment plans to the industry's level of expansion (as Figure 5.3 argues) then capacity restraint on the part of 4 carriers representing over 30% of the domestic trunk traffic probably induced additional restraint throughout the industry. Were New York Insurance Law not enough, it is clear from Table 1.14 that the major insurance companies lend across the board to carriers which compete in a large number of overlapping markets (Table 6.5). Financing one carrier to "victory" in a capacity war might thus endanger an insurance company's loan to some other carrier. This fact undoubtedly moderates the enthusiasm of insurance company lenders for excessive carrier equipment purchases. All of these facts pertaining to credit availability help to demonstrate the significance and operation of points I (b) and II (a) mentioned earlier.

While insurance company lending practices provided a significant constraint on airline debt, the attractiveness of investment tax credit leases to banks (page 40) may have caused bankers to be more generous in granting this form of financing in the 1967–1970 period than they had been in granting ordinary term loans during the 1960 airline profit squeeze. This generosity may have detracted from the significance of insurance company lending restraint, thereby adding significantly to the depth of the plunge in carrier profits in 1970.[23]

Internally Derived Capacity Constraints

Another source of capacity restraint derives first from considerations of firm survival, and second from the notion suggested in Table 5.5 that market share in a nongrowth business may not be worth a costly fight. Traffic growth for the domestic trunk carriers between 1969 and 1971 was very close to zero. Given the carriers' propensity to extrapolate a one- or two-year pattern of traffic growth into the more distant future (Table 5.9), in 1970 it would not be difficult to understand

---

[21] Trans World Airlines, Inc., *Preliminary Prospectus*, November 7, 1969, p. 5.

[22] In early 1971 United's president told a U.S. Senate subcommittee that "4 of the 12 major airlines were ineligible for insurance company borrowings in 1970, 7 would be ineligible in 1971, and 9 are expected to be on the list [for 1972] . . . ," *Wall Street Journal*, February 3, 1971.

[23] By June 30, 1970, the value of leased aircraft operated by the 12 major air carriers had grown to $2.6 billion, up from $1.0 billion some 18 months earlier. (Selig Altschull, "Aircraft Leasing Flies Into Storm," *New York Times*, December 27, 1970.)

a marked reduction in capacity aggressiveness on the part of most carriers for this reason alone. In addition, however, the three largest domestic trunk carriers sustained a combined pretax loss of $101 million in their domestic operations in the first six months of 1970. The severity of this financial pressure was sufficient to induce worry about firm survival.[24]

Under this kind of stress TWA, United, and American were able to reach an agreement[25] in August 1970, aimed at reducing seat capacity in 15 major city-pair markets. It was estimated that the proposed reduction would yield a cost saving in excess of $50 million. Although the CAB held this proposal in abeyance for nearly a year, the carriers (each acting alone) did manage to achieve significant reductions in their scheduled flight frequencies with consequent savings. These actions demonstrate.an ability on the part of carrier managements to exercise some capacity restraint internally under conditions short of receivership.

CAB Assistance Via Fare Increases

A final factor which normally reduced the depth of valleys in the cycle of airline profitability (but which may in fact have contributed to the capacity problem as will be discussed in Chapter 6) was the CAB's tendency to assist the carriers via fare increases when the industry ROI dipped below 5%. This loss moderating factor was less important in the 1970 airline profit collapse since the CAB responded then with smaller fare increases at a lower point on the industry ROI graph than might normally have been expected. The CAB adopted a "get tough" attitude toward the carriers at that point in time primarily because load factors were well below previous historic lows. The regulatory body feared that the industry was moving into an endless spiral which the Board later described as follows:

Schedules cannot be added indefinitely if the load factors achieved are insufficient, at the prevailing fare levels, to permit the carriers to cover costs and return a profit. But this economic incentive loses its force if the carriers are able to raise their fares to cover declining load factors. In that event, the pressure of competition to add

---

[24] In the second half of 1970, CAB chairman Secor Browne made the following comment:

My conclusion is that the airlines are all right for about a year, then some of them could run out of cash. Meanwhile, we have to work out their problems. If we can't, there will be bankruptcies.

(T. Alexander, "Is There *Any* Way to Run An Airline?" *Fortune*, September 1970, p. 117.) A look at the deterioration in operating funds flows versus the size of equipment purchases for two large but financially weak carriers underscores this comment.

	TWA			*Pan American*		
	1968	*1969*	*1970*	*1968*	*1969*	*1970*
	(Millions of Dollars)			*(Millions of Dollars)*		
Funds Provided by Operations	116	120	22	175	92	69
Capital Expenditures	187	244	273	159	244	466

[25] Agreement among American Airlines, Inc., Trans World Airlines, Inc., and United Air Lines, Inc., U.S. Civil Aeronautics Board, Docket #22525, August 28, 1970.

schedules will become virtually irresistible and will inevitably lead to a long-term decline in load factor, rising fares to support higher levels of unused capacity, and, because of regulatory lag, a chronically depressed profit level for the industry as a whole.[26]

The CAB's response to this and other regulatory dilemmas will be taken up in Chapter 6.

[26] U.S. Civil Aeronautics Board, Docket #21866-6B, Board Order #71-4-54, April 9, 1971, p. 5.

PART III

Altering the Competitive Environment

CHAPTER 6

Strategic Alternatives in Managing and/or Responding to the Competitive Environment

IN THE FOUR PREVIOUS CHAPTERS we have tried to zero in on the process by which the domestic trunk carriers respond to their environment in seeking a competitive advantage. Chapter 2, for example, demonstrated that carrier managers have a very narrow choice of directly controlled parameters to which an effective competitive strategy might be tied. Indeed, this chapter argued that *CAB* decisions in the areas where it exercised direct control were more important to an individual carrier's overall profitability than the decisions of that carrier's *own management* team in the areas where they exercised direct control.

Chapter 3 discovered that the fight for competitive advantage in the area of fares operated to encourage collective paralysis among the carriers, thus leaving the CAB in a position to exercise near total control over the structure and level of the industry's fares.

Chapter 4 discovered a similar pattern in the area of route awards. Route structure variables were found to be crucial to a carrier's profitability in Chapter 2, but Chapter 4 found that about the only effective management response to competitive challenge in the route authority area was one of delay on the part of the incumbent carrier(s) on routes being investigated for adding needed service.

Chapter 5 presented an altogether different situation. In the area of equipment acquisition decision making and flight scheduling, carrier managements held complete sway. This was the arena where the competitive energies of the trunk carriers were unleashed, and where the boom and bust cycles of airline profitability were causally linked to the competitive environment.

While Chapters 2–5 explained how the carriers responded to the competitive environment in their efforts to gain a competitive advantage, these chapters did nothing to explain (1) why the competitive environment is structured the way it is, (2) whether that structure is efficient in terms of the results produced, and (3) how the structure of the competitive environment might be changed for the better[1] by any or all of four[2] major groups with a role to play in domestic air transport. Chapter 6 will move on to consider, in the order presented, these three important questions.

Maintaining the Balance of Power

Almost all the regulatory problems confronting the CAB relate back to the pattern of industry competition which is dictated by the economics of air transportation. As shown in Chapter 5, a somewhat unique but very powerful economic force is at work constantly driving the industry (and in particular its weakest participants) to the verge of bankruptcy. Given this dynamic, the CAB's position has been one of (1) attempting in the long run to achieve a balance of power between carriers by giving smaller carriers a relative profitability advantage as an offset to the overall financial strength[3] advantage enjoyed by the larger carriers; and (2) attempting to level, or at least reduce, the size variance (measured in terms of industry market share or total industry asset share) among the industry's participants via route awards. When and if this second goal is accomplished, the CAB will presumably shift its emphasis to equalizing profit opportunity among carriers.

THE POLICY CHOICES

Figure 6.1 shows for the route award area the mix of policy choices available to the CAB in dealing with the dual carrier size and profitability issues. As appointed officials of a regulatory body, the Board members of the CAB must strike a balance

---

[1] "Better" here refers to overall benefit to the *user* as well as the *producer* of air transportation.

[2] The groups referred to here include the CAB, the Big 4 carriers, the Little 7 carriers, and the national administration. While the Congress might be included as a separate group, it is included in the administration for purposes of this analysis.

[3] This overall financial strength consists of (1) greater access to capital markets, (2) greater bargaining strength with airframe manufacturers, and (3) insulation from potential damage caused by a single competitor with markedly greater resources and a lower concentration of routes which are competitive with any one other single competitor. This third factor is a measure of the firm's ability to withstand a price war (or in the case of air carriers a capacity war) against a specific competitor and/or in a specific market. See for an example, U.S. Federal Trade Commission, *Economic Report on Corporate Mergers,* U.S. Government Printing Office, 1969, pp. 406–420.

FIGURE 6.1

CAB INFLUENCE ON THE MARKET SHARE SPLIT AND THE RELATIVE PROFITABILITY OF THE DOMESTIC TRUNK AIR CARRIERS—A POLICY CHOICE

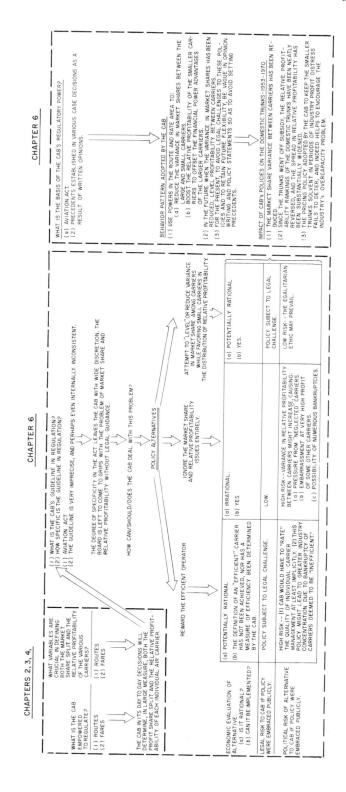

among the economic, legal, and political issues raised by the policy choices confronting them. The choices are essentially three in number: (1) To reward the efficient operator with the opportunity for high relative profitability and new routes to bolster its market share, (2) To ignore the market share and relative profitability issues entirely and choose to base important decisions (on routes for example) solely on some other criteria (such as historic interest), and (3) To "level" the carriers as outlined earlier.

The first alternative, while attractive from an economic point of view (at least in the short run), carries some very serious risks, particularly if it were publicly embraced. First, it would demand some definition of "efficiency" by the CAB. Second, it would require the CAB to at least implicitly "rate" the quality of individual carrier management. Third, it would force the CAB to *acknowledge* direct responsibility for allocating profit among the industry participants.[4] Politically, the alternative is extremely unattractive for these three reasons. Legally, it would be very difficult to implement since the definition of efficiency alone would take years to adjudicate. Finally, with or without public acknowledgment, economically such a policy might have long-run drawbacks since it might lead to a high degree of industry domination by one or two once highly efficient but soon-to-become monopolistic carriers.

The second alternative has little to recommend it along any dimension save the legal one, where Board decisions might gain predictability and consistency. In general, such a policy might lead to having large carriers get larger and the smaller carriers fall into bankruptcy.

Finally, the third alternative, the "leveling" strategy has some clear advantages to the CAB in terms of its low political risk.

> As many theorists have observed, governmental action in economic regulation through legislation is shaped, as a political phenomenon, by egalitarian pressures. In administrative action the egalitarian ethic is no less effective as an institutional

---

[4] The CAB generally denies any suggestion that it plays a major role in defining individual carrier profitability. In fact, the highly profitable small carriers are often held up by the Board as models for large carrier emulation—a fact which the large carriers find particularly galling. In 1971, for example, one Board member lauded the fact that the Little 7 carriers had earned a profit in 1970 with the following remark:

> Thus, we find a kindly and encouraging light emanating from this segment of the industry in the encirclement of darkening gloom from their bigger brothers.

The same speech carried these additional coments:

> In looking at the trunkline industry, it is paradoxical that the bulk of the losses this past year were incurred by the largest carriers— carriers that account for about 70% of the traffic and revenues and which have access to the largest and most lucrative markets both here and abroad, possessing and enjoying route systems productive of the longest range of nonstop mileage. This has led some observers to question whether there is not a diseconomy of scale which makes the largest air transportation corporations more vulnerable to the buffeting of adverse economic winds of change. (R. T. Murphy, Speech to the Traffic Club of New England, February 16, 1971, p. 6).

phenomenon. The regulation of equals is inherently easier. Hence a regulated industry is faced with continued pressure for homogeneity.[5]

A "leveling" strategy could hardly be embraced publicly, however, since this policy objective might expose the CAB to considerable legal risk. As outlined in the next few pages the CAB must always be conscious of the potential for having its decisions judged strictly on legal rather than economic grounds, and thus having them overturned or returned to the agency for review and redecision.

The CAB as a Legal Body

While the CAB is a regulatory rather than a judicial body, its role is quasi-judicial and, in rate and route proceedings, it acts much like a court of law.

> The Board's decisional process resembles that of an appellate court in many ways. The Board hears the various parties, applicants, corporate and community intervenors, and the Bureau of Operating Rights, representing the public interest, in an adversary proceeding. It also considers its hearing examiner's recommended decision and then prepares an opinion making findings of fact, discussing law, and some policy, making a decision and setting out an order. Since the CAB writes reasoned opinions like a court, its opinions can be treated much like a court's would be.[6]

Indeed, the CAB's opinions not only *can* be but actually *are* treated like those of a court.

> Sec. 1006 (a) Any order, affirmative or negative, issued by the Board or Administrator under this Act, except any order in respect of any foreign air carrier subject to the approval of the President as provided in Section 801 of this Act, shall be subject to review by the courts of appeals of the United States or the United States Court of Appeals for the District of Columbia upon petition, filed within sixty days after the entry of such order, by any person disclosing a substantial interest in such order. After the expiration of said sixty days a petition may be filed only by leave of court upon a showing of reasonable grounds for failure to file the petition theretofore.[7]

Each year many of the CAB's decisions have such significant consequences to individual carriers that they are appealed to the U.S. courts. In these courts the CAB's opinions have to be able to withstand the test of consistency with the Aviation Act and whatever precedents have been established in prior Board opinions. This

---

[5] Alan H. Silberman, "Price Discrimination and the Regulation of Air Transportation," p. 228.

[6] B. Hall, "The Civil Aeronautics Board Policy Favoring Subsidy Reduction to Local Service Carriers: Its Role and Implementation in the Decisional Process," *Journal of Air Law and Commerce,* Autumn 1968, p. 85.

[7] U.S. Senate, Committee on Interstate and Foreign Commerce, "Federal Aviation Act of 1958," U.S. Government Printing Office, 1959, p. 92.

legal test of consistency has placed the Board in a very delicate position. Legally and politically a formally declared policy of leveling carriers' market shares and deliberately adjusting relative carrier profitability via rate and route proceedings might be difficult to defend. At the same time any legally defensible rationale (or set of rationales) would either frequently point to decisions different from those reached under a "leveling" doctrine, or be defined in such nebulous terms as to be operationally useless. The Board has clearly chosen to meet this legal problem with obfuscation.

> It would seem then, that in avoiding elaboration upon the roles and significance of various factors of decision and the Board's own relevant policies, the Board has managed to keep its options open for future decisions. It is now able to alter directions with minimal resistance from its previous decisions.[8]

This policy, which emerges from some rather compelling environmental forces which are outlined in Figure 6.1, has caused legal scholars considerable grief. In his classic work on regulatory bodies, Friendly observed this phenomenon, but either failed to notice (or refused to accept as relevant) the environmental factors compelling such behavior.

> My quarrel is with the decisional process and the opinion writing. If most airline executives and lawyers thought that the Board had no standards as to the grant or denial of competitive [routes], that the elaborate hearings had almost no effect on the outcome, that the factors truly motivating decisions were quite other than those stated, that as was later to be said by one of the wisest of airline counsel "instead of the decision of a case being based upon the findings of fact and determination of policy disclosed in the agency opinion, the findings and determinations are based on the decision," the two [route case] opinions amply warranted such views.[9]

Allison has made the point which justifies the CAB pattern of behavior most succinctly.

> The necessity that [an arbiter of interests] build a consensus behind his preferred policy frequently requires fuzziness. Different people must agree with different things for quite different reasons. When a government decision is made, both the character of the choice and the reasons for the choice must often remain vague.[10]

Indeed, the basis of Board decisions is usually outlined in such nebulous form that on a few occasions the sketchiness of the opinion was in and of itself enough to have a decision overturned.

---

[8] B. Hall, *op. cit.*, p. 85.

[9] Henry J. Friendly, *The Federal Administrative Agencies,* p. 91.

[10] G. T. Allison, "Conceptual Models and the Cuban Missile Crisis: Rational Policy, Organizational Process, and Bureaucratic Politics," RAND Corporation Publication #P3919, 1968, p. 43.

The First Circuit pinned its decision on a failure of the Board to develop standards for deciding such cases and on the confusion created by its failure to properly articulate reasons employed in its decision.[11]

Such reversals were extremely rare, however, as the courts generally had no desire to tread in such complex areas.

The dissent pointed out the folly of the court's pursuit. He emphasized that the CAB is attempting to answer *economic* questions which are difficult enough to decide by an educated guess, without the criticism of an equally educated guesser.[12]

The Impact of CAB Policy Choices

The effect of the Board's slow and deliberate policy of leveling carrier market shares can be seen in Table 6.1. Since 1957 (by which time subsidy had effectively ended as shown in Table 3.1) the share of total revenue received by the Big 4 carriers (in spite of the acquisition of the relatively large but nearly bankrupt Capital Airlines by United in 1961) has dropped from about 77 to 67 percent. Without the Capital acquisition, the Big 4 total would probably have been lowered by an additional 4 or 5 percentage points.

At the same time, the Board's influence on the relative profitability issue can be seen in Tables 6.2 and 6.4. Table 6.2 shows the changes in relative profitability for all individual trunk carriers (and the Big 4 and Little 7 as groups) between 1953 and 1970. Without exception the members of the Big 4 have seen their relative profitability substantially eroded. The Little 7 carriers, on the other hand, enjoyed a truly dramatic boost (line 14 of Table 6.2).

In addition to letting the profitability distribution favor the smaller carriers (since they went off subsidy after the Korean War), the CAB has also allowed the spread in airline profitability to diverge widely from that normally found in other industries.

To show this effect, the profitability performance data of the firm members of several different industries have been arranged (by industry). For comparative purposes, data for domestic trunk air carriers, railroads, cement companies, integrated oil companies, and steel producers have also been included.

Table 6.3 (columns 1 and 4) shows the domestic trunk carriers arranged in order of relative profitability for the year 1967. If the revenue and profit shares of successive carriers are totaled cumulatively, as we move down this list (thus generating column 5 from column 2, and column 6 from column 3) we arrive at a profitability profile for the air transport industry. This profile shows the width of the percentage point spread separating cumulative industry profit share from cumulative industry revenue share. The profit distribution inequality across firms is measured in this way.

---

[11] Ronald D. Dockser, "Airline Service Abandonment and Consolidation," *Journal of Air Law and Commerce*, Autumn 1966, p. 521.

[12] *Ibid.*, p. 521.

TABLE 6.1

Two-Year Moving Average Market Shares* for the 11 Domestic Trunk Air Carriers—Domestic Operations
1953–1970

	1954	1955	1956	1957	1958	1959	1960	1961	1962	1963	1964	1965	1966	1967	1968	1969	1970
American	23.7%	23.3%	23.8%	23.2%	22.3%	21.9%	22.5%	21.9%	20.5%	19.8%	19.3%	18.8%	19.0%	18.8%	18.3%	17.9%	17.4%
Braniff	3.7	3.7	3.7	3.9	4.2	4.1	4.0	4.0	3.8	3.6	3.5	3.4	3.8	3.9	3.8	3.8	3.8
Continental	1.3	1.4	1.5	1.7	1.9	2.4	3.0	3.2	3.1	3.1	3.2	3.4	4.0	4.3	4.2	4.3	4.6
Delta	5.1	6.4	5.5	5.7	6.1	6.2	6.6	7.4	8.3	8.6	8.5	8.5	9.3	9.4	9.1	9.5	10.1
Eastern	16.9	17.5	17.7	18.1	17.1	16.0	15.2	13.8	12.3	12.1	13.0	13.4	12.6	12.5	12.9	12.9	13.0
National	4.1	4.3	4.4	4.1	4.0	4.1	3.8	3.7	4.2	4.5	4.6	4.9	4.8	4.7	4.9	4.8	3.9
Northeast	1.0	1.0	.9	1.0	1.6	1.9	2.0	2.3	2.4	2.0	1.7	1.5	1.6	1.7	2.0	2.2	2.1
Northwest	5.0	4.7	4.4	4.2	4.5	4.9	4.9	4.1	4.1	4.5	4.8	5.1	5.1	5.2	5.2	5.2	4.7
Trans World	16.0	15.1	14.6	14.7	14.8	15.5	15.6	14.6	13.7	13.7	14.6	14.9	14.1	13.8	13.6	13.2	12.8
United	20.2	20.7	20.8	20.5	20.9	19.9	19.0	21.7	24.5**	24.1	22.8	22.4	21.9	22.0	22.6	22.9	23.7
Western	2.7	2.8	2.6	2.8	2.7	2.9	3.5	3.2	3.3	3.6	3.8	3.7	3.7	3.7	3.5	3.5	3.9
Big 4	76.8	76.6	76.9	76.5	75.1	73.3	72.3	72.0	71.0	69.7	69.7	69.5	67.6	67.1	67.3	66.8	66.9***
Little 7	23.2	23.4	23.1	23.5	24.9	26.7	27.7	28.0	29.0	30.0	30.3	30.5	32.4	32.9	32.7	33.2	33.1

* Two-year moving average market share calculations are based on revenues for the year indicated plus the prior year.
** Includes Capital Airlines which merged into United in 1961 and which accounted for 5.6% of domestic trunk revenues in 1960.
*** Data for 1970 show a rising market share for the Big 4 carriers. This was due to strikes at National and Northwest which temporarily but significantly reduced their market shares during the year.

TABLE 6.2

TWO-YEAR MOVING AVERAGE OF RELATIVE PROFITABILITY* FOR THE 11 DOMESTIC TRUNK CARRIERS—DOMESTIC OPERATIONS
1953–1970

		1953	1954	1955	1956	1957	1958	1959	1960	1961	1962	1963	1964	1965	1966	1967	1968	1969	1970
1	American	1.21	1.12	1.16	1.38	1.57	1.46	1.18	1.50	5.86	2.71	1.56	1.28	.99	.98	.99	.93	.99	.67
2	Braniff	.15	.47	.91	.86	1.25	1.88	1.51	1.48	5.31	4.01	1.68	1.15	1.00	1.06	.74	.55	1.03	1.16
3	Continental	.53	.62	.61	.61	.79	.67	1.04	2.32	10.46	4.83	1.97	1.52	1.48	1.72	1.86	1.55	1.11	2.39
4	Delta	.63	.66	1.01	1.11	1.26	1.38	1.02	1.50	.14	7.93	3.50	1.91	1.51	1.75	1.88	2.11	2.75	5.21
5	Eastern	1.01	1.06	1.12	1.25	1.27	.80	.70	.28	-6.78	-5.16	-1.94	-.47	.37	.44	.44	.28	.14	.99
6	National	1.18	1.09	1.15	1.60	1.80	.95	.31	-1.33	-6.03	4.82	2.53	1.59	1.68	1.67	1.82	2.38	2.56	1.71
7	Northeast	.22	.48	.14	-.20	-3.11	-3.80	-2.55	-4.07	-18.32	-8.99	-4.23	-1.80	-.18	.07	-.29	-.26	-1.15	-3.25
8	Northwest	.15	.60	.77	.71	.39	.64	.80	.84	2.25	3.40	2.24	2.02	2.06	2.09	2.27	2.67	2.72	4.72
9	Trans World	.86	.98	.85	.19	-.41	-.03	1.00	1.11	-5.17	-3.45	.36	1.10	.95	.70	.44	.10	-.33	-2.74
10	United	1.31	1.14	.93	.91	1.08	1.50	1.29	1.02	2.21	1.31	.86	.75	.73	.66	.72	.91	1.13	.96
11	Western	.85	.92	1.04	1.18	1.86	1.71	2.10	3.29	6.79	4.02	3.29	2.49	1.66	1.52	1.56	1.38	.04	-.68
12	Industry	1.00	1.00	1.00	1.00	1.00	1.00	1.00	1.00	1.00	1.00	1.00	1.00	1.00	1.00	1.00	1.00	1.00	1.00
13	Big 4 Carriers	1.12	1.09	1.03	1.00	.99	1.03	1.07	1.03	.15	-.30	.47	.74	.78	.72	.68	.63	.53	.18
14	Little 7 Carriers	.58	.71	.91	1.01	1.04	.92	.82	.92	3.19	4.17	2.24	1.62	1.50	1.59	1.65	1.76	1.95	2.65

*Relative profitability is defined as: $\dfrac{[\text{carrier operating income/carrier operating revenue}]}{[\text{industry operating income/industry operating revenue}]}$. Data used in calculating the two-year moving average include the year indicated plus the prior year.

NOTE: (a) Negative values appear when a carrier suffered a loss.
(b) Wide variations in year to year results for some carriers were caused by labor strikes.
(c) Some very high values for the period 1960–1962 resulted from the fact that carrier profits during this period were very close to zero, making the denominator in the equation noted above very small.

TABLE 6.3

Cumulative Industry Profit Share Related to Cumulative Industry Revenue
Share with Individual Firm Data Ranked in Descending Order
of Relative Profitability Domestic Trunk Carriers—1967

1	2	3	4 = 3/2	5	6
				Cumulative Industry	
Carrier *(In Order of* *Relative* *Profitability)*	*Carrier* *Revenues* *(Percent of* *Industry)*	*Carrier* *Operating* *Profit* *(Percent of* *Industry)*	*Carrier* *Relative* *Profitability*	*Revenue* *(Percent)*	*Operating* *Profit* *(Percent)*
Northwest	5.3	13.3	2.5	5.3	13.3
National	4.8	9.8	2.0	10.1	23.1
Continental	4.3	7.9	1.8	14.4	31.0
Delta	8.9	16.0	1.8	23.3	47.0
Western	3.5	5.1	1.5	26.8	52.1
American	18.2	17.0	.9	45.0	69.1
United	22.5	20.1	.9	67.5	89.2
Eastern	13.0	7.3	.6	80.5	96.5
TWA	14.0	3.9	.3	94.5	100.4
Braniff	3.8	.8	.2	98.3	101.2
Northeast	1.7	(1.2)	−.7	100.0	100.0

When Table 6.3 is extended to include the five industries mentioned earlier, and
is simplified in order to show the cumulative data broken out at 10 percentage
point revenue increments rather than after data from each individual firm have
been introduced, then Table 6.4 is generated.

This table points up some interesting contrasts in the profit structures of high
fixed cost oligopoly industries. It is clear from the table that the regulated industries (airlines and railroads) face a significantly sharper intraindustry revenue-share
profit-share spread than do the unregulated cement, oil, and steel industries. The
inference here is that in the absence of regulatory constraint, profit opportunities in
an industry will be exploited in a way that tends to limit (to a surprisingly narrow
band) the spread between cumulative revenue and cumulative profits. This pattern appears to be true in all stages of the business cycle as the four years examined
in the table indicate. It is also true that the inequality of profit distribution in the
air transport industry has increased sharply since 1955, in keeping with the hypothesis regarding CAB profit redistribution activity. While the data of Chapter 2
indicate that the CAB was responsible in large measure for most of the difference
in relative profitability between various carriers, the data of Table 6.4 seem to
indicate that the CAB, in a policy decision made to bolster the smaller carriers
competitively, has opted for a far wider intraindustry spread between cumulative
revenue and cumulative profit than is found in any of the other oligopoly industries examined.

TABLE 6.4

INDUSTRY PROFIT SHARE RELATED TO INDUSTRY REVENUE SHARE
FOR HIGH FIXED COST OLIGOPOLISTIC INDUSTRIES

(Regulated Versus Unregulated, 1955-1967)

Cumulative Revenue	Air Transport Cumulative Income	Railroads Cumulative Income		Cement Cumulative Income	Oils Cumulative Income	Steel Cumulative Income
	Regulated			Unregulated		
			1955			
10.0%	13.2%	14.2%		13.1%	16.0%	12.2%
20.0	26.4	27.3		25.3	28.3	23.8
30.0	39.3	39.3		36.5	39.3	35.3
40.0	51.0	50.3		47.3	50.3	46.7
50.0	62.5	60.6		57.9	61.2	57.6
60.0	72.0	70.5		67.9	70.2	67.9
70.0	80.2	79.3		77.0	78.5	77.4
80.0	88.4	87.2		85.6	86.0	86.5
90.0	94.8	94.3		92.8	93.5	94.6
			1959			
10.0	20.4	22.2		14.1	17.6	14.9
20.0	35.8	38.1		26.9	31.3	27.2
30.0	48.1	51.9		39.0	42.0	38.9
40.0	58.8	63.9		49.9	51.6	50.5
50.0	69.2	74.3		59.5	61.1	61.9
60.0	78.9	83.0		68.7	70.3	71.5
70.0	88.0	88.9		77.7	78.5	80.7
80.0	95.6	94.4		86.1	86.7	89.0
90.0	102.7	98.7		93.6	94.0	96.0
			1963			
10.0	30.7	20.2		15.0	16.9	13.9
20.0	52.1	37.6		31.9	31.0	26.9
30.0	69.4	51.1		39.6	41.9	38.0
40.0	86.7	62.2		51.2	52.6	48.4
50.0	100.1	72.7		62.6	62.8	58.8
60.0	109.8	82.5		72.7	71.7	68.7
70.0	118.7	89.6		81.7	79.2	78.0
80.0	127.5	94.7		88.7	86.3	87.0
90.0	124.0	99.2		94.9	93.3	95.2
			1967			
10.0	22.9	19.8		17.1	15.7	16.0
20.0	41.1	36.7		32.8	30.0	28.6
30.0	55.1	50.5		45.7	41.2	40.4
40.0	64.4	61.5		56.9	51.3	51.5
50.0	73.6	71.7		66.6	61.3	61.7
60.0	82.5	81.4		76.3	71.3	71.5
70.0	90.6	89.6		85.7	80.0	80.1
80.0	96.2	96.0		92.9	87.1	88.8
90.0	99.1	100.9		97.8	93.5	96.9

NOTE 1: Income is defined as (1) operating profit for the airlines, (2) income available for fixed charges for the railroads, and (3) after-tax profits as reported to shareholders for the industrials.

NOTE 2: The sample sizes for each industry are as follows: airlines = 11 firms
railroads = 30 firms
cement = 12 firms
oils = 16 firms
steel = 33 to 35 firms

NOTE 3: In calculating the above data, firms were rank ordered within each industry by their income/revenue ratio in descending order. Firm revenues and profits were then added cumulatively, and cuts were made at the revenue deciles shown above.

THE GAME THEORY ASPECTS OF CAPACITY COMPETITION

The clear rationale for balancing high relative profitability and limited relative financial strength against lower relative profitability and greater relative financial strength can be seen from casting the capital budgeting problem of Chapter 5 into a game theory framework. When cast in the game theory mold, the airline industry's overcapacity problem appears to be the result of a set of environmental circumstances which closely approximates the Prisoner's Dilemma. The classical Prisoner's Dilemma problem of game theory has been outlined as follows by Luce and Raiffa:

> Two suspects are taken into custody and separated. The district attorney is certain that they are guilty of a specific crime, but he does not have adequate evidence to convict them at a trial. He points out to each prisoner that each has two alternatives: to confess to the crime the police are sure they have done, or not to confess. If they both do not confess, then the district attorney states he will book them on some very minor trumped-up charge such as petty larceny and illegal possession of a weapon, and they will both receive minor punishment; if they both confess they will be prosecuted, but he will recommend less than the most severe sentence; but if one confesses and the other does not, then the confessor will receive lenient treatment for turning state's evidence whereas the latter will get "the book" slapped at him. In terms of years in a penitentiary, the strategic problem might reduce to:[13]

PAYOFF MATRIX 1

PRISONER 1:	PRISONER 2:	
	NOT CONFESS	CONFESS
NOT CONFESS	1 YEAR EACH	10 YEARS FOR 1 AND 3 MONTHS FOR 2
CONFESS	3 MONTHS FOR 1 AND 10 YEARS FOR 2	8 YEARS EACH

The rational strategy[14] in such an environment is for each prisoner to confess, since a confess strategy minimizes each prisoner's maximum loss (8 years), and maximizes his minimum gain (3 months). There appears to be no way around this dilemma, in spite of the fact that it leaves the two prisoners with a "stupid" final outcome.

In relating this environmental situation to the airlines, attempting to expand market share by overbuying equipment becomes equivalent to "confess" while attempting to retain or increase profitability by preserving load factors via capacity restraint becomes equivalent to "not confess." While the punishment equivalents are difficult to quantify for the airlines, return on investment data might provide a hypothetical basis for approaching the problem.

If we look at a game payoff matrix for two air carriers (of markedly unequal

---

[13] R. D. Luce, and H. Raiffa, *Games and Decisions,* p. 95.

[14] This statement assumes a linear preference function for the possible payoffs.

size, but equal return on investment) which compete on a substantial fraction of the smaller carrier's routes, we can see rather clearly the competitive capacity problem faced by the carriers and the CAB. In Payoff Matrix 2 each carrier shows a 10% accounting return on investment for its total system operation (matrix elements 1 and 2). The competitive routes in question are significantly more important to the smaller carrier, however, since if the larger carrier could be forced into a poor minority position in these markets, the smaller carrier's system return on investment would climb to 20% (matrix element 4). If the smaller carrier were forced into a poor minority position in these markets (or bankrupted), however, the larger carrier's system return would rise to only 12% (matrix element 5) since the routes in question are not large in relation to the bigger carrier's overall operation.

PAYOFF MATRIX 2

LARGE CARRIER	SMALL CARRIER			
	CAPACITY RESTRAINT		CAPACITY AGGRESSIVENESS	
CAPACITY RESTRAINT	10%, 10% ① ② L S		7%, 20% ③ ④ L S	RETURN ON INVESTMENT MATRIX ELEMENT # CARRIER SIZE #
CAPACITY AGGRESSIVENESS	12%, 0% ⑤ ⑥ L S		8%, 1% ⑦ ⑧ L S	

SOURCE: Hypothetical example.

The downside situation for each carrier shows similar variability. While the larger carrier's return would drop to 7% if it were forced into a loss position in those markets (matrix element 3), the smaller carrier's return would drop to 0% overall (matrix element 6) if it were forced into a similar loss position in these markets.

If both carriers expanded their capacities in these markets substantially ahead of demand, the smaller carrier's system return would drop to 1% (matrix element 8), while the larger carrier's return would only drop to 8% (matrix element 7). Rational play given an environmental situation of this type would inevitably lead to overall excess industry capacity followed by bankruptcy for many of the smaller carriers,[15] just as it led to a "stupid" final outcome in the Prisoner's Dilemma.

---

[15] One recent example of a capacity war involves Braniff, Texas International, and Southwest Airlines on a number of intrastate routes in Texas. On entering these markets, Southwest's president made the following comments:

We went into business with nearly $6 million in cash in the bank, so were ready for any kind of war Braniff starts. . . .

They're just . . . [trying] to bankrupt us. That's why we got the capital we did. We can fight as long as they want to. (*Business Week,* June 26, 1971, p. 25.)

The CAB as a Social/Economic Umpire

Luce and Raiffa observed that,

> . . . some hold the view that one essential role of government is to declare that the values of certain social "games" must be changed whenever it is inherent in the game situation that the players, in pursuing their own ends, will be forced into a socially undesirable position.[16]

There is certainly no shortage of opportunities for government to act in areas so described. Indeed, a partial enumeration of those social problems with Prisoner's Dilemma similarities might lead one to suspect that most major social problems have this basic characteristic. For example, the problems associated with escalation in military conflicts,[17] arms control and disarmament,[18] segregation[19] (resulting from neighborhood tipping), and air pollution[20] can all be cast in the Prisoner's Dilemma game situation.

How one defines wasteful "excess capacity" in air transportation is subject to enormous dispute. This is true because there are some clear social and economic tradeoffs which can be made between (1) profitability, (2) fare levels, (3) utilization, (4) service frequency, and (5) load factors (Equations 1.1, 1.2). By way of example, one can speculate concerning what would happen if some great technological advance occurred which allowed a 105-seat[21] aircraft to be manufactured which would earn a 10% return on investment (at the 1968 fare level) with only a 20% passenger load factor. At one end of the spectrum of possible industry outcomes, competitive pressure might force a 2.5-fold [22] expansion of flight frequencies, which would force passenger load factors down to about 20%. At the other end of the spectrum, the CAB could force a reduction of fares to a level requiring a more historically "normal" 55% load factor in order to reach a 10% return on investment. Which of these results (or mixture) would ultimately obtain might be as much a social and political as an economic choice.

While the definition of an ideal load factor standard may be as elusive as the magic fare formula jointly sought by counsel for National Airlines and the CAB's vice chairman,[23] it is certainly possible to talk in a general way about some costs associated with changes in load factors over time.

A look at Table 1.10 shows a 12-point decline in passenger load factors between

---

[16] R. D. Luce, and H. Raiffa, *op. cit.*, p. 97.

[17] In conjunction with the Vietnam war, for example, President Lyndon Johnson was quoted as follows:

> When we add divisions, can't the enemy add divisions? If so, where does it all end? *(New York Times,* The Pentagon Papers, July 7, 1971.)

[18] See for instance, Donald C. Brennan, *Arms Control, Disarmament, and National Security,* or R. Gilpin, and C. Wright, *Scientists and National Policy Making,* p. 250.

[19] Thomas C. Schelling, *Models of Segregation,* RAND Corporation Memorandum, RM-6014-RC.

[20] Henry Ford, as quoted in *New York Times,* December 3, 1969.

[21] The average number of seats per aircraft in use in the industry was about 105 in 1968.

[22] This assumed no expansion of traffic and a 1968 passenger load factor of 50%.

[23] See Chapter 3, page 106.

1959 and 1970. With one load factor point equaling revenue of more than $100,-000,000 in 1970, it is clear that arguments vis-à-vis appropriate industry load factors in the 50%–60% band involve annual payments by users of air transportation in the many hundreds of millions of dollars, with this amount growing annually, percentagewise, as fast as traffic.

It is also clear that in the late 1960s many long haul high density markets were being served with a frequency volume that most industry spokesmen would be embarrassed to try and justify purely on an "improvement in quality of service" basis. (See Figure 6.2 for an example of one such route.)

FIGURE 6.2

FILLED VERSUS EMPTY SEATS ON TYPICAL LONG HAUL NONSTOP FLIGHTS
(*Typical Week, 1968*)

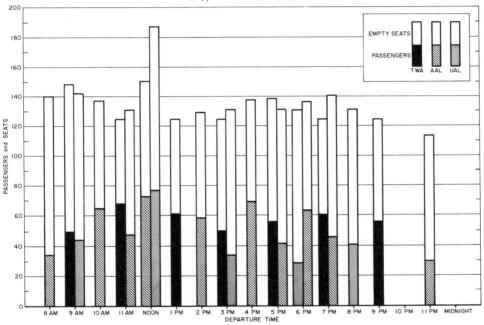

SOURCE: Private Carrier Data.

Excess Capacity as a Regulatory Problem

While the cost of excess capacity in air transportation, however defined, could potentially be enormous, the CAB had, until 1971 geared its "payoff matrix" management effort generally in the direction of avoiding potential carrier bankruptcies rather than attacking the capacity problem directly. At least some of its policies had the effect of muting capacity competition at the route and carrier level, but at least three of its policies have had the exact opposite effect, i.e., that of encouraging capacity competition.

The CAB has given the smaller carriers greater ROI potential by refraining from authorizing competition on the smaller carriers' monopoly routes as quickly as it might have done if a larger trunk carrier were involved. This has generally raised the fraction of highly profitable monopoly traffic carried by the smaller carriers substantially above that carried by the larger carriers (Table 2.2). The impact of this policy viewed in the game context is to raise matrix elements 2, 4, 6 and 8, thus making it far more costly for the larger carrier to achieve dominance on the routes in question.

Another tool used by the CAB to change the payoffs in the capacity game has been the Board's merger and route authorization policy. The Board has tried to make it clear (particularly in the Capital Airlines case) that by forcing a bankruptcy a strong carrier will probably not reduce the number of competitors on its routes for very long.[24] New authority will usually be granted to a larger and stronger carrier, and this possibility tends to lessen matrix element 7.

None of the regulatory tools described thus far offer the small carriers relief if the industry is depressed from the outset[25] of the analysis (i.e., each of the matrix elements 1 to 8 shown earlier is reduced by 5 percentage points). To prevent small carrier bankruptcies under these circumstances, the CAB has usually responded by permitting fare increases which have, from competitive necessity (see Chapter 3), been shared by all carriers, not just the financially weaker ones. This factor, which places a floor under matrix elements 7 and 8, tends to defeat meaningful regulatory response to the overcapacity problem (Figure 6.3), a fact which the Board acknowledged in the statement referenced in Chapter 5, footnote 26.

Carriers must intuitively (if not explicitly) measure both the *probability* and *value* of a successful market share assault against the possible loss caused by an unsuccessful foray. If the carriers strongly presume that the CAB will have to "bail out" the industry with fare increases if the carriers individually initiate market share duels, then even a relatively low probability of success attached to an increased market share may warrant the risk. Given these circumstances, an attempt to buy market share is extremely rational in the operating environment of the industry.

The "bail out" guarantee which is a necessity if the CAB's policy of avoiding bankruptcies in the industry is to be effective (but which may have been eliminated by the CAB in 1971 as will be discussed later), is thus the first of three strong factors (mentioned earlier) which encourages industry capacity competition (Figure 6.3). The second CAB-controlled factor encouraging this form of competition relates to the regulatory body's use of its route authorization power to reduce industry profitability whenever it starts to approach the 10% ROI level. This

---

[24] Soon after the merger of Capital into United, an investigation was started into the need for new service in the 4 principal (out of 19) markets in which competition was eliminated by the merger. Two-carrier competitive service was restored in these markets by October 1964. (*Handbook of Airline Statistics,* U.S. Civil Aeronautics Board, 1967 Edition, p. 474.)

[25] This depression might be due to overcapacity caused by market share aggressiveness, misestimation of demand, or rising unit costs.

FIGURE 6.3

FACTORS LEADING TO EXCESSIVE CAPACITY COMPETITION
AMONG AIR CARRIERS

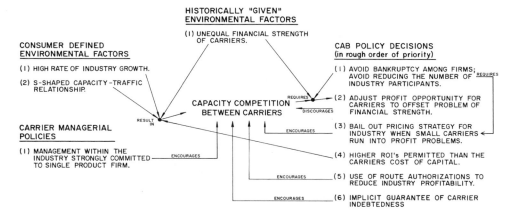

regulatory behavior pattern tends to make the "burying" of profit (as outlined in Chapter 5) via excessive equipment purchases during periods of high return appear to be an even more compellingly attractive business choice.

In a subtle but nonetheless powerful way, the CAB's concern for "maintaining the financial integrity of the entire airline industry" adds a third impetus to the overcapacity situation. In Chapter 5, it was stated that one of the most powerful forces acting to mute capacity competition was credit restraint on the part of industry creditors during periods of low profitability. The CAB has encouraged lenders to be more aggressive with air carriers than with their unregulated borrowers by in effect implicitly guaranteeing loans to the trunk carriers.

> Although lenders are primarily concerned with the economic potential of the particular company with which they are dealing, the prospects of an individual company can never be divorced from the prospects of the industry of which it is a part. We find that the bankruptcy and liquidation of Capital would adversely affect the ability of the air carriers to borrow money or to raise equity capital through the sale of capital stock or other equity securities to the public.
> Rejection of efforts of a carrier in financial trouble to protect its creditors and instead allowing that carrier to "go down the drain" would not be lost upon lending institutions and would be considered by them in fixing terms for the financing which the airline industry is going to require both for the present jet equipment and for future supersonic transport equipment expected in the next few years.[26]

In order to save the credit standing of the industry, the CAB allowed Capital and United to merge in spite of the fact that the two carriers were direct competitors on a substantial number of routes.

---

[26] United-Capital Merger Case, Board Order #E16605, April 3, 1961, pp. 15–16.

This fact has undoubtedly led the industry's creditors to "go a little further" in financing capacity duels than they might otherwise be inclined to do if they could not look in some way to the credit standings of the industry and the United States government for security on their loans.

A summary of all the principal forces acting to create the overcapacity spiral in air transportation is shown in Figure 6.3.

Grand Strategy, Profitability Distribution, and Overcapacity

At this point it is reasonably clear that a combination of industry economics, CAB policy choices aimed at preserving the financial integrity of all the trunk carriers, and carrier management decisions responding to this environment have led to (1) the encouragement of overcapacity, and (2) a pattern of profit allocation which may well be independent of management effectiveness. As outlined earlier in the chapter, prior to 1971 the CAB had made a relatively clear choice as to how both of these problems would ultimately be resolved. In answer to the *first* problem, the CAB had at least implicitly decided (1) that the cost of overcapacity was not too high when measured against the value of preserving the number of independent trunk carriers and (2) that this cost would get lower and lower, relatively, as carrier market shares converged due to CAB route award policies. The *second* problem, that of profit allocation, while troublesome would eventually become moot once the first problem was solved.

This pattern of regulation confronted the Big 4 and Little 7 carriers with a long-run profitability split that was weighted heavily in favor of the Little 7 carriers (Table 6.2). While the "industry" might earn an average return on investment of about 8%, that 8% was allocated as 6% on the $\frac{2}{3}$ of total investment controlled by the Big 4 carriers versus 12% on the $\frac{1}{3}$ of total investment controlled by the Little 7 carriers. Presumably the profitability advantage enjoyed by the Little 7 would be erased over time as each of the Little 7 carriers increased its market share to a size matching that of the slowly eroding individual shares of the Big 4 carriers. As shown in the trends of Table 6.1, however, this promised to be a lengthy process. The large carriers could look forward to having their hides removed slowly, while for an equal time span the small carriers could bask in an environment of regulatory largess.

An excellent contrast in the map of opportunity facing the smallest large carrier (Eastern) and the largest small carrier (Delta), for instance, can be seen from a comparison of Tables 6.1 and 6.2. The essence of this contrast was exquisitely penned by Frankel 24 years ago in his study of the petroleum industry.

> There is no more enthusiastic satellite than the biggest operator outside the ring —But, alas! the more successful he becomes the greater his danger of cutting off the branch upon which he is sitting. For, beyond a certain point, . . . he is faced with . . . joining the inner circle himself. Thus, while the position of the biggest "outsider" is the most desirable, the lot of the smallest "insider" is the most uncomfortable.[27]

---

[27] P. H. Frankel, *Essentials of Petroleum,* p. 86.

In terms of their broadest strategic choices ("grand strategy" as defined by Hart),[28] the four groups of participants with an important stake in the industry had a number of alternatives in responding to and improving upon the existing competitive environment.

Strategic Alternatives for the CAB

The CAB, for its part, had opted for one alternative in structuring the competitive environment that was, until the 1970 collapse in airline profitability, a low risk strategy. That alternative was (1) to let the course of its route award policy combine with growth in the industry to ultimately reduce the disparity in carrier sizes, and (2) until that goal was accomplished, to solve the threat of bankruptcies precipitated by capacity wars between carriers by means of occasional fare increases.

Politically this policy worked reasonably well between 1955 and 1968 because production economies flowing from the introduction of jet aircraft and stretch jets led to sharp reductions in carrier breakeven load factors. These economies permitted passenger load factors to fall significantly with little increase in airline prices (columns 6 and 11, Table 1.10). By 1969, however, inflation began to run ahead of productivity savings (Table 1.8) suggesting that fares would have to start to rise even with *constant* passenger load factors. Since the carriers had widely overestimated RPM demand (Table 1.5 compared with Table 1.10), when they had placed their orders for aircraft to be delivered in the 1969–1971 period, passenger load factors promised to be nowhere near constant during this period.

The CAB in early 1971 was thus confronted with carrier proposals calling for fare increases ranging to more than 30% [29] over the already sharply inflated October 1969 level (Figure 3.4). Faced with this type of pressure, the Board began giving its blessing to carrier-initiated capacity limitation discussions (page 151) as a way of holding down fares, and began to take a tentative step away from its long-standing informal fare bail-out guarantee by establishing an industry-wide load factor standard. In its opinion relating to load factor standards in the Domestic Passenger Fare Investigation rendered in April 1971, the Board decided that in future fare proceedings, fare levels permitted would be based on an assumed 55% industry passenger load factor, rather than actual industry experience. This would result in a disallowance of expenses and an assumed increase in income, for ratemaking purposes, where the actual industry load factor was below the standard load factor established. For the case at hand in 1971, however, a lower load factor standard was to be in effect since the carriers in making their earlier equipment plans had suffered from a . . .

lack of guidance which would have been available had the Board been in a position to establish load factor standards earlier.[30]

---

[28] B. H. L. Hart, *Strategy*, p. 335.
[29] U.S. Civil Aeronautics Board, Board Order #71-4-59, April 12, 1971, p. 6.
[30] *Ibid.*, p. 49.

Whether the Board will stick to its 55% load factor standard in the next down-cycle of industry profitability (if the industry falls below it and a few smaller carriers face bankruptcy without a fare increase) remains to be tested. In any case, this apparent change in tactics at the CAB (should it stand the test of the next profit downturn) could present the larger carriers with a potent weapon in their fight for a fair share of industry profits.

Strategic Alternatives for the Big 4 Carriers

One can hardly expect that without external pressure the CAB will suddenly judge its policy of the last 15 years vis-à-vis the structure of the competitive environment and the distribution of industry profits to have been a costly error. The impetus for change will probably have to come from outside this body. Clearly the Little 7 carriers, as prime beneficiaries of the CAB's existing policies, cannot be expected to lead or even encourage the challenge. Since the national administration (in the form of the Department of Transportation) has more pressing *social* problems in the urban mass transit area, and more pressing *economic* problems in the railroad area, not much help can be expected from that source. A response would more logically flow from the group whose ox was being gored most grievously by the existing situation—the Big 4 carriers.

The Big 4 carriers have two alternatives regarding their response to the competitive environment and the pattern of regulation established by the CAB.

(1) These carriers can individually acknowledge the inevitability of the existing pattern and accept reduced returns for 10–15 years until the industry is "leveled" by a combination of route awards and the rare merger of a failing participant such as Northeast and Capital, or

(2) They can individually attempt to hasten the leveling process (and thus limit the time period over which they must earn reduced returns) by assisting the small carriers to grow quickly via mergers. Since no two small carriers in the 12% return opportunity class would happily merge in order to move up into the 6% opportunity class, such mergers would require strong encouragement. This might be provided in one of two forms:

(a) The large carriers could individually try to convince the CAB (and/or the public) of the high cost in terms of excess capacity of the CAB's policy of protecting the smaller carriers by a wide profitability spread. The CAB, if convinced, could presumably respond by strongly encouraging the smaller carriers to merge amongst themselves or face greater competition on their routes, eroded profitability, and ultimate merger on less attractive terms.

(b) If the effort outlined in (a) failed (as it almost certainly would) the large carriers might individually choose to make future flight scheduling decisions with an eye toward the competitive impact on a smaller carrier already encountering profit problems for some other reason. A total industry route-scanning procedure (perhaps using 2-year-old data collected by the CAB as a result of its improved reporting methods outlined on page 116) might be set up independently by each of these larger carriers which would, at a glance, indicate an ordered array of competitive routes[31] on which added flights might do the greatest profit damage to any selected weak carrier at the lowest expected cost to the stronger carrier planning the assault. The hope here of the larger carrier would be to add impetus for the smaller carrier to seek a merger partner, and consequently reduce the total fraction of the overall industry investment requiring an abnormally high return. As indicated in Chapter 5, page 130, the CAB has in the past demonstrated an inability or reluctance to respond directly to this form of competition.

If the CAB has in fact moved away from providing a bail-out guarantee, the next downturn in industry profitability might present a unique opportunity for the Big 4 carriers to induce Braniff and Continental to merge with other carriers. With the potential absorption of Northeast, Western, and National, in 1972,[32] this could produce a domestic trunk industry of six roughly equal sized carriers (Table 6.1). This would remove the need for either the CAB's bail-out guarantee or its informal profit allocation activity.

Strategic Alternatives for the Little 7

The Little 7 carriers, since they already enjoy a somewhat privileged status among the domestic trunks, have little to gain and much to lose from any such restructuring of the competitive environment. Their competitive strategy will thus have to be basically defensive if the Big 4 carriers act as outlined previously. The Little 7 carriers can be expected to (1) appeal to the CAB if the Big 4 carriers compete in a manner that they interpret as "unfair," [33] or (2) appeal to the national administration (in the form of the Justice Department) if the CAB fails to offer protection as page 131 indicated might well be the case.

Strategic Alternatives for the National Administration

The actions of the Justice Department as they reflect national administration policy are clearly the key to the success of the Big 4 carriers in any effort to restruc-

---

[31] The total number of city-pair markets in which each carrier is authorized to compete against each of the other carriers is shown in Table 6.5.

[32] These acquisitions had not been complete at the date of the writing, but were in an advanced stage.

[33] The appeal might be made under Sec. 411 of the Federal Aviation Act of 1958 which reads as follows:

The Board may, upon its own initiative or upon complaint by any air carrier, foreign air carrier, or ticket agent, if it considers that such action by it would be in the interest of the public, investigate and determine whether any air carrier, foreign air carrier, or ticket agent has been or is engaged in unfair or deceptive practices or unfair methods of competition in air transportation or the sale thereof. If the Board shall find, after notice and hearing, that such air carrier, foreign air carrier, or ticket agent is engaged in such unfair or deceptive practices or unfair methods of competition, it shall order such air carrier, foreign air carrier, or ticket agent to cease and desist from such practices or methods of competition.

TABLE 6.5

Number of Total City-Pair Markets in Which Each Domestic Trunk Carrier Is Authorized to Compete with Each of the Other Domestic Trunk Carriers

Airlines	Total Individual Participation	American	Braniff	Continental	Delta	Eastern	National	Northeast	Northwest	Trans World	United	Western
American	562	0										
Braniff	359	48	0									
Continental	149	28	48	0								
Delta	995	112	32	8	0							
Eastern	1,375	139	34	8	325	0						
National	351	30	5	3	105	144	0					
Northeast	107	7	1	0	8	15	13	0				
Northwest	293	16	5	1	16	49	5	4	0			
Trans World	413	176	29	23	72	74	29	10	0	0		
United	1,580	125	19	7	108	204	64	12	18	121	0	
Western	228	6	2	4	3	1	3	0	7	7	48	0

Source: U.S. Civil Aeronautics Board, *Competition Among the Domestic Trunk Carriers.*

ture the competitive environment so that it yields economically rational performance. Insofar as the Justice Department's views were taken into account in a set of
merger guidelines[34] for the United States air carriers drafted by the Department
of Transportation in late 1969 (and finally issued in mid-1971), the outlook is favorable that the Big 4 carriers acting individually could accomplish some restructuring of the industry. Indeed, it appears that the smaller carriers might not only
be permitted to merge among themselves (Table 6.6), but that some of the weakest
of the Little 7 carriers might even be allowed to merge with some of the smaller
Big 4 carriers.

> Indicating the possible degree of concern over a concentration of the market as
> a result of the merger, Cherington [the Assistant Secretary of Transportation] said,
> for example, that an American merger with Western would only raise the share of
> the domestic trunk traffic held by the Big 4 airlines from 70.3% to 73.7% based
> on 1968 data. "I wouldn't think this would cause us to lie awake at night," Cher-
> ington said.[35]

While a strategy of benign neglect may have unfavorable connotations in solving some social/economic problems, in the air transport area it could represent a
socially and economically beneficial posture for the Justice Department to assume.[36]

THE ECONOMIC BENEFITS RESULTING FROM LEVELED CARRIER SIZES

The alternatives outlined above sketch the paths which (1) the CAB appears
to have chosen to date, and (2) the Big 4 carriers have available in responding to

---

[34] While these guidelines were "not [to] be interpreted as an encouragement of mergers," they
had evidently been coordinated with the Justice Department.

> Cherington said it also is the department's hope to coordinate at the CAB views of the
> various executive agencies, such as Justice and State, that might be interested in airline
> mergers. He said his department had no mandate for this but that it was endeavoring more
> and more to take on this role so that the Administration spoke with one voice in transpor-
> tation matters.

[35] *Aviation Week and Space Technology,* December 22, 1969, p. 28.

[36] The Justice Department was under some pressure from the Congress not to take this position, however. In a letter to the Attorney General, Rep. Emanuel Celler, Chairman of the
House Judiciary Committee, wrote that he found it "incomprehensible" that the Department
of Justice had not challenged the American-Western merger proposal, then in hearings at the
CAB. Rep. Celler felt that "the merger of Western and American will trigger a wave of mergers
that will virtually eliminate effective competition as a vital force in the airlines industry" *(Wall
Street Journal,* July 2, 1971). On August 31, 1971, the Department of Transportation issued its
"Executive Branch Criteria for Domestic Airline Merger Proposals" (which was prepared in
consultation with the Department of Justice). On that same day the Department of Transportation intervened at the CAB in favor of the American-Western merger proposal, and the Department of Justice intervened in opposition. While the Board and the President (both of whom
must approve the merger before it can be consummated) have yet to be heard from, the recommended decision of the CAB hearing examiner opposed the merger. (American-Western Merger
Case Docket #22916, Recommended Decision of William J. Madden, Hearing Examiner, December 20, 1971.)

TABLE 6.6

NUMBER OF TOP 135* CITY-PAIR MARKETS IN WHICH EACH DOMESTIC TRUNK CARRIER IS AUTHORIZED TO COMPETE WITH EACH OF THE OTHER DOMESTIC TRUNK CARRIERS

1970

Airlines	Total Authorization in Top 135 Markets	American	Braniff	Continental	Delta	Eastern	National	Northeast	Northwest	Trans World	United	Western
American	0	0										
Braniff	7	11	0									
Continental	26	10	10	0								
Delta	68	39	19	11	0							
Eastern	4	37	18	7	44	0						
National	5	19	5	3	26	21	0					
Northeast	21	14	3	0	13	21	15	0				
Northwest	52	24	8	10	23	27	10	10	0			
Trans World	5	47	11	10	41	33	22	16	30	0		
United	100	45	14	17	46	44	30	18	50	63	0	
Western	20	3	1	8	1	1	4	0	10	8	18	0

Author's Interpretation of Potential Merger Situations Which May Be Acceptable Under Department of Transportation Guidelines

Airlines	Number of Potential Merger Partners	American	Braniff	Continental	Delta	Eastern	National	Northeast	Northwest	Trans World	United	Western
American	4	0										
Braniff	7	√	0									
Continental	9	√	√	0								
Delta	3	x	x	√	0							
Eastern	2	x	x	√	x	0						
National	4	√	√	√	x	x	0					
Northeast	6	x	√	√	√	x	x	0				
Northwest	5	x	√	√	x	x	√	√	0			
Trans World	3	x	x¹	x¹	x	x	x	x	x	0		
United	0	x	√	√	√	x	x	x¹	x	x	0	
Western	9	√	√	√	x	√	√	√	√	√	x	0

Key: √ indicates combination involves less than 15 overlapping city-pair markets in top 135; merger may be acceptable.
   x indicates too many overlapping common city-pair markets; merger probably challenged on this basis.
   x¹ indicates merger passes overlapping city-pair test, but fails total market share test; merger probably challenged.

* The top 135 city-pairs include the top 100 city-pairs on an annual *RPM generation* basis, plus the top 100 city-pairs (35 of which are unduplicated) on an annual *total passengers emplaned* basis.
SOURCE: U.S. Department of Transportation, "Executive Branch Criteria for Domestic Airline Merger Proposals," August 31, 1971.

the competitive environment and in resolving the overcapacity and profitability distribution dilemmas. Each of the paths mentioned leads to a rough leveling of the carriers in terms of size equality. The alternatives differ in terms of the speed with which the goal of size equality is realized (and overcapacity thus reduced), and the "end point" market share held by each carrier once the rough size equality goal is achieved. The following pages of the chapter will be concerned primarily with explaining, in the Prisoner's Dilemma framework, why equalizing market shares should lead to reduced overcapacity and a more equitable profitability pattern.

An industry structured as described earlier would permit the CAB to generate a payoff matrix of the following variety (Payoff Matrix 3).

PAYOFF MATRIX 3

CARRIER 2		CARRIER 1			
	CAPACITY RESTRAINT		CAPACITY AGGRESSIVENESS		
CAPACITY RESTRAINT	10%, 10%		Y%, 12%		— RETURN ON INVESTMENT
	① ②		③ ④		— MATRIX ELEMENT #
	2 1		2 1		— CARRIER #
CAPACITY AGGRESSIVENESS	12%, Y%		X%, X%		
	⑤ ⑥		⑦ ⑧		
	2 1		2 1		

SOURCE: Hypothetical example.

The Xs at matrix elements 7 and 8 represent the CAB's willingness to "bail out" the industry when it gets into profit stress induced by capacity aggressiveness. If the Xs are replaced by a number substantially below that found in matrix elements 3 and 6, and the carriers individually are not permitted to earn a return substantially above their cost of capital (i.e., matrix elements 4 and 5 are reduced to the level of matrix elements 1 and 2), then the behavior pattern encouraged by the CAB is one of greater capacity restraint.

Asset Redeployment

Each individual carrier management team can also make a significant future contribution to solving the overcapacity problem while simultaneously benefiting their existing shareholder group. In the future, when equity prices rise in response to reduced capacity pressure (such as is projected for the 1972–1973 period), air carrier managers could take the opportunity to diversify substantially (perhaps to the extent of 30%–40% of their net profits) into areas unrelated to air transportation.

The asset redeployment issue is a key one for the airlines. None of the carriers has made a really major effort to diversify into other business activities. A few carriers have made minor diversification moves into the most obviously related areas like hotels and food catering. The effort has been half-hearted, however, and the particular timing of these moves (in 1967 when airline stock prices were at their peak—Figure 1.5 and Table 6.7) makes the transactions look as much like opportunistic efforts to transform inflated securities into hard assets as strategically motivated product line extensions.

Aside from the obvious corporate strategic and/or shareholder benefits resulting from opportunistic timing in equity transactions, diversification moves could also have an extremely beneficial impact on the overcapacity problem. In effect, airline managements' past unwillingness to explore outlets for investment capital outside the air transportation business has helped to depress the values for "Y" found in matrix elements 3 and 6. When industry profits were poor, no opportunity existed for redeploying any assets freed up by capacity restraint into other business areas. Similarly, when industry profits were high, there simply was no outlet for expansionary exuberance save in gearing up for future capacity duels.

The value of "Y" in the game matrix elements 3 and 6 need only be low if carrier management[37] sees its investment opportunity "map" confined to air transportation. Once this inward looking managerial bias has been overcome, however, the alternative to matching capacity aggressiveness is no longer a retreat to a successively smaller and smaller asset base. It is simply a redeployment of assets into more lucrative areas of investment opportunity. In addition, if the CAB and the carriers were to adopt the policy prescriptions mentioned earlier, competition along the excess capacity dimension (if it persisted at all) would be far less rational and for that reason probably would be quite limited in scope.

The prescription for reducing or ending the excess capacity problem is thus to alter first the structure of the industry and then change the payoffs from capacity competition to those outlined in Payoff Matrix 4.

---

[37] Since the CAB exercises some control over air carrier diversification, its concurrence may be required in some diversification decisions. This fact could be troublesome. For example, in 1971 the CAB agreed to let TWA acquire the Sun Line Companies only on the condition that TWA seek CAB approval for any additional investments in the company exceeding $500,000. This limitation was imposed because

> . . . The Board also has a responsibility to insure that the carrier's assets are not jeopardized in this tangential enterprise.

(U.S. Civil Aeronautics Board, Board Order #71-1-4, January 4, 1971, p. 5.) In this instance, the Board sounded much like the Interstate Commerce Commission which (in matters involving railroad diversification) seems to view rational economic behavior as a conspiracy.

> . . . Given alternative investment oportunities, if management arrives at the conclusion that there is no future in railroading, it may be expected to shift its investment to nontransport activities. . . . The Commission's existing reporting requirements are inadequate to provide the information necessary to *prevent* such disinvestment of rail assets. (Emphasis mine.)

(U.S. House of Representatives, Emergency Rail Services Legislation, Part 2, Serial No. 91-87. 1970, pp. 1058, 1059.)

TABLE 6.7

CARRIER INVESTMENT IN AFFILIATED OR WHOLLY OWNED COMPANIES, 1957–1970

(*Thousands of Dollars*)

	1957	1958	1959	1960	1961	1962	1963	1964	1965	1966	1967	1968	1969	1970
American	$1,737	$1,592	$1,584	$1,586	$1,609	$1,746	$1,737	$1,848	$1,835	$1,811	$15,106***	$20,334	$26,622	$34,932
Braniff	89	72	75	110	139	140	140	139	188	15,194**	669	5,660	1,227	2,594
Continental	17	18	17	23	25	26	33	59	2,825	2,901	3,733	4,795	6,914	11,630
Delta	93	108	140	139	109	132	122	130	145	144	153	183	243	310
Eastern	292	321	316	317	311	307	289	245	208	317	24,555†	29,369	29,021	32,323
National	1,117	9,903*	9,821	9,639	9,911	9,842	1,453*	419	365	333	268	221	211	220
Northeast	39	44	43	42	41	44	43	21	29	32	32	33	33	33
Northwest	249	112	240	220	178	187	202	226	236	240	264	232	290	268
Trans World	359	358	350	344	374	343	336	337	343	380	22,675††	28,202	34,714	39,871
United	592	595	711	945	1,261	1,258	1,253	1,271	1,765	2,115	1,211	1,317	14,368	16,999
Western	19	21	42	42	42	75	75	77	114	117	124	139	144	145
Industry Diversification Investment	$4,976	$13,512	$13,699	$13,688	$14,000	$14,100	$5,693	$4,782	$8,052	$23,584	$68,590	$90,482	$113,787	$139,327
Diversification Investment/Industry Net Worth	.8%	2.0%	1.8%	1.9%	2.0%	1.9%	.7%	.5%	.6%	1.3%	3.0%	3.8%	4.4%	5.6%

* Includes $8,300,000 of Pan American Airways common stock which the carrier was forced to divest in 1963.

** Includes investment in Panagra Airlines which was merged into the carrier in 1967; in 1968 includes advance of $4.87 million to LTV (parent company).

*** Reflects a write-up of investments to cost plus equity in retained earnings; includes Sky Chefs, Inc. ($16.8 million in 1968) and Heritage Inns, Inc.

† Principally represented by the Dorado Beach Hotel acquired for $21,600,000 of 3.75% preferred stock convertible @ $63; and Dilrock-Eastern ($4.1 million).

†† Principally represented by the Hilton International Hotel chain acquired in a pooling of interest transaction for a package of securities valued at slightly more than $90,000,000 including 511,000 shares of common stock @ $90 plus $46,500,000 of 4% preferred stock convertible @ $100/share.

In addition to transforming the real cost of excess capacity (which may amount to hundreds of millions of dollars in 1971) into passenger savings or higher airline profits, the alternative CAB and Big 4 carrier management strategies mentioned earlier could also yield two very important corollary benefits. *First* these changes could remove the need for most of the CAB's current informal profit allocation

PAYOFF MATRIX 4

CARRIER 2			CARRIER I		
	CAPACITY RESTRAINT			CAPACITY AGGRESSIVENESS	
CAPACITY RESTRAINT	10%, 10% ① ② 2 1		10%, 10% ③ ④ 2 1		RETURN ON INVESTMENT MATRIX ELEMENT # CARRIER #
CAPACITY AGGRESSIVENESS	10%, 10% ⑤ ⑥ 2 1		0%, 0% ⑦ ⑧ 2 1		

SOURCE: Hypothetical example.

activity. The problem associated with direct government profit allocation to private business was well described by a Presidential task force studying the United States Oil Import program.[38]

> No single aspect of the present system has engendered as much controversy as the allocation of valuable import rights among recipients. Some of the more dubious features of past practice can no doubt be corrected, but there are inevitable strains and distortions in the administrative process of favoring some at the expense of others. The hazards of fallible judgment, combined with the ever present risk of corruption, counsel strongly in favor of getting the government out of the (profit) allocation business as rapidly as possible.[39]

---

[38] The government directly and with high public visibility gave cash benefits in excess of $300,000,000 yearly to the U.S. oil industry under this program. While the size of this benefit is large in absolute terms, in relation to total industry profit it is relatively modest and its allocation does not lead to an unusually great spread in industry profitability (Table 6.4). In many ways the Department of the Interior (as administrator of the Oil Import program) in making the allocation faces problems similar to those faced by the CAB in its fare and route policies. The allocation function of both agencies are seen by the industry participants as zero sum games, but the public arguments on oil import allocations are more vicious possibly because of the transparency of the game. See, for instance, U.S. Senate, *Oil Import Allocations,* Hearings Before the Select Committee on Small Business, August, 10, 11, U.S. Government Printing Office, 1964.

[39] *New York Times,* "Fight On Over Oil Imports," Section 4, 12/28/69, p. 12.

Finally, these changes could return to the carrier managers some responsibility for being "masters of their own destiny" and not simply puppets dancing to the tune of a puppeteer with near total short-run behavioral unpredictability. The alternative strategies mentioned might also assure that a competitive advantage in management quality, if achieved, could redound to the benefit of the carrier achieving it, and not be offset by CAB action made to "level" the industry.

Bibliography

Index

Books and Pamphlets

Allison, G. T., *Conceptual Models and the Cuban Missile Crisis: Rational Policy, Organization Process, and Bureaucratic Politics*, RAND Corporation Publication #P3919, 1968.

Ansoff, H. I., *Corporate Strategy*, McGraw-Hill Book Company, New York, 1965.

Bain, Joe S., *Barriers to New Competition*, Harvard University Press, Cambridge, 1956.

———— *Industrial Organization*, John Wiley and Sons, Inc., New York, 1959.

Bierman, H., Jr., and Smidt, S., *The Capital Budgeting Decision*, The Macmillan Company, New York, 1966.

Booz, Allen & Hamilton, *Supersonic Transport Financial Planning Study*, May 1967.

Bower, J. L., "Strategy as a Problem Solving Theory of Business Planning," BP 894, Harvard Business School, Boston, 1967.

———— *Managing the Resource Allocation Process*, Division of Research, Harvard Business School, Boston, 1970.

Brealey, R. A., *An Introduction to Risk and Return from Common Stocks*, MIT Press, Cambridge, 1969.

Brennan, Donald C., *Arms Control, Disarmament, and National Security*, George Braziller, Inc., New York, 1961.

Burns, Arthur L., *Power Politics and the Growing Nuclear Club*, Princeton University, 1959.

Butters, J. K., *Case Problems in Finance*, Richard D. Irwin, Inc., Homewood, Illinois, 1969.

Caves, Richard E., *Air Transport and Its Regulators*, Harvard University Press, Cambridge, 1962.

Chamberlin, E. H., *The Theory of Monopolistic Competition,* Harvard University Press, Cambridge, 1933.

Chandler, A. D., Jr., *Strategy and Structure,* Doubleday and Co., Inc., Garden City, New York, 1966.

Cherington, P. W., *Airline Price Policy,* Division of Research, Harvard Business School, Boston, 1958.

Cookenboo, Leslie R., *Crude Oil Pipe Lines and Competition in the Oil Industry,* Harvard University Press, Cambridge, 1955.

Donaldson, Gordon, *Strategy for Financial Mobility,* Division of Research, Harvard Business School, Boston, 1969.

Frankel, P. H., *Essentials of Petroleum,* Chapman and Hall, Ltd., London, 1946.

—— *Oil: The Facts of Life,* George Weidenfeld and Nicolson, Ltd., London, 1962.

Friendly, Henry J., *The Federal Administrative Agencies,* Harvard University Press, Cambridge, 1962.

Fruhan, W. E., "Midland-Ross Corporation (B)," EA–F 329, Harvard Business School, Boston, 1968.

—— "General Electric 1970," EA–F 383, Harvard Business School, Boston, 1971.

Gill, F. W., and Bates, G. L., *Airline Competition,* Division of Research, Harvard Business School, Boston, 1949.

Gilpin, R., and Wright, C., *Scientists and National Policy Making,* Columbia University Press, New York, 1964.

Gordon, Robert J., "Airline Costs and Managerial Efficiency," *Transportation Economics,* National Bureau of Economic Research, 1965.

Hart, B. H. L., *Strategy,* Frederick A. Praeger, New York, 1954.

Henderson, B., *Perspectives on Corporate Strategy,* The Boston Consulting Group, Boston, 1968.

Kohlmeier, Louis M., *The Regulators,* Harper & Row, New York, 1969.

Learned, E. P., Christensen, C. R., Andrews, K. R., and Guth, W. D., *Business Policy,* Richard D. Irwin, Inc., Homewood, Illinois, 1969.

Luce, R. D., and Raiffa, H., *Games and Decisions,* John Wiley & Sons, New York, 1957.

MacIntyre, Malcolm A., *Competitive Private Enterprise Under Government Regulation,* New York University, 1964.

McArthur, J. H., and Scott, B. R., *Industrial Planning in France,* Division of Research, Harvard Business School, Boston, 1969.

Markham, Jesse W., *Competition in the Rayon Industry,* Harvard University Press, Cambridge, 1952.

Miller, R., and Sawers, D., *The Technical Development of Modern Aviation,* Routledge & Kegan Paul, London, 1968.

Murray, Roger F., *Economic Aspects of Pensions: A Summary Report,* National Bureau of Economic Research, 1968.

National Planning Association, "The 'Nth Country' Problem and Arms Control," 1959.

Richmond, Samuel B., *Regulation and Competition in Air Transportation,* Columbia University Press, New York, 1961.

Salter, M. S., "Stages of Corporate Development," unpublished manuscript, Harvard Business School.

Schelling, Thomas C., *Models of Segregation,* RAND Corporation Memorandum RM–6014–RC, 1969.

Scott, B. R., "A Stage of Development Model and Its Proposed Role in Business Policy II," unpublished manuscript, Harvard Business School.

Shaffer, E. H., *The Oil Import Program of the United States,* Frederick A. Praeger, New York, 1968.

Siegel, S., and Fouraker, L. E., *Bargaining and Group Decision Making,* McGraw-Hill Book Company, Inc., New York, 1960.

Solomon, E., *The Theory of Financial Management,* Columbia University Press, New York, 1963.

Straszheim, Mahlon R., *The International Airline Industry,* The Brookings Institution, Washington, D.C., 1969.

Thayer, F. C., *Air Transport Policy and National Security,* University of North Carolina Press, Chapel Hill, 1965.

Trans World Airlines, *Domestic Passenger Air Fares, The Time and Course for Change,* December 6, 1969.

U.S. Civil Aeronautics Board, *A Study of the Domestic Passenger Air Fare Structure,* January 1968.

U.S. Federal Trade Commission, *Economic Report on Corporate Mergers,* U.S. Government Printing Office, Washington, D.C., 1969.

U.S. Federal Trade Commission, *Economic Report on Mergers and Vertical Integration in the Cement Industry,* U.S. Government Printing Office, Washington, D.C., 1966.

U.S. Joint Economic Committee, Congress of the United States, *The Analysis and Evaluation of Public Expenditures: The PPB System,* U.S. Government Printing Office, Washington, D.C., 1969.

U.S. Senate, Committee on Interstate and Foreign Commerce, *Federal Aviation Act of 1958,* U.S. Government Printing Office, Washington, D.C., 1959.

——— Hearings Before the Select Committee on Small Business, August 10–11, *Oil Import Allocations,* U.S. Government Printing Office, Washington, D.C., 1964.

Von Clausewitz, Carl, *On War,* Penguin Books, Baltimore, 1968.

Weingartner, H. M., *Mathematical Programming and the Analysis of Capital Budgeting Problems,* Prentice-Hall, Englewood Cliffs, New Jersey, 1963.

Articles, Speeches, and Government Documents

Ackerman, Robert W., "Influence of Integration and Diversity on the Investment Process," *Administrative Science Quarterly,* September 1970.

Adams, John G., "U.S. Commercial Aviation," Speech to the New York Society of Security Analysts, January 12, 1968.

Alexander, T., "Is There *Any* Way to Run an Airline?" *Fortune,* September 1970.

Altschull, Selig, "Aircraft Leasing Flies Into Storm," *New York Times,* December 27, 1970.

Averch, Harvey and Johnson, Leland L., "Behavior of the Firm Under Regulatory Constraint," *American Economic Review,* December 1962.

Aviation Daily, Ziff-Davis Publishing Co., Washington, D.C.

Aviation Week and Space Technology, McGraw-Hill, Inc., New York.

Barcun, S., et al., "Airline Seat Share: An Optimizing Model," unpublished manuscript, 1970.

Bibeault, D. B., "Market Share Dependency Study," unpublished manuscript, March 31, 1969.

Business Week, "Why Northwest Puts on the Ritz," July 5, 1969.

Business Week, January 11, 1969.

Dean, Joel, "Measuring the Productivity of Capital," *Harvard Business Review,* January–February 1954.

Dockser, Ronald D., "Airline Service Abandonment and Consolidation," *Journal of Air Law and Commerce,* Autumn 1966.

Eastern Airlines, "Proposal For A Revised Fare Structure," July 1969.

Forbes magazine, "So Rich It Hurts," January 15, 1969.

Hall, B., "The Civil Aeronautics Board Policy Favoring Subsidy Reduction to Local Service Carriers: Its Role and Implementation in the Decisional Process," *Journal of Air Law and Commerce,* Autumn 1968.

Homer, Sidney, "Stocks Versus Bonds: A Comparison of Supply and Demand Factors," *The Institutional Investor,* August 1968.

Jones, William K., "Licensing of Domestic Air Transportation," *Journal of Air Law and Commerce,* Spring 1964.

——— "Licensing of Domestic Air Transportation, Part II," *Journal of Air Law and Commerce,* Spring 1965.

Kerley, J. J., and Brunie, C. H., "Industry Report, The Airlines," *The Institutional Investor,* March 1967.

——— "Spotlight: Finance," *Airline Management and Marketing,* January 1968.

Lazara, Joseph H., "Administrative Law—Ashbacker Doctrine—CAB Discretion," *Journal of Air Law and Commerce,* 1969.

Lin, Chi-Yuan and White, William L., "Four Procedures for Testing Linear Hypotheses," *Industrial Management Review,* Fall 1968.

Lorie, J., and Savage, L. J., "Three Problems in Capital Rationing," *Journal of Business,* October 1955.

Murphy, C. J., "The Airlines' Turbulent New Economics," *Fortune,* March 1968.

Murphy, R. T., Speech to the Traffic Club of New England, February 16, 1971.

O'Hanlon, Thomas, "The Fertilizer Market," *Fortune,* June 1, 1968.

Rice, Robert, First National City Bank, "Speech to Wings Club," December 13, 1967.

Silberman, Alan H., "Price Discrimination and the Regulation of Air Transportation," *Journal of Air Law and Commerce,* Summer 1965.

Taneja, N. K., "Airline Competition Analysis," Massachusetts Institute of Technology Flight Transportation Laboratory, *FTL Report R–68–2,* September 1968.

Tipton, Stuart G., "Air Transportation in 1967: The Opportunities and the Pressures," Air Transportation Association of America, October 16, 1967.

Trans World Airlines, Inc., *Preliminary Prospectus,* November 7, 1969.

——— "Domestic Passenger Air Fares, The Time and Course for Change," December 6, 1969.

U.S. Civil Aeronautics Board, Board Order #E16605, April 3, 1961.

——— Board Order #E20421, January 31, 1964.

——— Board Order #69–1–11, January 4, 1969.

——— "Report on Meetings Between the Civil Aeronautics Board and the Domestic Trunk Carriers on Domestic Passenger Fares," February 6, 1969.

——— Board Order #69–5–28, May 8, 1969.

——— "Letter to Airline Presidents," May 29, 1969.

——— Board Order #69–7–105, July 21, 1969.

——— Board Order #69–8–108, August 19, 1969.

——— Docket #21322, Delta Airlines, Statement of Position and Request to Present Oral Argument, August 28, 1969.

U.S. Civil Aeronautics Board, Docket #21322, Statement of National Airlines, Inc., August 28, 1969.

———— Docket #21322, Hearing Transcript, September 4, 1969.

———— Board Order #70–1–147, January 29, 1970.

———— Board Order #70–4–12, April 2, 1970.

———— Docket #21866–6, Domestic Passenger Fare Investigation Phase 6—Load Factor and Seating Configurations, Report of Prehearing Conference, April 7, 1970.

———— Agreement Among American Airlines, Inc., Trans World Airlines, Inc., and United Airlines, Inc., Docket #22525, August 28, 1970.

———— Docket #21866–2, Notice of Proposed Rule Making, September 10, 1970.

———— Board Order #71–4–54, April 12, 1971.

———— Board Order #71–4–58, April 12, 1971.

———— Board Order #71–4–59, April 12, 1971.

———— Board Order #71–8–91, August 1971.

———— Board Order #E24202.

———— Southern Transcontinental Service Case, 33 CAB, 701, 837–899.

U.S. Department of Transportation, "Executive Branch Criteria for Domestic Airline Merger Proposals," August 31, 1971.

U.S. House of Representatives, *U.S. Congressional Record,* U.S. Government Printing Office, April 23, 1969.

———— "Emergency Rail Services Legislation," Part 2, Serial No. 91–87, 1970.

Watkins, H. D., "New Routes, Costs, Test Local Airlines," *Aviation Week and Space Technology,* March 18, 1968.

Statistical Sources

Air Transport Association of America, *Facts and Figures,* 1968–1971.

——— *Major U.S. Airlines 1967–1971, Financial Projections and Requirements,* November 28, 1967.

——— *Major U.S. Airlines, Financial Requirements and Projections 1968–1971,* June 26, 1968.

——— *Major U.S. Airlines, Economic Review and Financial Outlook,* June 1969.

——— Origin—Destination Surveys of Airline Passenger Traffic, *Competition Among Domestic Air Carriers.*

"Bank and Quotation Record," William B. Dana Company, New York.

Board of Governors of the Federal Reserve System, *Flow of Funds Accounts, 1959–1970,* May 4, 1971.

U.S. Civil Aeronautics Board, *Handbook of Airline Statistics,* U.S. Government Printing Office, Washington, D.C., 1961–1969.

——— *Air Carrier Financial Statistics,* U.S. Government Printing Office, Washington, D.C.

——— *Air Carrier Traffic Statistics,* U.S. Government Printing Office, Washington, D.C.

——— *Air Carrier Analytical Charts and Supplemental Carrier Statistics,* U.S. Government Printing Office, Washington, D.C.

——— *Airline Industry Economic Report,* U.S. Government Printing Office, Washington, D.C.

——— *Annual Report to Congress,* U.S. Government Printing Office, Washington, D.C.

——— *Subsidy for United States Certificated Air Carriers,* U.S. Government Printing Office, Washington, D.C.

"Value Line Investment Survey," Arnold Bernhard and Company, New York.

Index